Palgrave Macmillan's
Postcolonial Studies in Education

Studies utilizing the perspectives of postcolonial theory have become established and increasingly widespread in the last few decades. This series embraces and broadly employs the postcolonial approach. As a site of struggle, education has constituted a key vehicle for the "colonization of the mind." The "post" in postcolonialism is both temporal, in the sense of emphasizing the processes of decolonization, and analytical in the sense of probing and contesting the aftermath of colonialism and the imperialism that succeeded it, utilizing materialist and discourse analysis. Postcolonial theory is particularly apt for exploring the implications of educational colonialism, decolonization, experimentation, revisioning, contradiction, and ambiguity not only for the former colonies, but also for the former colonial powers. This series views education as an important vehicle for both the inculcation and unlearning of colonial ideologies. It complements the diversity that exists in postcolonial studies of political economy, literature, sociology, and the interdisciplinary domain of cultural studies. Education is here being viewed in its broadest contexts, and is not confined to institutionalized learning. The aim of this series is to identify and help establish new areas of educational inquiry in postcolonial studies.

Series Editors:

Antonia Darder holds the Leavey Presidential Endowed Chair in Ethics and Moral Leadership at Loyola Marymount University, Los Angeles, and is professor emerita at the University of Illinois, Urbana-Champaign.

Anne Hickling-Hudson is associate professor of Education at Australia's Queensland University of Technology where she specializes in cross-cultural and international education.

Peter Mayo is professor and head of the Department of Education Studies at the University of Malta where he teaches in the areas of Sociology of Education and Adult Continuing Education, as well as Comparative and International Education and Sociology more generally.

Editorial Advisory Board

Carmel Borg(University of Malta)
John Baldacchino(Teachers College, Columbia University)
Jennifer Chan(University of British Columbia)
Christine Fox(University of Wollongong, Australia)
Zelia Gregoriou(University of Cyprus)
Leon Tikly(University of Bristol, UK)
Birgit Brock-Utne(Emeritus, University of Oslo, Norway)

Titles:

A New Social Contract in a Latin American Education Context
Danilo R. Streck; Foreword by Vítor Westhelle

Education and Gendered Citizenship in Pakistan
M. Ayaz Naseem

Critical Race, Feminism, and Education: A Social Justice Model
Menah A. E. Pratt-Clarke

Actionable Postcolonial Theory in Education
Vanessa Andreotti

*The Capacity to Share: A Study of Cuba's International Cooperation in
Educational Development*
Edited by Anne Hickling-Hudson, Jorge Corona González, and Rosemary Preston

A Critical Pedagogy of Embodied Education
Tracey Ollis

Culture, Education, and Community: Expressions of the Postcolonial Imagination
Jennifer Lavia and Sechaba Mahlomaholo

*Neoliberal Transformation of Education in Turkey: Political and Ideological Analysis
of Educational Reforms in the Age of AKP*
Edited by Kemal İnal and Güliz Akkaymak

Radical Voices for Democratic Schooling: Exposing Neoliberal Inequalities
Edited by Pierre W. Orelus and Curry S. Malott

*Lorenzo Milani's Culture of Peace: Essays on Religion, Education,
and Democratic Life*
Edited by Carmel Borg and Michael Grech

Indigenous Concepts of Education: Toward Elevating Humanity for All Learners
Edited by Berte van Wyk and Dolapo Adeniji-Neill

Indigenous Concepts of Education

Toward Elevating Humanity for All Learners

Edited by
Berte van Wyk
and
Dolapo Adeniji-Neill

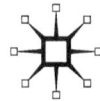

INDIGENOUS CONCEPTS OF EDUCATION
Copyright © Berte van Wyk and Dolapo Adeniji-Neill, 2014.

All rights reserved.

First published in 2014 by
PALGRAVE MACMILLAN®
in the United States—a division of St. Martin's Press LLC,
175 Fifth Avenue, New York, NY 10010.

Where this book is distributed in the UK, Europe and the rest of the world, this is by Palgrave Macmillan, a division of Macmillan Publishers Limited, registered in England, company number 785998, of Houndmills, Basingstoke, Hampshire RG21 6XS.

Palgrave Macmillan is the global academic imprint of the above companies and has companies and representatives throughout the world.

Palgrave® and Macmillan® are registered trademarks in the United States, the United Kingdom, Europe and other countries.

ISBN: 978–1–137–38217–7

Library of Congress Cataloging-in-Publication Data

    Indigenous concepts of education : toward elevating humanity for all learners / edited by Berte van Wyk and Dolapo Adeniji-Neill.
      pages cm.—(Postcolonial studies in education)
    Includes bibliographical references and index.
    ISBN 978–1–137–38217–7 (hardback)
     1. Indigenous peoples—Education—Case studies. I. Van Wyk, Berte.

LC3715.I459 2014
371.829—dc23   2013039986

A catalogue record of the book is available from the British Library.

Design by Newgen Knowledge Works (P) Ltd., Chennai, India.

First edition: August 2014

10 9 8 7 6 5 4 3 2 1

To my late husband and best friend
Albert Russel Neill
1927–2012
(from Dolapo)

Contents

List of Illustrations — ix

Foreword — xi
Carol D. Lee

Acknowledgments — xv

Introduction — 1
Berte van Wyk and Dolapo Adeniji-Neill

Part I Education and Identity

1. The Khoisan Indigenous Educational System and the Construction of Modern Khoisan Identities — 17
   Berte van Wyk

2. Imagined Geographies and the Construction of the *Campesino* and *Jíbaro* Identities — 31
   Bethsaida Nieves

3. How Indigenous Concepts Guide Education in Different Contexts: Tsilhqot'in Culture Course Development — 43
   Titi I. Kunkel and Blanca Schorcht

4. Self-determination and the *Indian Act*: The Erosion of Indigenous Identity — 55
   Georgina Martin

Part II Knowledges and Epistemologies

5. "Being at Home in the World": Philosophical Reflections with Aboriginal Teachers — 73
   Marjorie O'Loughlin

6	Indigenous Relatedness within Educational Contexts *Frances Kay Holmes*	87
7	Indigenous Knowledge, Muslim Education, and Cosmopolitanism: In Pursuit of Knowledge without Borders *Nuraan Davids and Yusef Waghid*	101
8	Curriculum Leadership Theorizing and Crafting: Regenerative Themes and Humble Togetherness *Vonzell Agosto, Omar Salaam, and Donna Elam*	113
9	Taking an Indigenist Approach to Research: Engaging Wise Ways of Knowing toward a Vision of Stl'atl'imicw Education *Joyce Schneider, Kicya7*	125
10	The Politics of Loyalty and Dismantling Past-Present Knowing *Ingrid Tufvesson*	139
11	Seal Meat in the Classroom: Indigenous Knowledge and School Mathematics *Melissa Kagle*	157

Part III Culture, Histories, and Language

12	I Will Chant Homage to the Orisa: Oriki (Praise Poetry) and the Yoruba Worldview *Dolapo Adeniji-Neill*	173
13	Containing Interwoven Histories: Indigenous Basket Weaving in Art Education *Courtney Lee Weida*	185
14	An African Philosophy for Children: In Defense of Hybridity *Amasa Philip Ndofirepi*	197
15	Language Ideology and Policy in an American "Hot Spot": Perspectives on Native American Language Education *J. Taylor Tribble*	209

Bibliography	223
Notes on Contributors	245
Index	249

Illustrations

Figures

4.1 Does the Band you are registered to have an existing membership code?   63
4.2 The RCAP report says that a minimum blood quantum as a general requirement for citizenship is unconstitutional under section 35. It is wrong in principle and it is perceived to be inconsistent with the evolution and traditions of the majority of Aboriginal Peoples. Do you agree with this statement?   64
4.3 The RCAP report says that Aboriginal people in Canada should enjoy dual citizenship, that they can be citizens of an Aboriginal nation and citizens of Canada. Do you agree?   65
4.4 Do you think that dual citizenship should be permitted between Aboriginal nations?   66
6.1 Indigenous epistemologies   88
6.2 The intersectionality of Indigenous epistemological notions: relatedness   93
11.1 Example of a design from Sarah's lesson   162

Tables

15.1 Master list—categories and themes from national-level documents   215
15.2 Master list—categories and themes from state-level documents   216
15.3 Master list—categories and themes from local-level documents   216
15.4 Master list—categories and themes from tribal nation-level documents   216

Foreword

Carol D. Lee, PhD

Indigenous Concepts of Education takes on a compelling and challenging set of issues in education. These issues are both historical and contemporary. In many ways, the historical antecedents emerge out of the history of Western colonialism and imperialism in Africa, North and South American regions, and the Asian Pacific region. When these Western invasions occurred, these regions were populated largely by groups of people who had occupied the land for long stretches of time prior to the invasion, and, in some cases, from the beginning of our knowledge of human history. Charles Mills (1997) offers a comprehensive examination of the philosophical rationales for these invasions, reconciling Christian values by ascribing less than human status to the peoples of these regions and the systematic institutionalization of practices that would denigrate, indeed destroy as much as possible, existing practices among these populations—religion, language, family structure, political structures, and institutions of socialization. In the United States and Australia, these efforts went so far as to remove forcibly children from their families and send them to boarding schools that would resocialize them in the dominant culture of the colonizing force (Churchill, 2003). Within the colonial and postcolonial territories, there have been persistent movements to sustain traditional practices and belief systems despite overt efforts to destroy them. Within the last several decades, these movements have coalesced across national borders to have an international presence and organizational structures, such as the World Indigenous Knowledge Network, the World Conference on Indigenous Peoples, the International Conference on Indigenous Knowledge Systems, and the International Conference of Indigenous Archives, Libraries, and Museums. These institutions represent one set of foci on indigenous knowledge and education, namely articulating, archiving, and sustaining indigenous practices and examining their uses in education, health, ecology of the land, and other domains.

There is another set of conditions that embody the landscape of indigenous knowledge and education and that are reflected in this volume. One of the impacts of Western colonialism and imperialism was to structure the boundaries of nation-states these colonial countries created to encompass ethnic groups that had previously existed as autonomous political entities. This was certainly true in the United States where tribal communities, even with current legal status with the US government, were, prior to their conquest, independent and sovereign nations. In countries across the African continent such as Nigeria and Ghana, again ethnic communities existed as autonomous regions prior to the English takeover, and sometimes ethnic communities existed alongside one another in political confederations. However, there are interesting differences between the circumstances of indigenous communities in the United States, Australia, and New Zealand, for example, where the colonial powers or their descendants took and continue to control the state versus countries such as Nigeria and South Africa where some confederation of the indigenous communities now control the political state. While the original invasions of what became the United States involved the British, the French, and the Spanish, the British won out in that competition but then the British colonists rebelled against the British crown and formed the United States of America. A similar complexity exists in the South African context, as the colonial invasions originally involved the British, the Portuguese, and the Dutch, with the Dutch Boers eventually taking political control until the defeat of apartheid in 1994.

I point out these historical antecedents because it helps us to understand some of the dilemmas of conceptions of indigenous membership, culture, and knowledge systems, and to what they are being contrasted, and the circumstances under which efforts to institutionalize and sustain indigenous practices in education must operate. First, conceptions of the indigenous inevitably invite weighing what may be tensions and disjunctures among different groups of original populations who now exist within common national borders. In the US context, for example, this means such efforts will typically address both what is Cherokee and what is Native American or First Nations. In the South African context, there are additional complexities as the original peoples are the Khoisan, with migrations starting around 1000 BC, of Bantu peoples from the North culminating in the dominant Black ethnic communities in South Africa such as the Nguni peoples (e.g., Zulu, Xhosa, Swazi, Ndebele), the Sotho-Tswana peoples, the Venda, the Lemba, and the Shangaan-Tsonga peoples. And in contemporary South Africa, the Khoisan peoples are a black minority who struggle to reestablish their own indigenous practices within the context of contemporary South African education.

To the extent that indigenous knowledge and education on the African continent involve attention to a broad conceptualization of African or Pan African indigenous knowledge in contrast to a Eurocentric focus in education, these efforts are complicated not only conceptually but also politically as these states are now run by Black people. In contrast, communities typically associated with the idea of First Nations are, on the whole, existing in nation-states that are run essentially by the descendants of the original colonizing forces.

In addition, one must consider in these multiethnic states the cultural challenges around class distinctions within indigenous communities that are often associated with different levels of assimilation into the dominant culture of the nation-state. Sometimes, these issues are heightened by transnational migration of persons educated in Western institutions, such as what has been described as the brain drain of continental Africans who are college educated in the West and choose not to return home. These variations in assimilation within indigenous communities can also intensify debates about the definition, significance, and utilization of indigenous knowledge systems and practices in hybrid nation-states. These variations can also impact efforts to articulate, support, and sustain indigenous knowledge systems and practices (Goncalves & Araujo-Olivera, 2009). Sometimes, these efforts will be centralized in the indigenous communities themselves. For example, there are a number of examples of school projects on Navajo, Cherokee, and Menominee reservations in the United States where efforts at language maintenance and revitalization, incorporation of indigenous knowledge and practices into the curriculum of schools take place (McCarty, 2002; Lomawaima, 2004). Sometimes, these efforts will be centralized in institutions of the nation-state, for instance, public and or private colleges and universities such as the Department of Māori Studies (Te Wānanga o Waipapa) at the University of Auckland in New Zealand (Miller & Thomas, 1972; Phillips, 1983; Grande, 2000).

Finally, a significant conundrum in the twenty-first century has to do with tensions between the traditional and the demands of modernity (Sampson, 1988; van Wyk & Higgs, 2007). Sometimes, particularly with regard to indigenous communities around the world, the traditional is positioned as problematic. This often has to do with practices that involve rituals. This positioning is highly hegemonic because frequently this same lens on the traditional is not vetted with regard to practices such as one finds in the Roman Catholic Church, or the rituals that surround monarchies in places like Britain or the inauguration of presidents in countries such as the United States. The fact is that, as humans, we live and make meaning in a world of symbols and rituals (Some, 1995; Wahlman, 2001). It is just that institutions of power informed by hegemonic ideologies are more likely to normalize certain rituals over others. The bearskin hats worn by the Queen's Guards at Westminster Palace in London serve a prized symbolic function that is no less meaningful than the leopard skin worn by the chief of the Zulu Nation in South Africa.

One area where there have been interesting efforts to connect the traditional indigenous and the modern has been in the area of ecology and sustainability (Kawagley, 1995; Bang et al., 2007). This work is interesting, in part, because it exemplifies a set of practices that are typically tied to allegiances to historical land, connect with spiritual beliefs about the nature of relationships between humans and the natural world, and create potential shared conceptual spaces between modern science, modern schooling, and indigenous knowledge systems. This shared space is further exemplified in a number of chapters in this volume. It is a space of potential hybridity that is nuanced and complex, but in many ways represents the challenge of indigenous knowledge systems in the twenty-first century.

This volume is unique and raises some of the most important issues facing indigenous communities around the world. Its scope represents a significant range of indigenous communities from around the globe and interrogates topics that will invite substantive reflection across communities and institutions.

Acknowledgments

We gratefully acknowledge the help of our graduate assistants, Bettina Fantal-Pinckombe and Brian Cyriac of Ruth S. Ammon School of Education, Adelphi University.

Introduction

Berte van Wyk and Dolapo Adeniji-Neill

This volume explores philosophical, sociological, as well as political perspectives on how Indigenous communities develop concepts that serve as drivers for (the) education that articulates their aspirations. In the light of colonial and postcolonial legacies, many Indigenous communities are confronted with the challenge of revisiting, reviving, and reasserting unique, and sometimes precolonial, perspectives with the purpose to educate and construct knowledge. These perspectives acknowledge the power of words/concepts/definitions and how they can be constructed and used for the purpose of domination (or liberation or reinvention of self and knowledges); the affirmation and promotion of other ideas, knowledges and ways of knowing that are non-hegemonic and may be anti-systemic; the acknowledgement of the validity of a people's lived experiences and the fact that these experiences vary from group to group and from time to time even within the same society although they are connected to one another (see Okolie, 2003, p. 245).

Moreover, this volume explores the variety of ways in which communities draw on both their traditional virtues and their resourcefulness to navigate the contours of (post)modern living. Several responses are evident: there is a tendency to romanticize the past and the opposite is also evident (a complete break from tradition). Of course, there are many positions between these two poles. Broadly speaking, such responses are closely aligned with the influence of globalization and what people understand as "the local" and the attempts to polarize and/or find synergy between the global and the local. Contributors to this volume explore the cultural virtues, ways of knowing, knowledge traditions, interaction between what is regarded as Indigenous and postmodern Western cultures, and seek to emphasize that which is distinct in Indigenous communities or has remained more or less largely unaffected by the influence of Western, colonial or postcolonial cultures, and yet the stress on the humanity of all peoples. We, the contributors and the editors of this volume, explore knowledge(s) unique to a given culture or society characterized by the common-sense ideals, thoughts, values of people formed as a result of the sustained interactions of society, nature, and culture (see Sefa Dei, 2002).

Some of the questions explored in this volume include: What is the relevance and usefulness of Indigenous concepts? How do Indigenous concepts guide education in different contexts? What research is being conducted vis-à-vis Indigenous concepts around the world? What are the implications of epistemologies that result from Indigenous concepts? How do discourses on Indigenous concepts disrupt ideas on education, and assist communities to confront and/or (re)discover their humanity, human experiences, prejudices, racism, and (dis)advantagement?

The above guiding questions elicited certain responses, which are captured in the chapters of this volume. In the following chapters, we highlight and analyze various Indigenous concepts in many different contexts, such as Africa, Australia, Alaska, Canada, and the United States of America. These contexts can be regarded as diverse, complex, unstable, unpredictable, and, sometimes, even messy. Smith (2008) suggests that educational research takes place within a framework in which the search for *findings* (results and outcomes: "what works"?) is treated as unproblematic. He contends that such an approach is driven by the demand for accountability, which often seems to involve the fantasy that an exhaustive audit might be made of reality: that reality could be completely known. This volume indicates that despite various publications on the theme, we cannot claim that we can completely know Indigenous perspectives to education nor that there is any one perspective that will surface on the topic. According to a Yoruba adage, "Wider than the brightest skies and deeper than any ocean are the ways and knowledges of humankind; and no child can have more used clothings or rags than his/her parents." We conclude that this approach is the major strength of the present volume: it provides new and contemporary understandings of various Indigenous approaches to education that seek to elevate humanity.

One of the strengths of the volume is its courage to articulate the everyday lives of otherwise marginalized and silenced communities and showcase these communities and contexts as arenas of knowledge production. The five critical questions mentioned earlier provide solid grounding for the volume (1) by locating its theory in the relevance and usefulness of Indigenous concepts; (2) by confronting the role of Indigenous knowledge and education; (3) by exploring areas of research; (4) by indicating the implications of Indigenous knowledge for wider and deeper understandings of education; and (5) by emphasizing the restorative function of Indigenous knowledge for our humanity. Ultimately, the volume speaks to a desire to foster ways of learning and being that will promote and elevate our humanity.

A major challenge for this volume has been to organize the contributions in a coherent way without compromising on their distinctiveness. Starting with the guiding questions, we work within a critical theoretical paradigm where we highlight past and present conceptions of Indigenous concepts in order that conceptions of Indigenous concepts are grounded in them. Then we identify and explore Indigenous concepts from different parts of the world by constructing their constitutive meanings. Charles Taylor remarks that a society is, among other things, a set of institutions and practices, and these cannot exist and be carried on without certain self-understanding on the part of the participants. Taylor argues that these self-descriptions can be called constitutive (1985, p. 93). We conclude that constitutive meanings are appropriate in the sense that they provide, at any point in the critical analysis, the best focus for deconstructing and reconstructing the phenomenon (Indigenous concepts) in its sociohistorical context. From our research into indigenous concepts, it became evident that this method of exploration has been largely ignored in writings on the theme. Thus we decided that the present volume should address this gap in literature by introducing a new way of thinking about Indigenous concepts.

As expected, when researchers from so many different contexts make contributions to a volume of this kind, perspectives and interpretations of guiding questions turn out to be wide and varied. This can be a weakness if chapters are not organized tightly under themes that cohere and knit them. To this end, we reflected on how to construct a robust theoretical introduction to tie all the strands together into a coherent line of argument. Special attention had to be paid to the current literature on Indigenous studies, cultural studies, and decolonizing research. In addition, the relationship between the global and the local had to be clearly articulated in the light of the aforementioned references. Also, while these concepts may, on the surface, look similar to others in different contexts, their meanings, understandings, and currency with communities may be very specific. With this in mind, we turned to the work of Lee Harvey who asserts that where there are multiple meanings it may be difficult to work with a large number (1990, p. 29). Harvey notes that where there is a large list of concepts in practice, it is not necessary to attempt a separate critical analysis of each. They are interrelated, and so the "key" is to locate a central concept and critically analyze it. The other concepts can be reconstructed on the basis of the analysis of the central concept. Harvey's idea guided us and provided a framework for organizing the chapters into a very coherent line of argument. Harvey suggests that some meanings embed multiple connotations and it may be difficult to work with such a large number. Each part of this volume thus presents constitutive meanings that provide the intellectual spine around which many other meanings can be built, to accommodate various understandings of Indigenous concepts as reflected by the various contributors.

Part I: Education and Identity

The constitutive meanings of "education" and "identity" stand out in this part of the volume, and the contributors highlight the dynamic interplay of these meanings. For starters, there is a very clear argument that any attempt to understand ways of education of an Indigenous community cannot solely rely on western notions and understandings of education. Education in this context takes on a different meaning; a meaning that is sometimes at odds with a western notion. The western notion is primarily a formalized one that refers to the institutionalized, chronologically graded and hierarchically structured educational system, spanning lower primary schools and the upper reaches of the university (Rasmussen, 1998).

Berte van Wyk (chapter 1) points out that Khoisan education during the early years of colonization of South Africa can best be described as informal and nonformal and based on the oral tradition. The oral tradition also comes out very strongly in other chapters—for instance, Dolapo Adeniji-Neill's (chapter 12) assertion: I am a child of the oral tradition. Van Wyk posits that early settlers to South Africa used their Eurocentric traditions to view the Khoisan people. An example of this is a comment by Pascal Dubourg Glatigny and Estelle Alma Maré (2002) on the Khoi in seventeenth-century European representations:

Thus They Were Soon Subjugated and Finally,
As Could Be Expected, Became Extinct

This European proclamation points both to the absurdity of European understandings of Indigenous Khoisan people, and a very one-sided claim of extinction that is mirrored in many Indigenous communities around the world. A vivid reminder of ill-treatment of Khoisan people is the case of Sarah Baartman (belittled and humiliated by Afrikaners and Europeans by calling her "Saartjie"). This chapter illustrates how Khoisan education is organized through community (togetherness, harmony, caring, the well-being of the community above that of the individual), leadership (fairness, consultation, healing), and the land (the land is not ours, we belong to the land; communal life). The story of Sarah Baartman illustrates the worst of European invasion into Khoisan life, and illustrates what can happen when a person is taken away across an ocean and separated from her community, her leaders, and her land. The chapter concludes that the plight of Indigenous Khoisan communities in South Africa after 1994 can be characterized as a silent cultural revolution.

The dynamic interplay between "education" and "identity" is evident when Bethsaida Nieves (chapter 2) discusses *how* the *campesino* and *jíbaro* identities in Puerto Rican education at the turn of the twentieth century were constructed. Nieves takes a different and Indigenous turn when she introduces what she calls "eugenic notions." She argues that these constructions were based on an emerging concept of eugenics that both American and Puerto Rican educators believed would improve Puerto Rican education. She further critically discusses the conceptual and historical constructions of *jíbaro* and *campesino* identities, and how such constructions of identity pervade the contemporary notion of what it means to be Puerto Rican. As such, the chapter analyzes how knowledge about the self and the "Other" was socially and biologically constructed. For Nieves, the history and historiography of Puerto Rican education at the turn of the twentieth century has been constructed to talk about the difference in terms of development and assimilation under United States' colonial rule. She contends that although the processes of development and assimilation were to construct an identity of sameness and resemblance, they were based on an underlying principle of creating and effacing difference. Thus the cultural construction of difference would serve as a legitimizing force for education intervention policies aimed at ameliorating the educational "crisis" in Puerto Rico. The limits of such histories and historiographies are twofold: discussions regarding the emerging eugenic discourses influencing Puerto Rican education are few, and discussions about the conceptualization of the *jíbaro* and *campesino* children are also rare.

Titi I. Kunkel and Blanca Schorcht (chapter 3) argue that First Nations people continue to practice contemporary forms of their cultures, drawing on teachings from past generations and passing these down to the new. However, their cultures remain largely oral, and cultural knowledge is passed on to the next generation through land-based activities, stories, and legends. First Nations languages have been, and remain, the vehicle for transmitting culture. Since colonization, First Nations people have lost some of their languages and cultures. Hence the Tsilhqot'in people, through various initiatives, including teacher education, are working to preserve their language. Kunkel and Schorcht further describe that Indigenous knowledge is inherently tied to particular landscapes, landforms, and biomes where ceremonies are properly held, stories properly recited, medicines properly gathered, and transfers of knowledge properly authenticated. The traditional lands of the Tsilhqot'in people have sustained them through hunting, fishing, trapping, and gathering. These activities provide both sustenance and other intangible values such as learning to live off the land and the ability to transmit oral traditions from generation to generation. The process also ensured the communal validation and vetting of claims to oral traditions and culture.

The erosion of Indigenous identity is the subject of chapter 4 by Georgina Martin. In her contribution, she prefers to use Indigenousness as an identity marker that expresses her affinity with people globally who have similar backgrounds. Noting that the use of this term is supported by the United Nations, she also uses other labels such as Aboriginal, Indian, Native, and First Nations when citing authors or referring to policy. Martin argues that identity cannot be separated from modern-day treaty making in British Columbia because both identity and Band membership are vital factors in the movement toward self-determination. She keeps in mind the difficulties faced in terms of membership when the legal definition connecting people is legislated by an external government. The loss of identity threatens the identity of a people because it severs the individual from their community and culture. Although the issue of identity loss through the *Indian Act* is a source of personal pain for Aboriginal women and their children in particular, identity loss applies to both female and male persons who are disconnected from their communities. Aboriginal men can be denied membership and excluded if their mothers were excluded.

Introduction 7

Part II: Knowledges and Epistemologies

This part of the volume focuses on Indigenous philosophies that Frances Kay Holmes (chapter 6) describes as "ways of knowing," "ways of being," "Indigenous knowledges," "worldview," and "epistemologies." Several philosophical contributions are included in this part of the volume.

Marjorie O'Loughlin (chapter 5) initiates the discussion on knowledges and epistemologies when she briefly addresses the possibilities of an "interface" between Indigenous and nonindigenous understandings of knowledge, country, and the concept of The Dreaming (Tjukurrpa) in contemporary Australia. Drawing upon discussions with Aboriginal teacher education students, she raises some key issues generated out of an engagement with the notion of "being at home in the world." The focus is upon philosophical accounts of Aboriginal approaches to the natural world and to being. Critical comments on the prospects for an interface are made throughout the chapter and possible points of contact suggested. According to O'Loughlin, Indigenous knowledge is a generally understood term referring to the beliefs and practices of peoples of non-Western origin that, following the example of the United Nations Organization, some nations have recognized as a fundamental dimension in the lives of Indigenous peoples around the world. Australian Aboriginals are an identifiable group having had a very long association with places across the continent. Such knowledge is said to be social, physical, and spiritual in character and is inextricably interwoven historically with their survival as hunter-gatherers, their sense of being at home in their place or *country*. At the very centre of their worldview is undoubtedly the knowledge of the land, country, environment that is, in nonindigenous terms, environmental and ecological knowledge. Because of the focus upon the land or country, questions about the nature of Aboriginal knowledge in relation to science have been foregrounded in different ways with different emphases.

Frances Kay Holmes (chapter 6) explores several, but not all, notions of Indigenous relatedness. She argues that the current state of many US dominant systems is symptomatic of a lacking in relatedness, which is inherent in an evolving market economy. Not only is relatedness missing from colonial models of instruction, but dominant forces of industrialization and corporatization have also worked to extinguish relatedness from education to achieve homogeneity. In exploring notions of Indigenous epistemology, Holmes suggests it is important to recognize that mainstream society, from the time of invasion, has dismissed, romanticized, and reduced Native philosophies leaving academia and western society in general, with little understanding of the experiences, worldviews, and perspectives of Native Peoples today. She states that her work is not just about the research; it is about deeply considering Indigenous epistemologies, internalizing them, and examining preconceived notions, while recognizing that learning about Native philosophy cannot be a substitute for living it. Another identity and epistemological driven stance is taken by Holmes when she introduces the concept of "Whitestream researchers" who have often diminished Indigenous philosophies referring to them as "worldviews," in contrast to designations such as "ontologies" and "epistemologies" frequently used to describe western thought. She finally asserts it is important to approach Indigenous research through a tribally specific epistemology, the latter being the foundation that allows discussion of generalities in Indigenous epistemologies.

Earlier we alerted readers to the diverse, rich, and original contributions of this volume. This is exactly what Nuraan Davids and Yusef Waghid (chapter 7) do when they pose the question: what form of knowledge, then, is constituted by knowledge in Islam? This question ties in neatly with our ideas as we conceptualize the volume and then present the parts of the volume in terms of constitutive meanings. For Davids and Waghid, part of the answer is located in their conscious distinction between knowledge of Islam and Muslim education—in other words, they draw a distinction between *knowledge of* Islam, and how this knowledge is enacted. They regard this as a crucial distinction, since, on the one hand, it draws attention to the heterogeneity of any community of Muslims, and, on the other, recognize that all communities of Muslims are as susceptible to other types of communities and forms of knowledge as any other community. By examining what is constituted by an Indigenous form of knowledge, Davids and Waghid argue that any form of education that is constituted by cultural norms and other ethnic practices cannot escape being couched as an Indigenous form of knowledge. Likewise, it would be difficult to consider a conception of knowledge of Islam without considering its indelible allegiances to cultural practices informed by both revealed and supposedly nonrevealed sources of education. For them, it would not only be extremely challenging to divorce cultural norms from any form of knowledge albeit of a social, political or ethical kind, but also equally difficult invariably to speak about nonindigenous forms of knowledge and, indeed, nonindigenous forms of education.

Vonzell Agosto, Omar Salaam, and Donna Elam (chapter 8) present personal reflections on a curriculum theory course that introduced doctoral students to Indigenous concepts through its set of programs and pedagogy. The focus is on how the professional development of culturally competent leadership supports the discussion of how curriculum theory and Indigenous knowledge might be brought to bear upon the development of (curriculum) leadership that is culturally emancipatory. They make reference to cultural imperialism in education that "involves the universalization of a dominant group's experience and culture, and its establishment as the norm" that marks the dominated group as both remarkable (Other, deviant beings) and relatively invisible. Contrasting cultural imperialism is the term "cultural emancipation," which has been associated with forms of critical multiculturalism. However, the term "cultural emancipation" may not include the analysis of Eurocentric hegemony over school and knowledge construction, leading some to prefer the term "critical emancipatory multiculturalism." Their term of choice, culturally emancipatory leadership, is grounded in critical and multicultural perspectives. This chapter makes reference to TribalCrit Theory. Of its nine tenets, two are most relevant here: the recognition that colonization is endemic to society, and the interrelationship between knowledge, culture, and change (the ability to recognize change, adapt, and move forward with the change). This chapter also draws on The Declaration for the Rights of Indigenous Peoples, which "emphasizes the rights of indigenous peoples to maintain and strengthen their own institutions, cultures and traditions, and to pursue their development in keeping with their own needs and aspirations" (United Nations, 2007).

Joyce Schneider Kicya7 (chapter 9) outlines/practices Indigenist knowledge seeking/making processes in the dissemination of a research approach that engages with Stl'atl'imicw ways of coming to know toward a collective vision of Stl'atl'imicw-controlled education. She asserts that Indigenous communities have important protocols that come with and prior to knowledge seeking and making. It is stated that Stl'atl'imicw communities believe that everything must begin and proceed in a good way if it is to result in good outcomes. These knowledge-seeking and making protocols are little known, let alone practiced in mainstream education and research. With reference to wise approaches/practices, Joyce recognizes the need to return to and invigorate ancestral "wise practices" and engage community members, from youth to Elders, in a reassertion of fundamental belief structures, values, and ceremonial practices. Taking back and revitalizing their own ways will ensure that Aboriginal peoples will continue to reconnect with our respective traditions and practices and strengthen the sacred circle of life that is evident in the Non-interference story. She further reflects on the beauty of Indigenous ways to demonstrate that there are other conceptions of education available to draw upon as we seek to transform mainstream systems in ways that move us to spaces where "new ways of thinking and being and new ways of being connected reshape all people."

Ingrid Tufvesson, in chapter 10, asks: How do Indigenous concepts foster education for humanity, where the very notion of what and who fitted into what constituted "humanity" was, and some would say still is, based upon systemized, institutionalized, legalized, and sermonized racism, sexism, and socioeconomic classism? She contends that given the South African history, the very notions of what is authorized and acclaimed as "knowledge" and "success" completely ignore Indigenous ways of being and defining, doing, living, sharing, imparting, and receiving education. Tufvesson explains how the politics of loyalty shapes, informs, and maintains historical status quos in taken-for-granted ways of doing and speaking in higher education institutions. She argues that when attempting to introduce Indigenous concepts to shape education for humanity, those who would do so must remain ever cognoscente of the fact and the accuracy of the assertions of Lordé (1984) and Hall (2010) in the titles of their works—"The Master's Tools Will Never Dismantle the Master's House," and "Nothing is Different, but Everything's Changed," respectively—in order to try to effectively elucidate the subaltern voice in relation to conceptualizations of "success" and "quality" as commonly verbalized by those dominant voices that have set the merited and accredited knowledge agenda for *all* South Africans. She concludes that it would be pointless to argue that marginalization, exclusion, and oppression as it relates to the conflating dynamics of racism, whiteness, sexism, religion, and socioeconomic classism were not, indeed are not, pivotal in today's Khoisan-erased South African education.

A fitting conclusion to this part of the volume is offered by Melissa Kagle in chapter 11 where she explores how traditional cultural practices such as eating seal can thrive within the mandated curriculum of schools. She argues that while we may have left behind the era of education as simply a vehicle for the assimilation of Native students, schools still have not found consistently meaningful ways to incorporate Indigenous knowledge in the classroom. She describes a successful approach to this task that gives teachers of Indigenous students the understanding that they need to become an *elitnauristet maklagtutulit*. This case demonstrates the complexity, challenges, and potential rewards of bringing Indigenous knowledge into the classroom. Kagle refers to a "third space" that occupies the borderland between Indigenous culture and mainstream school. Such a space "brings academic content into dialogue with indigenous cultural knowledge that has historically been left outside the schoolroom door," implying both a pedagogical shift toward Indigenous knowledge as well as a challenge to historic and current asymmetric power relations between indigenous communities and schools. The MCC curriculum facilitates the opening of a third space by making indigenous knowledge and pedagogies the basis of the mathematics curriculum. In Indigenous cultures, children traditionally learned through a process of observing skilled adults and then trying to accomplish small parts of what the adults demonstrated; learners were expected to be keen observers of the adults.

Part III: Culture, Histories, and Language

These three constitutive meanings conclude the introduction to this volume. The question arises: Can one understand culture and language outside the context of historical consciousness? We think it is very important to consider how and in what ways concepts of culture can enhance our understanding of education/concepts of education. The literature suggests that culture seems to be a very difficult concept to work with, and Välimaa (1998) cautions that "culture" is difficult to use as an instrument of research because it can be defined in far too many ways. He adds that culture may also be problematic as a general framework of analysis. Parekh (2000) provides further insights into understanding culture when he discusses the following aspects thereof: nature and structure, dynamics, cultural community, loyalty to culture, cultural interaction, cultural diversity, and evaluating cultures. When we speak of Indigenous people, we almost intuitively speak of culture, thus culture makes its presence known whenever a new leader appears or there is a change in managerial style. We conclude that "culture" is a very difficult concept to work with, and the concept lends itself to a variety of interpretations (see also CHE, 2007). Culture thus takes on many different meanings and directions, and finds its expression historically through the powerful medium of language.

Dolapo Adeniji-Neill (chapter 12) explores the role of "oriki," praise poem/songs, and folklore of the Yoruba culture in which she was born, raised, and educated. Notably, Yoruba culture is largely oral, and Dolapo positions and reaffirms her historical roots with the words. She says: I am a child of oral tradition. She explains how, through praise songs and folklore, people have learned basically how to live, what to value, and how to organize a life in a particular time and place. The word "Yoruba" in her culture refers to the people, the land, the language, and the culture. The examples of oriki, folklore, and folktales in the chapter are significant in that they can affect one's conception of oneself and one's role in society. To the Yoruba, oriki is a point of honor and pride, and the effect of oriki on the subject is enormous, for it infuses the recipient with a sense of self and connects the past with the present. The oriki poet informs people of things about society that can only be gleaned through the spoken word. It is stated that the oral knowledge of the Yoruba is neither authoritarian nor static; it is creative, adaptive, and can be highly personal. There is reference to the modern praise poet and artist, King Sunny Ade, who personifies this aspect of Yoruba culture best in his songs. It is concluded that oriki is the most used of all Yoruba poetic genres; no wedding, naming ceremony, or celebration of life after death is complete without copious use of oriki.

The incredible value in basketry and basket weaving is the focus of Courtney Lee Weida in chapter 13. From her perspective, it is commonly believed that baskets preceded and gave birth to the art of pottery, as clay was discovered within the dirt used to plug holes in the baskets. Theorizing basket weaving as an art form that is romanticized, misunderstood, and/or neglected in manners similar to the treatment of Indigenous studies, this chapter explores relationships between basket craft and Indigenous cultures. Writing from an outsider, Western perspective, she also problematizes her own positionality as an artist and educator and the troubled/troubling roles of colonial influences on basket traditions. By reclaiming aspects of gender, myth, and connections to other crafts, she makes a case for baskets as part of an inclusive, culturally rich, and socially just art curriculum. She points out the connection of women's baskets and white colonization and how women's "ingenuity with food and baskets" impressed European settlers and traders, and the resulting alterations in the design and decoration of their weavings came to signify the level of assimilation of artistic and cultural norms. She concludes that in order to bring crafts such as basketry into a more respectful, dynamic, and culturally nuanced educational space, there must be a willingness to push past oversimplified historical accounts and question what socialized perceptions of the Other—whether negative or idealized—shape educational approaches to looking and knowing.

Amasa Philip Ndofirepi (chapter 14) presents a theoretical argument for a hybridized Philosophy for Children program. He defends the contention that Africanizing education institutions should start from what is Indigenous to Africa by arguing for a transcendence of Eurocentric education, acculturation, and socialization. He acknowledges Matthew Lipman's initiative of doing philosophy with children in schools from an early age. For such a program to be relevant to the context, he submits that it must start from the existential circumstances of its consumers. He explains that a hybridized Philosophy for Children project for Africa, which amalgamates the western and traditional African ways of doing philosophy with children is not dismissal of the western paradigm. He contends that (1) "education always occurs in a specific ecological and cultural context"; (2) philosophy begins in a cultural milieu and to philosophize, one starts from one's existential circumstances; and (3) the twenty-first-century Africa is fundamentally in a state of cultural flux because of the absence of a truly "traditional African" culture or the existence of western culture living in a "third space." On the question, "In what context should African educational aims and objectives be fostered?" he argues for a hybrid model that involves "indigenising what is foreign, idealising what is indigenous, nationalising what is sectional and emphasising what is African."

J. Taylor Tribble, in chapter 15, observes that Native American tribes within the state of Oklahoma are faced with the loss of their heritage language at an alarming rate, much to do with monolingual English language ideologies that have been promoted within schools. The author identifies a clash of ideology and a confusing disconnect between policy intentions and actions on the ground, and highlights the relationship between language ideology, policy, and educational practices that impact student outcomes. This chapter discusses the four following distinct, yet interrelated, levels: nation, state, local, and tribal nation. Each level in this chapter is considered as a distinct interpretive community—holding unique perceptions, beliefs, and values that result in part from their particular involvement in the language and education policy environment. It is argued that the perceptions, beliefs, and values of one interpretive community may compete with, contradict, and/or reinforce that of other interpretive communities. The case is made that language ideologies represent the perception of language and discourse that is constructed in the interest of a specific social or cultural group. Expressed differently, the language of educational policies is a means to express thoughts, ideas, and feelings, hopes, and goals of the educational policy actors who are sociopolitical language users who construct and perpetuate their worldview through language and law.

Education and Identity

1

The Khoisan Indigenous Educational System and the Construction of Modern Khoisan Identities

Berte van Wyk

This chapter explores educational perspectives of the indigenous Khoisan people of South Africa. My argument is that any attempt to understand ways of education of the Khoisan people cannot solely rely on Western notions and understandings of education. To this end, I explore three key notions pertaining to Khoisan education, namely community, traditional leadership, and the land question. In these discussions, I briefly touch on initiatives aimed at promoting Khoisan culture, languages, heritage, and the struggles for the restoration of ancestral lands dispossessed under colonialism and apartheid. In doing so, I will also dispel and challenge myths and distortions by European settlers of the Khoisan people.

Khoisan (first recorded as "Koïsan") is the name by which the lighter-skinned indigenous peoples of Southern Africa, the Khoi (Hottentots) and the San (Bushmen), are known. The name refers to cultural, linguistic, and even traditional patterns among the people. *Khoi* (in old Nama orthography) or *khoe* (in modern Nama orthography) means "person." The Nama and Korana, the two herding peoples who have survived into the seventeenth century, use the compound *Khoekhoen*, "People of People," as their self-appellation (Barnard, 1992, p. 7). *Khoe* was first recorded as Quena (the -na is a common-gender plural suffix) by Jan van Riebeeck in January 1653 and is found as a generic term for people in most Khoe languages—that is, those of the Khoehkhoe, the Damara, and certain "central Bushman" groups. In Nama, the term requires a number-gender suffix (*khoeb*, a man; *khoes*, a woman; *khoera*, two women; *khoeti*, three or more women, etc). The term Khoisan is widely accepted among the indigenous people over the last few decades, and the different groupings embrace the term as they seek to restore their traditions and culture.

Education in the context of this chapter takes on a different meaning, a meaning that is sometimes at odds with a Western notion. The Western notion is primarily a formalized one, which refers to the institutionalized, chronologically graded, and hierarchically structured educational system, spanning lower primary school and the upper reaches of the university (Rasmussen, 1998). However, when the first Europeans came to the Cape Town, there were no structures among the Khoisan people that fitted this description of education. When van Riebeeck landed with three ships in Table Harbour in Cape Town on April 6, 1652, there were no written records (such as books) that could serve as references of Khoisan education, and the Europeans made no effort to understand the indigenous Khoisan people from a Khoisan perspective. They, instead, used their Eurocentric traditions to view the Khoisan people. An example of this is a comment by Pascal Dubourg Glatigny and Estelle Alma Maré (2002) on the Khoi in seventeenth-century European representations:

> Thus they were soon subjugated and finally, as could be expected, became extinct.

The educational traditions of the Khoisan people in the seventeenth century, the time of the arrival of the Europeans, were characterized by an oral tradition although there were important writings such as the rock art. However, such paintings were regarded as primitive and invariably were interpreted through foreign lenses, which distorted and devalued precolonial forms of education in South Africa. In contrast to Western views, Khoisan education during this period can best be described as informal and nonformal. Rasmussen (1998) describes informal education as the lifelong learning process by which every person acquires and accumulates knowledge skills, attitudes, and insights from daily experiences and exposure to the environment. Nonformal education is described as any organized, systematic education activity carried on outside the framework of the formal system to provide select types of learning to particular subgroups in the population, adults as well as children.

South Africa after 1994 is characterized as a silent cultural revolution. There are also attempts to downplay the indigeneity of the

Khoisan people, and from some quarters there are even attempts to group all the African and black people in the country as being indigenous. It is not the aim of this chapter to explore such claims, but suffice it to say such claims are accompanied by silence on the part of the African National Congress (ANC)–led government in recognizing and giving First Nation status to the Khoisan people.

I will next explore key areas of Khoisan education and will interweave these with my experiences growing up on the ancestral lands in the Northern Cape province of South Africa. This is done in an attempt to draw on contemporary practices to inform historical interpretations.

Community

The Khoisan people were hunter-gatherers in the past, living largely off game, honey, and the roots and fruits of plants. They lived—and some still do today—in total harmony with nature, posing no threat to wildlife and vegetation by overhunting or gathering. The seminomadic existence of the San was (and is) governed by the seasons and the movement of game. Thus, Khoisan ways of life were built on a strong sense of community. In such a community, the well-being of the community came first, as opposed to that of the individual. Since the community was dependent on natural resources, there were no permanent towns or places of living. For instance, during periods of drought, food became scarce and the survival of the community depended on moving to greener pastures where food was plentiful. To move an entire community was no mean feat. Given the terrain (semi-desert in large parts of the country), it took skillful organization to manage and navigate their way. When game is scarce, the group splits up into smaller parties to search for food. During severe, prolonged droughts, the women chew the bark of a particular tree, which acts as a contraceptive, so preventing an increase in the number of mouths to feed. Many animals such as snakes, lizards, and even scorpions are eaten when food is scarce.

To provide liquid in dry areas and at times of drought, the San store water in ostrich shells, which they bury deep below the sandy desert surface. They recover the shells with uncanny accuracy. Skin kaross, loin cloths, and aprons are the San's only adornments. Their seminomadic life makes it impossible to possess anything that is not easy to carry. Their shelters are built of sticks and form roughly a circle, 150 mm high. Some cover the sticks with mats woven from reeds.

Most groups today are less nomadic than their forebearers were. However, the desert San live much as their ancestors did. They move in small clans, each with its clearly defined territory. The women gather wild melons such as tsamma (a source of food and water), roots, and edible berries. The men hunt with wooden bow and arrow and use clubs and spears if necessary. The arrowheads are tipped with poison made from insect grubs. It acts slowly on the victim's nervous system.

I attended primary school in the small town of Kenhardt and my mother, Maria van Wyk, left for work before I went to school and returned when the school was closed for the day. During those years, we were allowed to go home to eat during school intervals, as my home was just across the school. Very often I was asked by neighbors to join with their children for a meal. At that time I took these gestures for granted as my mother always served food to other children visiting my home. Reflecting back, I now realize that this sense of community epitomized the way of life for us. At that time if I was at somebody else's house, they almost automatically would provide me a meal as well. In this way the community took care of the children, and at that time incidents of child abuse and violence against children were almost unheard of.

Caring for neighbors is an integral part of community life. Next to ours lived a poorer family, and they always came to our house asking for small things, from matches to paraffin and sometimes for food. My mother always reminded us that if someone comes asking for something that we have in the house, we should give what they asked for. So when we served food, there would be extra plates for them, and sometimes people will be seen crisscrossing the neighborhood taking food to other families—it was at times quite funny to see this!

Wedding ceremonies in our community are occasions when the community spirit is also manifested, and I remember the wedding of my cousin in the small town of Rietfontein in the Kalahari. After the church service, the celebration in the hall went on from about 3 in the afternoon till about 11 in the evening. Nobody needed an invite, but guests kept on arriving in stages, had their meal, congratulated the couple, and then made way for the next round of guests to arrive.

While this sense of community still prevails in many parts of the country, it is sadly lacking in many urban areas. Khoisan communities are in urgent need of the restoration of their sense of community. A sense of community characterized by the adage 'I am my brother's keeper' can make a significant difference to deal with modern social ills, such as school dropouts, teenage pregnancies, substance abuse, violence, and gangsterism, as well as to provide a safety net for struggling families.

Traditional leadership

Job Morris (2012) claims that San leadership cannot be understood by others and that it is elderly based. The leaders are known for their fairness and their ability to consult. The San believe that in the absence of a leader, leadership does not exist. Leaders should create an enabling environment and hear everyone's concerns. In this leadership structure, women, children, and men have different gifts, and everyone should contribute to the wholeness of the community.

San leadership is further described as one that is not coercive and one that is not imbalanced (Morris, 2012). The San have a history of their leaders acting as servants of their people. The principle is that leaders should not be hard, warrior-based, coercive, or directing. Leaders are those who seek advice from their people. A leader invites his people around a fire and establishes dialog about matters of interest to the clan or community. Very importantly, this is where healing takes place. He invites them to touch on their joys and sorrows as they tell their stories. Folklores or tales were passed on to many generations in this way, and such depictions can be seen in the rock art that had existed for centuries. San leaders also prosecute an offender depending on the nature of the offence but after an offender has been repeatedly warned. Trial judgment is passed only after consultation with other elders.

The clan system of the Khoi was somewhat more reformed than that of the San. Each group had a chief. Khois dwelled in beehive-shaped huts made with pliable sticks. Long mats with the strips sewn together covered the frame, leaving an opening at either end. A narrower mat to roll up or down was hung over these openings. The huts could be dismantled easily and transported on the back of oxen as people moved on. These mat-covered huts can still be seen in Namaqualand and other parts of the country.

Strong leadership has been pivotal to Khoisan's way of social life. The influence of leaders was also evident in my hometown, Kenhardt. In this town where I grew up, we had a Khoisan minister at our church. Through my research, I found that he was a contemporary of the late Chief Albert Luthuli, an ANC leader and recipient of the Nobel Peace

Prize. Due to the influence by this ANC minister, Rev. Saul Damon came to Kenhardt and, as part of the congress tradition, assessed the state of education in the community. He then earmarked funds of the church and paid for the studies of late D. A. Titus (affectionately called Dappie) to become a teacher. This move inspired others in the community to also choose teaching as a career. Readers should note that this happened under apartheid, and there were not many career options available to Khoisan people, with the result that teaching and nursing became popular choices.

Due to these developments, schools in the Northern Cape produced many professionals across careers. Matric results, which are a major focus of academic excellence in democratic South Africa, consistently place the Northern Cape in the top three (out of nine) provinces. A further point to note is that I was only taught by Khoisan teachers at school, and this must have protected me from the worst impact of apartheid. Typically of that period, our school was quietly resisting apartheid symbols and celebrations. I remember on one apartheid Republic Day celebration that I was surprised to see some children tear the apartheid flags and trample upon them on the ground. What made these children to display such a drastic action? I can only assume that the then Khoisan leadership had a hand in such actions and there was tacit approval by the community leaders.

The Land Question

When the Dutch settlers arrived in Table Bay in Cape Town, they had to encounter the indigenous Khoisan people. Early European records describe these pastoralists, with large herds of stock, as being more wealthier than the average European peasant of the time. However, their wealth and prosperity would prove short-lived in the face of increasingly aggressive European migration into the interior. Soon after their arrival here, the Europeans aggressively and through their superior military powers occupied traditional Khoisan land. Morris (2004) provides the following statement by Jan van Riebeeck:

> They strongly insisted that we had been appropriating more and more of their land which had been theirs all these centuries...They asked if they would be allowed to do such a thing supposing they went to Holland, and they added: "It would be of little consequence if you people stayed at the fort, but you come right into the interior and select the best land for yourselves..."

This excerpt from van Riebeeck's diaries describes with surprising honesty the sentiments expressed by the Khoikhoi leaders at the so-called peace talks in 1660, which brought to a close the first Dutch-Khoikhoi war in the Cape. It was the first of many wars waged by the settlers against the indigenous peoples of Southern Africa. Since then, the issue of land has remained the central and unresolved question in South Africa to this day.

What is the Khoisan philosophy toward land? It can best be described as: the land is not ours, we belong to the land. The Europeans exploited this philosophy and used this nonlegal position to their own advantage. Vinnicombe (1986, p. 287) posits that the question of the future of indigenous people in relation to their traditional land throws up several moral and political issues that researchers need to address. To her, the current conflict over land rights issues for the few existing hunter-gatherer peoples in the world derives from two different, culturally specific interpretations of the earth. One is based on the land as an inert, inalienable commodity—as a potential source of personal and corporate profits. The other is rooted in a view of the land as inseparable from the process of living (and may I add education) and as identical with communal human life. I agree with Vinnicombe that the basic controversy is whether the earth should be considered economic real estate or spiritual reality. If the latter philosophy holds a place in the modern world, then the issues of land rights and self-determination become matters of vital concern for hunter-gatherers espousing this philosophy.

San are perhaps the most profound human beings on earth who believe that nature has a spiritual and a symbolic relationship with them. In the transformation happening due to climate change and other human implications that contributed to the severe scarring and damage of the earth, San claim that their source of life has been destroyed as a result of those unfortunate events (Morris, 2012). According to the San, their mandate in this world is to bring balance to the ills of mother earth and heal the environment to be greener and fat. Believing that they have a phenomenal connection with the earth, they feel responsible for taking care of it. From time to time, they see people cut down trees, kill animals for their sport or for fun, burn down the environment, littering, digging gigantic holes to extract precious stones, and, as their population grows, expand into the territories of the San and occupy their land. Environment, veld (woods), Mother Earth is a source of life for the San, and their very existence is embedded in how they survive in that land. Mother Earth and the natural environment are integrated into the Khoisan system of education for children. Seeing other people take away their precious land is more like seeing their own people being killed. Their source of food is the ground—digging tubers and burying its roots so it can regrow and be a resource for others as well.

Under apartheid, land once again became a point of friction. The media sensationalized the story of District Six, which was inhabited by a mix of communities, at the centre of the city of Cape Town. The apartheid government declared this as slum area, forcefully removed all the inhabitants, and dumped them on the Cape Flats. For this purpose, Mitchell's Plain was built, and early inhabitants of this area described it as a patch of sand where the wind always blows.

More Khoisan people were forcefully and without compensation removed from the northern suburbs of Cape Town, such as Goodwood, Vasco, Parow, and Bellville. Families were dispossessed of their homes and acres of land. Some people living in Bellville-South described how painful it was to drive through the areas where they once lived and see their houses with the basic structures still intact. Once thought to be powerless, these people are now organizing themselves to fight land claims through courts and constitutional provisions.

For some time now, the ANC-led government has been dragging its feet to give back ancestral land to the Khoisan people. At the heart of the problem is the 1913 Land Act, promulgated under the Union of South Africa. The petitioners site weaknesses in the legislative framework for restitution and point out that Section 25(7) of the Constitution does not provide for an opportunity for the Khoisan people to lodge claims in terms of the Restitution of Land Rights Act of 1994. Both the Constitution and the Restitution of Land Rights Act prescribe that a person is entitled to restitution if he/she or a direct descendant lost land rights after June 19, 1913. Petitioners argue that some racially based land dispossessions that occurred prior to 1913 are impassive under the Act and the most affected are the Khoisan people who had reportedly lost land rights as early as 1652. It is quite clear that current legislation does not favor Khoisan people and it does not promote social justice. The approach of "willing buyer, willing seller" further rubs salt in the wounds of people as many of them never received compensation for their land but are now expected to buy their land at market rates. Current legislation thus perpetuates injustice.

The promise of land was also used as a tactic to lure people to defend one's own country. I remember being narrated by family members who fought in World War II about promises made especially to Khoisan soldiers. For the record, the Union of South Africa fought in the War under the British Commonwealth. Although many of the Khoisan soldiers were recognized for their bravery in battle, they were shocked and disillusioned on their return to South Africa. On the ships, the soldiers were separated based on race, and white soldiers were allowed to keep their weapons, but Khoisan soldiers had to hand in their arms. Of the promises made, Khoisan soldiers only received either a bicycle or a wheelbarrow (to do what?), while white soldiers were compensated with farms and land (land that was confiscated from the Khoisan people). I was told by a war veteran's family that when Queen Elizabeth visited South Africa on the occasion of her twenty-first birthday, she had met and actually danced with Willem Cloete, born in the Steinkopf district in the Northern Cape. A family member told me that the late soldier was informed by a representative of soldiers that he (the late soldier) was a very rich man because of his war exploits. However, to date this family has not received any compensation from relevant authorities. This raises the question of how funding earmarked for war veterans was administered.

Recently I had a discussion with students on the land question in one of my classes. A white female student remarked that her family bought their farm legally. When I asked her who they bought it from, she replied they bought it from the government and walked out of the class with the words "We will never have reconciliation in this country" when I reminded her that as far as my people are concerned we did not sell our land to white people. The land was stolen and sometimes violently confiscated by successive colonial and apartheid governments, and despite her claims, our ancestral lands are still being occupied illegally. How can there be reconciliation when ancestral lands of the Khoisan people are still being occupied by others? Surely reconciliation should not, and can never, mean that we just forget the atrocities committed against the Khoisan people and that we suddenly become friends. After all, who can be friends with person(s) who took away your land? I have to insist that true reconciliation can only take place when the land issue is resolved and the ancestral land is returned to its rightful owners. I am fully aware that the so-called Western world is dead set against what I advocate, but our birthright is ours alone. It is impossible to separate land from Khoisan understanding of education, and the unresolved land question seriously impacts on the construction of modern Khoisan identities.

Concluding Remarks

The first European travelers to South Africa found people there were very different from themselves, so different that the Europeans, in fact, described them as "savages" or "cannibals." A vivid reminder of ill-treatment of Khoisan people is the case of Sarah Baartman (belittled and humiliated by Afrikaners and Europeans who called her "Saartjie"). This chapter illustrates how Khoisan system of education is organized through community (togetherness, harmony, caring, and well-being of the community than that of the individual), leadership (fairness, consultation, healing), and the land (the land is not ours, we belong to the land; communal life). The story of Sarah Baartman illustrates the worst face of European invasion into Khoisan life and describes what could happen to a person who is separated from her community, her leaders, and her land.

Sarah Baartman was born in 1789 into the Griqua tribe of the Eastern Cape, and her family moved to a shack near Cape Town. At 20, while working as a servant to a local farmer, she attracted the attention of a visiting English ship's surgeon, William Dunlop. What caused the curiosity in the doctor's eyes was her steatopygia—the state of enlarged buttocks—and her unusually elongated labia, a genital peculiarity of some Khoisan women of the time (Davie, 2012). Dunlop persuaded her to travel with him to England. Davie suggests one can never predict what was in her mind when she boarded—of her own free will—a ship for London. But it is clear what Dunlop had in mind—to display her as a "freak," a "scientific curiosity," and make money from shows, which he promised to share with her (*The Guardian*, 2007).

In the early 1800s, Europeans were arrogantly obsessed with their own superiority and with proving that others, particularly blacks, were inferior and oversexed. They were obsessed with Sarah's physical features (not unusual for Khoisan women, but larger than normal), which were "evidence" of this prejudice, and she was treated like a freak exhibit in London (Davie, 2012). Needless to say, when she walked down a street among her own people, she would not raise any special interest as she would not stand out physically, and the greetings from friends and others would not raise any eyebrows.

She was called the "Hottentot Venus" in London, "Hottentot" being a name given to Khoisan people with cattle (thus people with a certain form of wealth). Ironically, Venus is the Roman goddess of love, a cruel reference to Sarah being an object of admiration and adoration instead of an object of leering and abuse that she became (Davie, 2012). She first performed in Piccadilly in London on September 24, 1810. Dressed in a figure-hugging body stocking, beadwork, feathers, and face-paint, she danced, sang, and played African and European folk songs on her ramkie (forerunner to the tin-can guitar). Slung over her costume was a voluminous fur cloak (kaross) enveloping her from neck to feet; it was an African version of the corn-gold tresses of Botticelli's Venus—and every inch of its luxuriant, curled hair was equally suggestive (*The Guardian*, 2007). To London audiences, she was a fantasy-made flesh, uniting the imaginary force of two powerful myths: Hottentot and Venus. The latter invoked a cultural tradition of lust and love; the former signified all that was strange, disturbing, and—possibly—sexually deviant. Almost overnight, London was overtaken by Sarah mania. Within a week, she went on from being an anonymous immigrant to one of the city's most talked-about celebrities. Her image became ubiquitous: it was reproduced on bright posters and penny prints, and she became the favored subject of caricaturists and cartoonists.

She spent four years in London before moving to Paris, where her degrading round of shows and exhibitions continued. In Paris, she attracted the attention of French scientists, in particular Georges Cuvier. Sarah arrived in France in 1814, a recognized icon preceded by her reputation as a scantily clad totem goddess. Napoleonic Paris greeted her as a celebrity. In France, as in Britain, her image proliferated—with a significant difference: where English representations exaggerated the size of her buttocks, French portrayals attempted to be more true to life. In the spring of 1815, Sarah posed for three days as a life model for a panel of Europe's leading enlightenment scientists, naturalists, and staff painters at the Muséum national d'Histoire naturelle. Georges Cuvier, Henri de Blainville, and Étienne Saint-Hilaire led the scientific team. Resident artists Léon de Wailly, Nicolas Huet, and Jean-Baptiste Berré produced delicate watercolor portraits of her figure. As well as integral to the "scientific" project, these illustrations became collectible popular art, copied and sold in great quantity. de Wailly's tactful portrait—used as her official image by the ANC—was drawn with evocative, poignant sensibility. In this image, Sarah stands in the antique pose of the Cnidian Venus, so beloved of Renaissance sculptors, a figure that was to reappear later in the nineteenth century in the Orientalist grandes odalisques of Ingres and Renoir (*The Guardian*, 2007).

Sarah Baartman was not only an African woman most frequently represented in racially marked British and French visual culture, she also had less immediately visible influences on Western art. In an age when art and science were commonly regarded as bedfellows, her image appeared in a proliferation of media, from popular to high culture. Sarah was depicted in scientific and anatomical drawings, in playbills and aquatint posters, in cartoons, paintings, and sculpture. Both during her life and after her death, caricaturists Thomas Rowlandson and George Cruikshank made her the subject of works typifying London life and the Napoleonic era. Sarah's body cast was one of the inspirations for Matisse's revolutionary restructuring of the female body in *The Blue Nude* (1907), prompted by African sculptures and conceived, as Hugh Honour argues, "as an 'African' Venus: that her skin is not black is hardly of significance in view of his attitude to colour" (*The Guardian*, 2007).

Sarah Baartman died by the end of 1815, at the age of just 26. Indignity followed her in death: within 48 hours, her body had been dissected, her bones boiled, and her brain and genitals bottled. Cuvier, the father of comparative anatomy and palaeontology, conducted the postmortem. Plaster casts were taken of her body. Once the whole figure was integrated, "sculptors and artists finished the lines to the mould, polished the model surface with oil of turpentine, and then skin, vessels were painted on; the whole covered in a coat of clear varnish." For nearly two centuries, these relics were kept in the Muséum national d'Histoire naturelle. Posthumously imprisoned in Paris, Sarah's violated body became one of Europe's most analyzed specimens. From these lifeless and fragile remnants, European scientists manufactured monstrous, crackpot pseudoscientific theories proposing biological differences between human groups.

Sarah's native land, South Africa, never forgot her. The end of apartheid was the crucial turning point in her afterlife. In 1994, when the ANC won the first free and fair national election, President Mandela raised the matter of Sarah with President Mitterrand during his first state visit to South Africa. Supporting the long-running campaign initiated by the anthropologist Professor Philip Tobias for the return of Sarah's remains, President Mandela told Mitterrand that it was time for her to come home. Claiming the right over Sarah's remains and honoring her as a heroic national ancestor was the first act of international cultural reparation made on behalf of democratic South Africa. The French people and politicians supported her repatriation, but museologists raised objections that she was still a viable object of "scientific" study and French patrimony. Henri de Lumley, director of the Musée de l'Homme, claimed insultingly that she would be "safer" and better "cherished in the home of liberty, fraternity and equality, than in South Africa."

Sarah's remains became central to the ongoing debate over the return of cultural heritage, plundered from formerly colonized nations, that fills European museums. Responding to the hysteria that Sarah's return would open the floodgates to similar requests, Ben Ngubane, minister of culture, wryly observed that South Africa was unlikely to request the return of all its plundered patrimony, as there is not enough space in Africa to store it. Brigitte Mabandla, deputy minister of culture, pointed out: "The end of colonialism is tied to the return of Africa's cultural heritage...Scholars argue that 200-year-old remains should be classified as ordinary artifacts, and tools for research, and that there is no need to attach emotions to them. This is a fallacy. Europe is littered with ancient heritage, and there is a lot of passion associated with heritage by Europeans themselves."

According to *The Guardian* (2007), it took a further eight years and the intervention of Mandela's successor, Thabo Mbeki, before Sarah's remains were released. In May 2002, her remains were flown back to South Africa, and on August 9, the National Women's Day, a state funeral was organized in the Gamtoos River Valley, in the town of Hankey in the Eastern Cape, her birthplace. President Thabo Mbeki gave the funeral speech. Today, Sarah Baartman is South Africa's most revered female historical icon of the colonial era.

The legacy of Sarah Baartman has been to carry the burden of racist representation for colonial and imperialist history. Visual representations of her body are fraught with the negative consequences of reproducing offensive iconography. These images persist as products of a white society that imposed perceptions, damaged and subordinated the lives, consciousness, and body images of millions of people. The history of "Hottentot Venus" raises vexing questions about intention and audience when reproducing racist representations, but it also highlights the dangers of censorship. Images of Sarah are part of her story: they will offend, but no good ever came of locking pictures in the attic. Images of subjected slaves kneeling or celebrating their release were unthinkingly reproduced long after abolition. Notably, Sarah was never shown in a classic slave image. However, her body was subjected to indignity and exaggeration. Hopefully, a new exhibition at the National Portrait Gallery, timed to coincide with the two-hundredth anniversary of the Abolition of the Slave Trade Act, will begin to challenge the omission of Sarah and recognize her influence on British culture. Just to demonstrate the prejudice of Europe during Sarah Baartman's time, her death in Paris coincided with the repatriation to Italy of the famous Roman statue known as the Medici Venus. Plundered from the Palazzo Uffizi by Napoleon in 1802, this celebrated Hellenistic statue was crated up and sent back to Florence in December 1815. Fleet Street, appreciating the coincidence, went for the bottom line, capturing the Platonic assertion that there are two Venuses in Western culture, one celestial, the other vulgar (*The Guardian*, 2007). Her story is a vivid reminder of how things could go wrong when people lose their humanity and treat the other as not being fully human, which was typical of the European attitude toward the Khoisan people. My conclusion is that when you treat others inhumanely, you also dehumanize yourself.

Despite claims that the Khoisan people have become extinct, contemporary researchers are rewriting the history of these proud people, and the ascendance of the Khoisan is undeniable. As an ascendant of the Griqua tribe of the Khoisan, I attempted to make a small and humble contribution to appreciate educational traditions of my people. I further pointed out how contemporary communities construct modern Khoisan identities, and all these serve the goal of restoring the cultural aspirations of the Khoisan people. This chapter makes a small contribution to the literature on the plight of the Khoisan people in the twenty-first century—which I prefer to call "The Silent Revolution."

2

Imagined Geographies and the Construction of the *Campesino* and *Jíbaro* Identities

Bethsaida Nieves

Puerto Rico is currently a commonwealth nation, and some would argue that it is the oldest colony in the world. The purpose of this chapter is to discuss *how* the *campesino* and *jíbaro* identities in Puerto Rican education at the turn of the twentieth century were constructed. It is argued that these constructions were based on an emerging concept of eugenics that both American and Puerto Rican educators believed would improve Puerto Rican education. This chapter critically discusses the conceptual and historical constructions of *jíbaro* and *campesino* identities and how such constructions of identity pervade the contemporary notion of what it means to be Puerto Rican. As such, the chapter analyzes how knowledge about the self and the "Other" was socially and biologically constructed.

The history and historiography of Puerto Rican education at the turn of the twentieth century has been constructed to talk about differences in terms of development and assimilation under United States colonial rule. Between 1898 and 2010, scholars of Puerto Rican education have framed the narrative of development at the turn of the twentieth century as one espousing the intellectual, economic, and social progress goals of US empirical rule. Folded into this narrative of development is the account of Puerto Rican cultural, linguistic, and racial assimilation under US colonial rule. Although the processes of development and assimilation were to construct an identity of sameness and resemblance, they were based on an underlying principle of creating and effacing difference. The cultural construction of difference would serve as a legitimizing force for education intervention policies aimed at ameliorating the educational "crisis" in Puerto Rico. The limits of such histories and historiographies are twofold: discussions regarding the emerging eugenic discourses influencing Puerto Rican education are few, and discussions about the conceptualization of the *jíbaro* and *campesino* children are also rare.

Teacher Training, Americanization, and Racial Regeneration

Scholars of Puerto Rican education development and assimilation have often cited teacher training as the locus of Americanization. For example, Navarro-Rivera's work focuses extensively on the US government using American teachers to both teach English and promote cultural assimilation in Puerto Rican schools. Navarro-Rivera (2009) explains: "Immediately after wresting Puerto Rico from Spain in 1898, the United States began opening schools throughout the country and importing teachers from different U.S. states. Puerto Rican teachers were also trained in the educational ways of the conquering nation" (p. 163). Adding to the complex discussion that teacher training was part of a colonial nation-building agenda is Mixer's (1926) argument that English language textbooks used by American and Puerto Rican teachers were not relatable to the Puerto Rican experience (p. 228). Moreover, Mixer points out that the translation of textbooks from English into Spanish was imperfect, and teachers using these textbooks were caught between Spanish and American standards of instruction (p. 228). Osuna (1949) also argues that the textbooks under US colonial rule were not adapted to meet the realities of Puerto Rican students. The result, according to Osuna, was that children copied books without understanding the words:

> Readers with stories on sleighing and skating parties or even picnics where the traditional roasted pig was the center of attention; and problems of arithmetic on apples, peaches, pears, bushels and what not, could not be appreciated by the children as if they had been on bananas, nisperos, aguacates, oranges, and fanegas or quintales. In writing it was a very common thing to see a child with a copy book copying down English words and phrases the meaning of which he did not know from Greek. (pp. 202–203)

The use of schoolbooks in English and Spanish languages simultaneously promoted American ways of understanding the world and erased Puerto Rican daily life from its pages.

While both teacher training and textbooks promoted Americanization, "elite" Puerto Rican teachers sought to hierarchize Puerto Rican society and reform the socially constructed "Other" for the betterment of self and nation. For example, Navarro-Rivera (2009) contends that the process of using American teachers to educate Puerto Rican children was one of "civilizing" the newly colonized populace: "According to principal leadership elements in the United States, Puerto Rico was an economically and militarily important country but was inhabited by inferior beings who needed to be 'civilized' in order to maximize the potential benefits of the conquest" (pp. 163–164). Moral, however, expands the narrative of development vis-à-vis assimilation with her discussion of "elite" Puerto Rican teachers racializing Puerto Rican education. According to Moral (2009), "The elite teachers' project of citizenship building was primarily a project of racial regeneration, which was based on a popular eugenic and scientific understanding of the concept of biological race in combination with social and cultural processes of racialization" (p. 141). Moral further affirms, "Elite teachers and American colonial officials hesitantly forged a space in which they negotiated goals of regenerating the citizenry" (p. 144). Race and intelligence would later become intertwined in the eugenic logic of who could and could not be educated.

As explicated by the aforementioned authors, both American and Puerto Rican teachers were instrumental in Americanizing and racializing Puerto Rican education. In addition to the public and private schools, religious institutions and economic societies played a significant role in Americanizing Puerto Rican education. Osuna (1949) argues that the church and economic society influenced education policy and curriculum during the second half of the nineteenth century: "These two agencies, the Church and the Economic Society, other private organizations, and the government, were the agencies active in secondary and professional education in Puerto Rico during the nineteenth century" (p. 104). According to Navarro-Rivera (2009), the Catholic Church was in charge of education during the time of Spanish colonial rule, but the shift to state-sponsored Americanization through education became the norm under US colonial rule (p. 163). Barreto (2009), however, makes the case that both Catholic and Protestant churches played a role in Americanizing Puerto Rico: "Both Catholic and Protestant churches established private schools, eagerly promoting Americanization, beyond encouraging language shift. Both church and state assumed that Anglo-American cultural norms and practices were imperative" (p. 146). The Catholic Church, according to Mixer (1926), expanded its role under

US colonial rule, thus confounding the idea that Americanization policies were invested solely in the secular classroom: "The activities of the Catholic Church have materially changed since the American occupation. Many American priests have been sent to the Island with the church's welfare work, particularly on the side of education, has been largely expanded" (p. 203). Complicating the expansionist role of the Catholic Church was the nationalistic counternarrative in which Puerto Ricans defined themselves as Catholic and Spanish-speaking (Barreto, 2009, p. 148).

The idea of teacher education being one of the primary forces of Americanization is limiting because Puerto Rican teachers, Puerto Rican nationalists, and nongovernmental institutions each played a significant role in fabricating Puerto Rican identity under US colonial rule. Another limit is that power relationships in these historical narratives are contextualized as a relationship between the colonizer and the colonized, and not between colonized subjects. Whether Puerto Rican students met the objectives of Americanization policies or that of racial regeneration, the outcome was still the assimilation of indigenous peoples under colonial rule. The identity of those in power changed, but the subjugation of autochthonous populations remained the same. The ideas presented in the literature contend that if educators could intervene in the life of the child, they could save that child. Within this framework was an embedded assumption of who the child was or could become.

Eugenic Discourses Influencing Puerto Rican Education at the Turn of the Twentieth Century

In 1901, President McKinley selected Martin Brumbaugh for the position of Commissioner of Education for Puerto Rico. Brumbaugh described the state of the Puerto Rican school system in three reports. In his second report, Brumbaugh declared that the Puerto Ricans needed to "awaken to the importance of preserving health and realize the methods dictated by modern science" (Solís, 1994, p. 54). As a Progressive, Brumbaugh believed in the "use of the public schools to improve health, vocation, and family and community living" (Solís, 1994, p. 65). According to Mixer (1926), health and hygiene rules implemented by the insular government had the potential to solve the social problems of Puerto Rican rural society:

A continuation of the excellent sanitary measures instituted by the Insular Government is also most important, including instruction as to proper foods and the means of securing them, and the proper care of the body. As the economic and physical conditions in country life are improved, the moral problems connected with rural family life will tend to solve themselves. (p. 170)

Furthermore, the school organization of the Red Cross—the Junior Red Cross—would also create programs to teach children about modern health and hygiene practices:

It [the Junior Red Cross] is entirely devoted to the health and welfare of school children and its efforts on their behalf have assumed a variety of forms such as free dental service, medical school inspection and children's clinics, prizes for school gardens and scholarships for advanced students. (Mixer, 1926, pp. 206–207)

By 1924, Home Economics Clubs, which taught home hygiene, care of the sick, as well as sanitation, had been established in the Puerto Rican rural education system (Mixer, 1926, p. 241). The Home Economics Clubs, Mixer (1926) explains, were

fundamentally designed to teach the maintenance of health through proper feeding and exercise and to instill the principles of service. Under the latter head the clubs aid the "Comedor Escolar," or school lunches; the "Zapato Escolar" or association to furnish shoes to school children; as well as all Junior Red Cross activities. (p. 241)

Moral (2009) posits that Puerto Rican "elite" teachers used health education as a way of promoting their racial regeneration agenda for Puerto Rican students: "Teachers were optimistic that they could regenerate and whiten the Puerto Rican national body through the teaching of health, hygiene, and sanitation" (p. 140). In this sense, health and hygiene practices became enveloped in discourses about race. Embedded into discussion of health and hygiene were beliefs of how members of a race lived, thought, and behaved. More problematic was the idea of a racial hierarchy and that some ways of being human were superior to others.

The limit of this discussion is that it places the responsibility of improving the health and well-being of the nation on the rural inhabitants. Health and hygiene were literally placed on a specific geographic location, but it was the imaginary of a particular type of individual that was being questioned, challenged, and targeted for reform. By doing so, the rural dweller became pathologized and vilified, and discourses of rural health would become transmogrified into discourses of eugenics and morality.

Conceptualization of *Campesino* and *Jíbaro* Children

Meléndez's (1916) differentiation of *jíbaro* and *campesino* identities created a discourse for eugenic intervention in the life of the *campesino* child. Meléndez, both an educator and a renowned essayist, introduced a discussion of eugenics into Puerto Rican education by focusing on the *campesino* population. Explicit in Meléndez's work is a link between eugenics and the health of the body and nation. Considering Meléndez's work within the frame of the early twentieth century, it can be argued that he was among the liberals who were "endorsing a modernizing program, to improve working-class families" (Schell, 2010, p. 488). One of the ideals of the eugenics movement was to maximize the potential of the human body for the economic survival of the nation, but cultural and moral discourses competed with the prevailing discourses of economic development and the globalization trends of the time.

Meléndez's recommendations for improving the state of the *campesino* included an examination of internal and external factors (1916, p. 14). He argues that the following factors were the sources of the *campesino*'s character problems: climate, intelligence, overpopulation, economics, social interactions, family, labor, hygiene and morality, diet, hereditary alcoholism, and illiteracy. The remedy, according to Meléndez, was a eugenic reconfiguration of the *campesino*'s existence. His theory begins with the idea that the fertility of the land made the *campesino* lazy and unable to adapt to modern methods of cultivating it (p. 15). Citing Adam Smith's book, *Wealth of Nations* (1776), Meléndez points out that an individual's occupation is reflected by his intelligence (1916, p. 24), and, therefore, the *campesino*'s occupation as farmers coupled with the climatic conditions under which they worked kept them in a sub-mental state (p. 27). From Malthus's (1798) *An Essay on the Principles of Population*, Meléndez (1916, p. 34) applies the idea of overpopulation and economic demise to the *campesino*'s condition. Layering the discussion of climate and intelligence, Meléndez rationalizes that overpopulation in the countryside was causing a state of crisis for the *campesino* and, by default, the nation (p. 32).

The *campesino*, in addition to presumably overpopulating the countryside and causing economic stress on the nation, are paradoxically described as isolated, socially inept, and without the pleasure of friendship (Meléndez, 1916, p. 49). Adding to this narrative of troublesome social relationships, Meléndez cites common-law marriages as a problem of the *campesino*'s moral state. While common-law marriages were more customary than civil marriages at the time, the reality was that many Puerto Rican couples living under Spanish rule were required to pay the priests for the right to marry, which many Puerto Ricans could not afford. With rates generally high, Puerto Ricans often avoided the fees for marriage and entered into unions on their own. As a result, marriages in wealthier classes were disproportionately higher than in poorer classes (Briggs, 2002, p. 57).

Continuing the argument from a macropolitical overview to an increasingly micropolitical critique, Meléndez discusses the *campesino*'s diet, health, and hereditary throwback status. With respect to diet, Meléndez alleges that caloric consumption was not sufficient, thereby leaving them malnourished (1916, p. 71). Moreover, hereditary alcoholism afflicting some *campesino* families was attributed to physiological degeneration, increased rates of mortality, and several other physical and mental pathologies (Meléndez, 1916, pp. 79–80). The conclusion of Meléndez's argument of external and internal factors affecting the life and well-being of the *campesino*, and inevitably the future of Puerto Rico, points toward illiteracy. Meléndez stresses, "Illiteracy in our campesino class is a problem of equal significance to pauperism, constitutional anemia, social anemia, illegitimate marriages and alcoholism" (1916, p. 85). With the illiteracy rates determined to be upwards of 79 percent in 1899, Meléndez reasons that immediate action through education is needed (1916, p. 88), which includes an understanding of hygiene and public sanitation by all *campesinos* (p. 107). At this point of his argument, Meléndez makes the case for the need of eugenics to solve the crisis of the *campesino* and the state of the nation (p. 120).

Imagined Geographies—"Urban" and "Rural" Spaces

Within the imagined spaces of "urban" and "rural," the *campesino* child became the site of intervention and the object of reform. While the process of Americanization created a student without a history and without a country, eugenic discourses created the *campesino* child as the subject of crisis. Imagined geographical territories such as "urban" and "rural" would become metaphors for speaking about the *campesino* who was believed to be intellectually, morally, and genetically degenerate. The epistemological limitations and the politics of the cultural construction of differences reveal how fields of power and knowledge intersect with governing and governance.

Quoting Dr. Paul G. Miller, the Commissioner of Education of Puerto Rico in 1919, Osuna notes that in June 1899, "there were reported 212 town schools and 313 rural schools...the total number of children between the ages of 4 and 16 years which was then the legal school age, who were without school accommodation, was reported as 268, 630" (1949, pp. 242–243). With regard to elementary school enrollment, "the school census of 1899 showed that the Island had a school population of 322, 393 and a total enrollment in the public schools of 29, 172, or only about nine per cent of the school population" (p. 184). Furthermore, the rural night schools initially established to educate adults were reorganized to serve a larger proportion of children (Meléndez, 1916, pp. 92–93). Within this configuration of student populations and spaces, the *campesino* child became an urgent problem requiring management, intervention, and reform.

According to educational historians, the conditions of colonialism and scientific racism were factors in establishing cultural differences. MacDonald points out, "The island of Puerto Rico was acquired during an era of U.S. history when scientific racism was gaining credence and conquered people were viewed as genetically inferior" (2004, p. 94). Negrón reviews the letters written by the commissioners of education at the Department of Instruction between 1900 and 1930 and argues that they reveal a process of Americanization (1977, p. 8). Moral's study builds on Negrón's work and analyzes how elite teachers in public education focused on discourses of national and racial regeneration, in addition to Americanization policies. According to Moral, teachers were instrumental in teaching Puerto Rican children how to behave and think under US rule: "Teachers were going to help their students evolve from colonial subjects into national citizens, from illiterates into intellectuals capable of comprehending and practicing their civic duties" (2006, p. 137). Furthermore, the students targeted for reform were the *campesino* children, the children who lived in the countryside and who had not been integrated into the developing mainstream societal ideals of modernity. As Moral observes, "Teachers and educators would reach into the island's most distant and isolated, rural, and traditional communities and incorporate them into a modern, progressive, and democratic nation" (p. 138). Meléndez and Huyke would also claim that schools needed to intervene in educating children because not all parents were capable of doing so (1927, p. 33). Osuna notes that during the first five years of US colonization, the number of rural schools in Puerto Rico increased by 54 percent:

> During the scholastic year ending June 1899, there were reported 313 rural schools, 426 barrios without any school facilities and 267, 630 children most of them from the country out of schools. Rural schools were established so that by 1903 there were 580 rural schools. (1949, p. 209)

Writing at the turn of the twentieth century, Meléndez does not consider discourses of colonialism and scientific racism, but instead investigates a complex web of science and morality. As previously mentioned, Meléndez argues that the *campesino*'s health and intelligence are determined by their heredity and mentions that, in 1899, 79.6 percent of Puerto Rico's inhabitants were illiterate (1916, p. 88). For Meléndez, governmental policies promoting eugenics and literacy could improve and eventually solve the health and hereditary problems that he viewed as endemic to the Puerto Rican *campesino*.

In order to improve the state and status of the *campesino*, he would have to be treated as a whole as explained by Meléndez. Meléndez identifies the life, body, mind, and environment of the *campesino* as the sites of rehabilitation and reform. He argues that hygiene and public health needed to be made available to those dwelling in the rural areas of Puerto Rico in order to improve the social conditions of Puerto Rico's population (1916, pp. 107, 120). Meléndez's solution was to create a medico-legislative apparatus in which police surveillance, hospitals, and schools would aid in bettering the society by bettering the *campesino*. In addition to a village plan housing these institutions, Meléndez introduced the use of eugenics as a way to create a better *campesino*, and thus a better citizen and citizenry. "And why not talk about 'eugenics' in this long chapter of 'means' to improve the social status of the Puerto Rican *campesino*?" (Meléndez, 1916, p. 119). Meléndez's rationale rests on the idea that the *campesino*'s maladies were hereditary and could be eradicated from the gene pool using the science of eugenics.

Eugenics, according to Meléndez, is the scientific technique for improving the intelligence and moral state of the *campesino* population. Osuna states, "According to the 1899 census, Puerto Rico had a total population of 953, 243 inhabitants of which 78.6 per cent was rural, that is, living in the country or in villages under 1, 000 inhabitants" (1949, p. 208). And it is this rural population that was the target of reform. These discursive practices of bettering the body through science were intertwined with a discourse of rural and urban that was not necessarily about geography but about a particular type of persons, the *campesino*. These discursive practices also contrasted with discourses about the *jíbaro*, the individuals constructed by an ambivalent notion of geography, but also of class and culture. While Meléndez would cite his concerns for the eugenic reform of the *campesino*, he would praise the *jíbaro* as the "true" Puerto Rican: "The Jibaro culture has the fire, heat, and vital substance that breathes life into our land" (1963, p. 495). The *jíbaro*, descended from the Spaniards and perceived as both racially pure and autochthonous, was described by Meléndez as, "white, well-behaved, and useful peasants of Spanish extraction" (Guerra, 1998, p. 284). Meléndez considered the *jíbaro*'s racial composition as a symbol of true Hispanic racial identity (1963, p. 494). Unlike the *jíbaro*, the *campesino* was thought to be uncultured: "The jibaro lacked education, but he was not uncultured, like he is now, actually, the adult campesino who did not attend school, or that the state could not offer the benefits of public education" (Meléndez, 1963, p. 493; 1966, p. 41). The *jíbaro*, Meléndez would argue, was poor but cultured (1963, p. 494). The *campesino*, not the *jíbaro*, declares Meléndez, needed to be the focus of eugenic reform.

Conclusion

This chapter demonstrates that, at the turn of the twentieth century, the discursive practices influencing the cultural construction of differences within Puerto Rican education relied heavily on eugenic notions of race and race betterment. Not only did individuals and groups become carriers of differences, but that differences also embodied specific ideas about what was scientifically and socially acceptable. Eugenic discourses produced a hegemony of "normal," and eugenic notions of "fit" and "unfit" determined which bodies were "able" and "unable" to participate in society. Differences based on eugenic categorizations allowed for the construction of the *campesino* child as the object of reform that needed to be made literate for the public good. Eugenics and race were contextualized within a larger salvific narrative that embodied notions about morality and citizenship. Teacher education, curriculum design and development, as well as student learning would come to rely on these discursive practices of differences based on eugenic thinking.

Today, the *jíbaro* remains a significant part of Puerto Rican national identity. From children's books to music, monuments, and modern art, the *jíbaro* represents the romanticized and mythologized pure past. The *jíbaro*, "the white male peasant from the inner highlands" (Duany, 2002, p. 24), has come to dominate the narrative of Puerto Ricanness. It transcends the island of Puerto Rico and lives in the imagination of the diaspora of Puerto Rican communities of Hawaii, New York, Chicago, and beyond. To self-identify as *jíbaro* means to have a cultural grounding that is uniquely Puerto Rican. In further studies, we might ask: Which histories are to be used for which contexts without looking at any one history as being more real than another?

3

How Indigenous Concepts Guide Education in Different Contexts: Tsilhqot'in Culture Course Development

Titi I. Kunkel and Blanca Schorcht

This chapter describes the processes involved in developing the curricula for Tsilhqot'in culture courses through the University of Northern British Columbia (UNBC) in collaboration with the Tsilhqot'in people. It also draws on the authors' experiences in developing textbook content and working with a community focus group. This chapter outlines the processes followed in the development and delivery of the curricula and how these have worked, including both successes and challenges, and examines how the challenges have been addressed. This chapter also reports on the ways that the Tsilhqot'in community ensures the validity of claims to oral history, reflecting on the use of language and the ability to translate from Tsilhqot'in to English and evaluating community review processes versus other forms of reviews such as "peer review" and "blind review."

The province of British Columbia (BC), Canada, has many First Nations cultures. These Aboriginal cultures, well established prior to the colonization of the province, have sustained the people for millennia. In the central interior of the province, the Aboriginal people include the Secwepemc (Shuswap), Dakelh (Southern Carrier), and Tsilhqot'in (Chilcotin) First Nations. These cultures are indigenous to the area, and each has its own language emanating from different language groups.[1] First Nations people continue to practice contemporary forms of their cultures, drawing on teachings from past generations and passing these down to the new. However, their cultures remain largely oral, and cultural knowledge is passed on to the next generation through land-based activities, stories, and legends. First Nations languages have been, and remain, the vehicle for transmitting culture. Since colonization, First Nations people have lost some of their languages and cultures. Hence, the Tsilhqot'in people, through various initiatives including teacher education, are working to preserve their language.

Initial delivery of the first course took place from September to November 2012; the translation from course development to successful delivery also forms a part of this chapter.

Involving Tsilhqot'in Community Members

As part of the Tsilhqot'in language and culture diploma, students are required to take two Tsilhqot'in culture courses. These courses needed to be developed further. Based on the first author's experience in developing and delivering course content for Aboriginal students and her own indigenous Yoruba[2] background, she was selected by the university and Tsilhqot'in National Government (TNG) to work with members of the Tsilhqot'in Language Group (TLG), a community-focused group, to develop and deliver the culture Level-1 and Level-2 courses.

The TLG consists of members from the six communities served by the TNG. Members of the TLG teach within their communities, working with children from preschool age through to teenagers in high school. They are fluent speakers of the Tsilhqot'in language; most of them are able to read and write in Tsilhqot'in. Some group members work as language translators, translating oral stories from the elders as evidence for court cases, traditional land use studies, community documents, and environmental assessment reports. One group member had translated a part of the Bible into the Tsilhqot'in language in a previous project.

Eight members of the TLG along with the first author, a university instructor, became the committee responsible for developing the courses, curricula, and the corresponding textbook. Five of these TLG members are elders and are recognized by their communities as knowledge keepers. These TLG elders are from different family groups. The committee was responsible for making decisions regarding topic selection, materials, content of the courses, and evaluation methods. The course evaluation methods, agreed upon by the committee, reflected individual and communal learning methods. Culturally appropriate evaluation techniques were used. These consisted of reflexive journal entries of in-class and field trip experiences, an oral presentation of understanding, student's interpretation of select legends, research into cultural items, as well as talking circles, oral story presentations, and final examinations. However, the decisions made by the group were still subject to review and approval by community chiefs. This unique process, in which collective decisions were made, reveals indigenous methodology at work on the ground.

Developing Culture Courses from Oral Traditions

As stated by Battiste (2002), indigenous knowledge is inherently tied to particular landscapes, landforms, and biomes where ceremonies are properly held, stories properly recited, medicines properly gathered, and transfers of knowledge properly authenticated. The traditional lands of the Tsilhqot'in people have sustained them through hunting, fishing, trapping, and gathering. These activities provide both sustenance and other intangible values, such as learning to live off the land, and the ability to transmit oral traditions from generation to generation. The landscape of the Chilcotin region consists of mountains, rivers, lakes, and rock formations; these provide a rich context for histories and visual evidence of stories, mythologies, legends, and beliefs. Visual evidence includes rock formations shaped in the forms of people and animals. These rock formations support belief systems and are also sites of sacred teachings. Community members visit these sites and landmarks, like pilgrimages, in order to reconnect with ancestral spirits, to pray, and to make offerings. Settler activities, such as resource development, continue to impact some of these landscapes. However, the Tsilhqot'in people have been able to maintain their culture and continue to resist some development activities within their territory. One such resistance of note is the Tsilhqot'in uprising of 1864, which prevented the construction of a road from Bute Inlet on the coast of BC into the gold rush region of the Cariboo (Hewlett, 1973). This lack of road resulted in reduced economic infrastructure within the region, which, in turn, paradoxically has helped to preserve the culture of the people.

The Tsilhqot'in, like many other First Nations, relies primarily on oral traditions. The works of anthropologists such as Livingston Farrand (1900), Robert Lane (1953), James Teit (1909), and James VanStone (1993) captured the early forms of Tsilhqot'in culture, written from anthropological perspectives. However, the people believe that these publications do not truly reflect the contemporary culture and practices of the Tsilhqot'in; rather, they give an historical, and sometimes Eurocentric, perspective. It was, therefore, necessary to develop a written curriculum, including a textbook, for these courses while, at the same time, paradoxically respecting the primacy of ongoing oral traditions. The Tsilhqot'in people themselves became key players in both the development and the teaching of the courses. The university instructor contributed to the translation of academic pedagogy, while community instructors brought in their knowledge of language and culture.

The course development process started with a review of outlines from the university's existing First Nations culture courses. These included course outlines for the Carrier, Tsimshian, Nisga'a, Metis, and Gitksan peoples. Relevant topics were selected from these outlines. These included arts and crafts, foods, traditional gatherings and celebrations, customs, and beliefs. The topics were then reviewed to ensure they were appropriate for public consumption and are accurate reflections of the contemporary culture of the Tsilhqot'in people. It was also necessary to ensure that the topics suggested for Level-1 transitioned smoothly into the Level-2 course. Committee members met weekly for a period of six weeks and contributed information and shared knowledge and narratives in all the topic areas selected. These were collated and edited and formed the foundation of the textbooks for the two courses.

Seven additional members of the Tsilhqot'in community, including three elders, made further contributions to the content of the course material and the textbook. It was decided that the textbook should reflect how the communities felt about their culture, emphasizing ancestral connections and contemporary practices. This was captured in the title, *Tsilhqot'in Culture: Sadanx, Yedanx, K'andzin—The Ancient, The Past, and The Present*. The content of the book also reflects ancestral connections to lands, wildlife, and past generations. The publication consists of personal material submitted by members of the committee, including photographs of past and present generations, landscapes, seasonal activities, traditional gatherings, and craft items. Contemporary forms of fishing, hunting, gathering, and trapping are included. It was important for committee members to feel comfortable with the content of the publication and to be able to answer questions relating to the publication. They also had to be able to justify the inclusion of items in the publication to their family members and to the chiefs. Four of the six Tsilhqot'in chiefs reviewed the content and provided feedback, recommending changes as required.

Tsilhqot'in culture has a wealth of stories and mythologies (Farrand, 1900; Lane, 1953) that have been passed down from generation to generation through oral traditions and narrations. These narrations function as instruction, correction, information, teaching, and entertainment (Sterling, 1997). However, some Tsilhqot'in mythologies, also known as legends, are considered sacred and should only be narrated in context. Tsilhqot'in stories can be narratives of events or about connections to the land, animals, or the cosmos. These are also treated with respect. There are protocols surrounding how and when legends can be told, however; these protocols are not typically applied to other stories. It is also important to note that some of these stories are not for the general public. Commercialization and losing control over the use of stories and their contexts as a result of textualization is an ongoing concern and was debated at length by the committee. With the understanding that it is difficult to control the use of printed text, it was decided to include only select short narratives and stories that were not considered sacred. It was also agreed that Tsilhqot'in elders would participate in the delivery of the courses, one as co-instructor and others as guest speakers, to teach sacred stories and legends that were not textualized. The elders would decide what to share, within the confines of the course content, based on the students in the classroom. This is also how an oral storyteller gauges which stories to perform and how much to tell the audience.

Stories and legends were originally told in the Tsilhqot'in language. Some stories and legends were recorded as a project at a community event prior to the development of the culture courses. The recordings were transcribed and translated into English. Transcription and translation were done by individuals who can both read and write Tsilhqot'in. The committee suggested the use of some of these transcriptions for the culture courses after verification by elders and chiefs. A number of other publications were included in the text as references to provide historical information. Of note is the work of Livingston Farrand who travelled through the Tsilhqot'in communities in the 1800s, accompanying the renowned anthropologist, Franz Boas. Farrand collected legends of the Tsilhqot'in people, which he published in 1900. His publication contains 32 legends, translated from Latin into English.[3] The publication, while comprehensive, did not acknowledge the narrators, however. Nevertheless, this collection was deemed a good reflection of some of the legends and included a Tsilhqot'in creation story. This publication was recommended as an additional resource for the classroom. Other resources included two video recordings of Tsilhqot'in cultural events and an award-winning short documentary of a legend directed by a member of one of the communities. The documentary provides visual representation of an oral legend, was filmed locally, and also featured actors known to the people.

Informed Consent, Ownership, Control, Access, and Possession

Select narratives from some families, primarily short oral stories, were included in the course material. These narratives were originally told in the Tsilhqot'in language and were translated into English by family members. There was consensus on which of these stories to be included in the textbook; the selected narratives were subject to approval from family members and Tsilhqot'in chiefs. Family members needed to be aware of the implications of publishing their stories and utilizing them in the classroom. The implications included losing control of where and how these stories are used and by whom. Families were informed before their narratives were used. It was difficult to get approval from family groups who were not represented during the development of the courses. Members of the committee were mindful of the lack of representation from two communities. They felt that course development should exclude cultural aspects unique to these communities because there would be no validation of information pertaining to them. Consequently, the information collected and used was limited to the works of members of the committee and family members who gave consent. It was also decided that all published information should be generic and applicable to all Tsilhqot'in people.

Questions regarding copyright and ownership of both written and oral source materials, and who has the right to teach this material, even in a university context, remained in the forefront while developing these courses. Many First Nations communities across Canada have adopted a research ethics code, which asserts Ownership, Control, Access, and Possession (OCAP) of research processes, data custody, secondary use of data, intellectual property rights, and outcomes (TCP, 2010). This adoption followed a long period of advocacy for OCAP principles in research (Schnarch, 2004). The need to apply the OCAP principles became apparent from the beginning of the project. The question of who owns the copyright to narratives, stories, and legends in the textbook was frequent. Typically, the copyright belongs to Tsilhqot'in family groups. The copyright of oral knowledge represented in a written context poses an ethical dilemma. Some members of the committee, while giving the consent, did not sign away their authorship and ownership of such material. In this particular project, the knowledge shared, the narratives, and the stories were treated as though they belong to the TNG. Family groups were acknowledged as sources, and consent was obtained prior to the publication of any information. While copyright is held by the TNG, some committee members expressed their desire to republish their family narratives and stories at a future date. Assurance was given that consent would not be unnecessarily withheld.

TNG assigned a dedicated language coordinator to manage all aspects of the project. The coordinator oversaw data collection and management, managed review processes, coordinated with the community members, and also provided the necessary reports to the funding organization. The coordinator ensured that the chiefs and members of the communities were kept informed of the development the work.

The aim of the Tsilhqot'in students taking the diploma program is to become certified language teachers within their communities. Some of these students have nonteaching degrees, diplomas, or certificates and currently teach or work as support staff at their community schools. Consequently, the TNG coordinator expressed the need to have the textbook written in a format easily adaptable to suit the needs of different levels of teaching within the communities. The textbook will also be used by community members for purposes beyond the diploma program.

Translation and Validation of Oral Narratives

In Tsilhqot'in culture, narrators of stories must be acknowledged, along with translators and the context. Acknowledging the various people is a form of citation. Questions were asked about the validity of stories and the credibility of some of the sources. Questions included asking permission to share information; the date when the information was shared, and the event; whether the narration was recorded or recalled from listener's memory; and the identities of transcribers and translators. Was the translator fluent in the language? Could the transcriber read and write the language fluently? Were these stories affirmed by other stories? The ability to answer these questions provided assurance and confidence as to the validity of the oral information.

Members of the committee expressed their difficulties and challenges in translating Tsilhqot'in into English. Despite the notion of the translator being invisible, English language ability and vocabulary played an important role in the translation process. A Tsilhqot'in word or phrase could be a concept in English, or there might not be any English equivalent. Translators were faced with the challenge of expressing these concepts or phrases without changing the meanings and intents. Consulting with different community members about a story, however, quite often yielded multiple versions of the same narrative. Committee members hypothesize that the different dialects among the Tsilhqot'in communities were a contributing factor in the multiple versions. The narrator of a story or a legend, typically an elder, is usually acknowledged. All transcribers, translators, and editors are acknowledged as well. This internal validation process serves to keep the originality of the story or legend and informs the listener of the source. The question arose as to which version of a narrative or story should be published. It was decided that multiple versions of certain narratives should be published to show how different people narrated and shared the same information. These translations of stories were not edited, thereby retaining the meaning and intent of the storytellers.

The First Delivery of the Tsilhqot'in Culture Course

The first delivery of the Tsilhqot'in culture Level-1 course was in the fall of 2012. The three-credit course consisted of 39 contact hours. The university instructor and one of the TLG elders, who were also involved in course development, instructed the class. This elder was well known and respected in the community and has done similar work for a different university. The instructors were able to develop lesson plans to accommodate people with advanced and experiential knowledge of Tsilhqot'in culture as well as those without that knowledge. Two other elders who participated in course development were invited as guest speakers. Three of the six chiefs visited as guest speakers. These visits were significant as they marked the communities' acceptance of the courses and the program. One of the visiting chiefs, in his address to the class, expressed the recognition of the Tsilhqot'in culture course as part of their journey in self-determination.

Traditionally, Tsilhqot'in people learned from elders and through land-based activities. The timing of the first course was such that the participants could not take part in seasonal harvesting activities such as fishing, hunting, gathering, or trapping. However, the students were able to participate in a community's opening ceremony of its new health centre. The opening ceremony provided students and instructors with the opportunity to experience other aspects of the culture first hand. Furthermore, students went on a field trip to the sites of three Tsilhqot'in legends. This combination of in-class learning, field trips, guest speakers, and participation in a community ceremony provided a rich context to learn and experience Tsilhqot'in culture.

Some Lessons Learned and Future Recommendations

The development and delivery of the Tsilhqot'in culture course was historic for the people. The publication of the textbook by the TLG was a major accomplishment. Elders and children joined the class for field trips to the sites of some of the legends. Some community members and elders randomly showed up for in-class discussions and to share information. Some of these discussions, however, were beyond the scope of the class or the course content. It was, therefore, a challenge for instructors to manage such discussions and keep the class on track. Considerations for future course delivery include a university setting or specifically designated classrooms.

There were, nevertheless, advantages in delivering the culture courses in context and on the ancestral lands. These advantages included the ability to travel to sites of community legends and to participate in cultural activities. Equally important was the comfortable setting for speakers and chiefs. Guest speakers felt more comfortable talking to university students within the community settings. The delivery of a culture course in context served as a reminder that Tsilhqot'in culture is very much alive in contemporary forms and has not been relegated to history.

Recommendations from a past work (Kunkel, Schorcht, & Brazzoni, 2011) were used from the outset in the development of this project. Kunkel et al. identified the social barriers that limit the ability of First Nations people living in remote communities to participate in education initiatives (2011). Some of these include the lack of transportation to travel to urban centres and the inability to afford tuition fees and textbook costs (Kunkel et al., 2011). The collaboration between the TNG and UNBC made it possible to address some of these social barriers through strategies such as the choice of delivery location, the development of a companion textbook, and a tuition fee waiver made possible by a funding obtained by the TNG. The TNG was also able to secure additional funds to provide honoraria and travel for members who participated in the course development. Equally commendable are TNG's efforts in the publication of the textbook. The books were supplied free of charge, bringing relief to the students as most of them live on a low income. As a result of these, student participation in the culture courses increased.

The combination of university instructors and community elders as course instructors was a success. In the classroom, the community elder would provide insight and instruction on legends and stories and ensured that Tsilhqot'in customs and protocols were observed, taught, and adhered to. The elder would also provide basic language training and translations in the classroom. The language component of the class provided additional insights and understanding of the culture. The presence of community elders in the classroom was beneficial to the students as there was reciprocal learning and intergenerational transfer of skills. However, some of these elders also expected to learn new things about their culture. This was a concern as the expectations for a first-year university course would not necessarily provide additional learning for elders. Some of these elders are interested in the language teaching diploma but feel that they should be exempt from the basic culture courses. At the time of this writing, the university has been looking at ways to address this challenge.

The history of native education in Canada shows government policies that served to assimilate, segregate, and then integrate Aboriginal people into mainstream Canadian society (Miller, 1996; Milloy, 1999). Aboriginal children had to attend residential schools, and this resulted in their removal from their communities (ibid.). This system had left behind a legacy of abuse, trauma, and social dysfunction. After the closure of residential schools, marginalization and systemic discrimination of Aboriginal students continued, and still continues, to limit their access to university level education (Clement, 2009; White & Peters, 2009). The majority of students in the diploma program were survivors of the residential school system. Their lives and communities have been and continue to be shaped by government policies that still marginalize them. This led to a lack of trust in external organizations and agencies. It was, therefore, important and necessary to build trust and follow the principles such as respect, relationship, responsibility, accountability, and relevance. These principles were identified as being important in Aboriginal education (Kirkness &Barnhardt, 1991; Kunkel et al., 2011) and were applied throughout course development and in the classroom.

Indigenous communities have unique ways of transmitting knowledge and verifying information. It is recommended that future course development in indigenous communities should start by acknowledging the unique ways of each community. It is also important that university instructors learn community protocols and adhere to these. This is essential in building respectful relationships.

Conclusion

The success of this project is a credit to the work and involvement of the TLG focus group and the TNG coordinator. The development of the course and the accompanying textbook also served to enhance and strengthen the TLG's research skills. While the members had worked together on projects in the past, the articulation and application of Tsilhqot'in ways of validating and verifying information were new. Working with a university instructor to document contemporary forms of culture was also very important to the people. The process affirmed the knowledge of the elders and gave ownership and control to the people. Joint authorship acknowledged the works, contributions, and the roles of the members of the TLG. This was a source of pride both for the members and their communities. As a result, other neighbouring First Nations communities are now seeking to embark on similar projects.

Lessons learned include the culturally specific ways in which the Tsilhqot'in people vet and verify information. The community's review process, which was very different from academic processes such as "peer review" and "blind review," was very thorough. The review process reflected the communal ways of how Tsilhqot'in knowledge is owned and generated. The process also ensured communal validation and vetting of claims to oral traditions and culture.

Notes

1. The Dakelh and Tsilhqot'in languages are both from the Athabaskan (Dene) language family, while the Secwepemc is from the Interior Salish language family.
2. This author is an indigenous African from the Yoruba tribe of West Africa. Her homeland is Nigeria.
3. Presumably, the legends were translated from Tsilhqot'in to Latin, or to English and then Latin, which was the practice in those days.

4

Self-determination and the *Indian Act*: The Erosion of Indigenous Identity

Georgina Martin

In 2003, I conducted research in partnership with the community of Canim Lake in the interior of British Columbia (BC) to assist in discussing the parameters of citizenship, membership, and self-governance associated with defining Band membership. Band membership is a creation of the Canadian federal government with exclusive authority to determine who is an "Indian" in accordance with federal legislation. Furthermore, only Band members are eligible to reside within one of the 203 Indian Bands in BC, which is also legislated by the federal government. My purpose was to explore how the erosion of the rights of Indigenous[1] Peoples to self-determine compromised their identities. I argued that the *Indian Act* of 1876 legally forced Indian Bands to construct Band membership codes in such a way that traditional identity is undermined. The research highlights how Canim Lake Band members responded to the concept of Indigenous identity; that identity cannot be separated from modern-day treaty making in BC because both identity and Band membership are vital factors in the movement toward self-determination.

Legislative Authority Governing Aboriginal People

In 1867, Canada was formed and Section 91(24) of the *Constitution Act 1867* (Canada's first constitution) gave the Parliament of Canada jurisdiction over Indians and lands reserved for Indians. The *Indian Act* was passed by the Parliament in 1876, which is currently administered by Aboriginal Affairs and Northern Development Canada (AANDC). The minister has the sole responsibility for the administration of the *Indian Act*. The *Indian Act* consolidated all existing laws in the provinces and territories concerning Indian people. The *Indian Act* focused on lands, membership, and local government. Alarmingly, the Act and subsequent revisions define who is an Indian. The *Indian Act* determines one's identity of Indian status and enables the Federal Ministry of Indian Affairs to provide services to those people who are defined as Indians.

The original Act governing Indian status remained intact from 1876 to 1985, a period of 109 years. The passages of the *Indian Act* relevant for the purposes of this chapter are sections 2(1) and 6, which outline how a person is entitled to be registered under the Act. Palmater (2011, pp. 33–34) describes the complexity as follows:

> Section 2(1) of the Indian Act defines an Indian as "a person who pursuant to this Act is registered as an Indian or is entitled to be registered as an Indian." Indigenous people who are registered as Indians today are divided into which section of the Act they are (or are not) registered under, section 6(1) or 6(2). Aboriginal people who are barred from registration, or who never applied, are called non-status. The major difference between those registered under section 6(1) and those registered under 6(2) is the latter's inability to pass on their Indian status to their children in their own right.

Canadian Aboriginals must satisfy the legislative criteria to be deemed an Indian by the federal government. With the Bill C-31 amendment to the *Indian Act* in June 28, 1985, Indigenous communities gained the authority to define Band membership. The federal government continued to determine the Indian status. Bill C-31 brought added complexity, according to Palmater:

> Even within the 6(1) category of status Indians, divisions were created among Bill C-31 reinstatees who are registered under section 6(1)(c) of the Act and those who are registered pursuant to section 6(1)(a), often referred to as the "acquired rights" group. Section 6(1) registrants are considered to have full status, while those under section 6(2) are considered to have half status. The fact that one cannot transmit one's status to one's children in one's own right is the reason most people do not want to be a section 6(2) Indian. (2011, p. 34)

In June 28, 1987, two years following the inception of Bill C-31, Bands could allow AANDC (previously Department of Indian Affairs and Northern Development, or DIAND) to control Band membership. If membership is controlled by the AANDC, anyone who held Indian status automatically kept the right to Band membership. Bill C-31 extended the option for people without membership to apply for it. Bands had the option to control their membership based on set criteria. According to Furi and Wherrett (2003), the rules respect the following two principles.

1. a majority of Band electors consent to the Band's taking control of membership, as well as to a set of membership rules (which must include a review mechanism); and
2. the membership rules cannot deprive a person of previously acquired rights to membership.

In spite of Bill C-31, the federal legislation's power to legally define an Indian remained. A person with a legitimate Indian status could be considered for membership in a Band. Palmater (2011) claims the situation has not improved because her Band defers to Indian status to determine membership. Bill C-31 entitled Palmater to both Indian status and Band membership, but it excludes her children. Her Band can include nonstatus Indians in Band membership, but they chose not to.

Identity definitions in the *Indian Act* are contrary to traditional Indigenous laws. The policies contained in the Act hindered the clan and matrilineal systems. The impact is destructive on Aboriginal women and their children. Many were displaced from their communities and homeland. Benefits and services such as community housing and education were lost. In addition, pre-1985 legislation permitted immigrant women of European descent to marry an Indian and inherit Indian rights and benefits. These rights and benefits were extended to the children of the mixed marriage. In contrast, while a full-blooded Indian woman lost her status when she married a non-Indian, a non-Aboriginal woman gained status when she married an Indian. Aboriginal women could keep their heritage intact by not marrying non-Indian men. Women experienced the loss of status under the *Indian Act* as an absolute injustice.

Positioning Myself Within the Research

My conviction with and interest in identity aligns with my descent as a *Secwepemc* person. The *Secwepemc* people in my vicinity include the communities of Canim Lake, Williams Lake, Dog Creek, Soda

Creek, and Esketemc. These are five of the 17 communities within the *Secwepemc* nation. I originate from the Williams Lake Indian Band, which is situated seven miles south of the city of Williams Lake in BC. Canim Lake is the site of the research. I lived and worked in Canim Lake for some time; therefore, a reciprocal relationship grew between the community and the researcher.

The erosion of kinship and identity only commenced with the arrival of the Europeans. The European settlers eradicated and replaced the original values and authority within Aboriginal communities. Eventually, the practice of traditional customs and protocols was displaced, which erased the authority of esteemed and trusted leaders and elders. The *Indian Act* and the federal citizenship policies altered customary laws and relegated Aboriginal communities to a place, both physical and emotional, of subordination and oppression by European ideologies. My inquiry reveals how Aboriginal Peoples' identity has been eclipsed into a hegemonic mind-set.

Research Community

Canim Lake Band is located 30 kilometers east of 100 Mile House. The main community is situated along Bridge Creek, west of Canim Lake. The *Shuswap People in Story* (1992) report confirms a population as 85 Band members living off the reserve and 380 living on the reserve, a total of 465 members. Canim Lake is comprised of six parcels of designated reserve land, totaling 5,074 acres, 100 acres of which is prime agricultural land.

Canim Lake Band members completed a semistructured questionnaire for my study. The survey responses from on-reserve and off-reserve Band members gaugeed their knowledge and thoughts about membership criteria. The information gathered is significant because many Indigenous communities in the province of BC are engaged in the tripartite treaty-making process, and both identity and Band membership are vital determinants in terms of self-determination.

Conceptualizing the Parameters of the Research Problem

To conceptualize the research problem, I kept in mind the difficulties faced in terms of membership when the legal definition connecting people is legislated by an external government. The loss of identity threatens people because it severs the individual from their community and culture. Although the issue of identity loss is a source of personal pain for Aboriginal women, and their children in particular, identity loss applies to both women and men who are disconnected from their communities. Aboriginal men can be denied membership based on the criteria that resulted in their mothers' exclusion.

Aboriginal Views on Citizenship and Band Membership

Alfred (1999) contends that contemporary community life is controlled by dual value systems that are fundamentally opposed. One is rooted in traditional teachings that construct social and cultural relations, while the other is imposed by the colonial state's political structures. The disunity between the systems caused factionalism within Indigenous communities. Alfred notes how Indigenous people made significant progress to reconstruct their identities. He admits the threat of assimilation into nonindigenous communities is not as overwhelming and ismanageable. He also affirms that the fundamental task facing Aboriginal communities is to overcome the racial, territorial, and "status" divisions that are features of the political landscape. The solutions to these divisions must come from within the nations based on the integrity of their traditions and their rejection of the divisive categories defined by the state. The author supports the move away from dependency. Movement is necessary to rectify over 200 years of colonial history. I realize that Indigenous societies were stronger in the past when there were no questions of cultural boundaries and people did not have to think about their group affiliation or whether or not they were truly Indian. The classifications forced the Indigenous people to categorize and define the quality of being Indigenous. To undo the damage, certainty must be achieved through a process of fairness and openness in Band member determination.

In *Journeying Forward*, Patricia Monture-Angus (1999) examines the path of Aboriginal people on the journey to reclaiming individual and collective identities. She states that as Aboriginal Peoples (Indian, First Nation, Inuit, and Métis) there is no regimented perspective on anything. Homogeneity is nonexistent within First Nations, Métis, or Inuit cultures. Monture-Angus (1999) explains that the "self-government," "self-determination," and "sovereignty" do not hold the same connotation from a single Aboriginal frame of reference. Yet, singular Aboriginal traditions or notions of self-governance appear to exist when juxtaposed against the dominant non-Aboriginal system. She believes that diametrically opposed worldviews move Aboriginal people further away from solutions as competing worldviews create distance rather than relationships. An example of distance is section 91(24) of the Canadian Constitution, in that the federal parliament has authority over Indians and lands reserved for Indians. Monture-Angus argues that as long as section 91(24) remains intact, Indigenous people will never be free from their subordinated position.

The subordinated position Monture-Angus (1999) refers to is evident by the Bill C-31 amendment, which provides Indian people with a new membership and status system that contains gender inequalities. The amendment denies Indian women who married non-Aboriginals the right to register their grandchildren, while Indian men who married non-Aboriginals do not suffer the same encumbrance. The separation of Indian status and Band membership through this Bill created a more complicated system for negotiating and securing registration for Indian children. The federal government avoids fair and equitable solutions.

Meanwhile, Bish and Cassidy (1989) find the ultimate justification for First Nation governments in the power of the creator. They maintain that the power of the creator originally determined First Nation activities including the subjects of jurisdiction, not the federal government. The citizens were empowered and they enjoyed a status equal to that of governments in their own systems. Ultimately, these authors reiterate that Indigenous identification is systemic and that the *Indian Act* reduces the autonomy of Indigenous communities to practice their own systems of identification to nonexistence. Through this study, my intent is to explore the possibilities for self-determination to evolve.

The Citizenship and Membership Debate

Many authors have come forward on the subject of citizenship and membership. However, in this chapter, only a few are mentioned, which led to the discussion to revolutionize the current mentality of oppression that affects Band membership. Poelzer (1996) indicates that while research has been concerned with constitutional and legal issues, insufficient attention has been given to the broader cultural or sociological foundations upon which the current struggle for Indigenous self-government is based. Youngblood Henderson, Benson, and Finlay (2000) add that more than two decades of commissions, inquiries, reports, special initiatives, conferences, and books have made it clear that the effects of colonization on Aboriginal Peoples in Canada have eroded their self-identity, and the only way to repair the damage is through reform that leads to decolonization. One of the commissions that produced a multivolume report is the 1996 Royal Commission on Aboriginal Peoples (RCAP). RCAP explained how individuals previously exercised personal autonomy in communities within frameworks of community ethics. Communities enjoyed autonomy within the larger network of what became tribes or nations. Nations were demarcated on the basis of language, dialect, or territory. Relationships within the nation were knit together by clan membership that went beyond immediate ties of blood or marriage. In terms of Aboriginal nations, RCAP's view upholds the right of an Aboriginal nation to determine its own citizenship as an existing Aboriginal and treaty right within the meaning of section 35(1) of the *Constitution Act* 1982. The rules and processes governing citizenship must satisfy certain basic constitutional standards from section 35. These standards prevent an Aboriginal group from unfairly excluding anyone from enjoying collective Aboriginal and treaty rights, and equality is guaranteed to both men and women. RCAP (1996) also acknowledged that citizenship does not only confer rights, entitlements, and benefits to individuals; it also implies responsibilities. The rights include civil, democratic, and political rights (e.g., the right to participate in the selection of a leader), cultural and economic rights (such as the right to pursue traditional economic activities), and rights to social entitlements (such as those that emerge from treaties and include education and health care). RCAP (1996) concludes that as nations rebuild citizenship codes, they will embrace all individuals who have ties to the nation but, for various reasons, had been excluded in the past. Therefore, new citizenship provisions would eliminate the aftereffects of Bill C-31, which created categories of "full" Indians and "half" Indians. My point of clarification is that Aboriginal people in their own communities have rights and responsibilities to enact regarding Band membership. I believe that membership responsibility is reciprocal between individuals, leadership, and community. The current understanding of Canim Lake Band member responsibilities is considered in this research project.

Canim Lake Community Survey

Methodology

The questionnaire was administered by personal interview between the researcher and respondents. The majority of qualitative/quantitative interviews took between 15 and 20 minutes to complete depending on the depth of the response. The study was designed to capture general information permitting the respondent to offer their views, beliefs, and attitudes in certain areas pertaining to the existing or potential arrangements applicable to citizenship and membership in their community.

Two groups of respondents were surveyed simultaneously over a period of two weeks between March 13 and March 25, 2003. The questionnaire consisted of three parts: the introductory questions collected demographics such as year of birth, gender, birthplace, confirmation of Indian status, and Band membership. The balance of the survey was divided into sets of structured and unstructured questions. The key respondents comprised of a sample group representing on-reserve and off-reserve Band members selected from the Band list using a systematic sampling technique. On-reserve and off-reserve refers to residency. This technique is simple wherein the kth element in the total list is chosen systematically for inclusion in the sample. The method guards against human bias by applying a random number between 1 and 10. The Canim Lake Band Administrator selected the start-up number, and then every tenth person listed on the Band register was chosen. Only Band members of 18 years and older were included in the survey. If a Band member could not be found, then the next person on the list was interviewed. At the time of the survey, there were 202 on-reserve Band members and 156 off-reserve members, a combined total of 358 for the sample. The survey sample consisted of 17 on-reserve members and 11 off-reserve members. Interestingly, the number of men was higher in the on-reserve pool while the number of women was higher in the off-reserve group.

Results and Discussion

Although the size of my sample is small, the results produced insightful information that can be utilized as benchmarks about how Canim Lake's membership felt toward certain aspects of membership within their community. In this chapter, I focus on certain parts of the survey

Self-determination 63

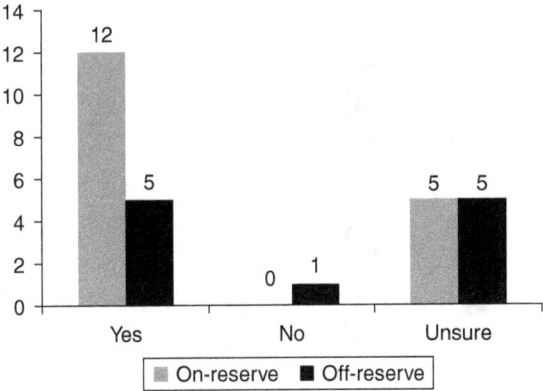

Figure 4.1 Does the Band you are registered to have an existing membership code?

that correspond with Band members' rights and responsibilities; the results are displayed in this section. The responses provided by the Canim Lake community members invoke important considerations for the future. The total combined respondents are 28, representing 17 on-reserve members and 11 off-reserve members. Incidentally, the off-reserve sample size reflects a growth from 85 in 1992 to 156 in 2003. The off-reserve movement had increased by 46 percent. This statistic is important because it coincides with the growth in numbers of Indigenous people moving away from reserves for economic or educational reasons. According to Statistics Canada (2006), "A smaller proportion of First Nations people lived on reserve than off reserve. In 2006, an estimated 40% lived on reserve, while the remaining 60% lived off reserve." In the following section, four questions from the community survey are discussed (figure 4.1).

Discussion

The results of question 5 shows that 71 percent of on-reserve members are aware that a Band membership code exists, while only 45 percent of off-reserve members declared knowledge of a Band membership code. The members in both on-reserve/off-reserve who are unsure about the code are 29 percent and 45 percent, respectively. The on-reserve community members are likely more involved or familiar with the code because they are called upon to exercise their vote in Band member decisions when someone is requesting membership in the Band. Quite often, off-reserve members rarely return to the community to

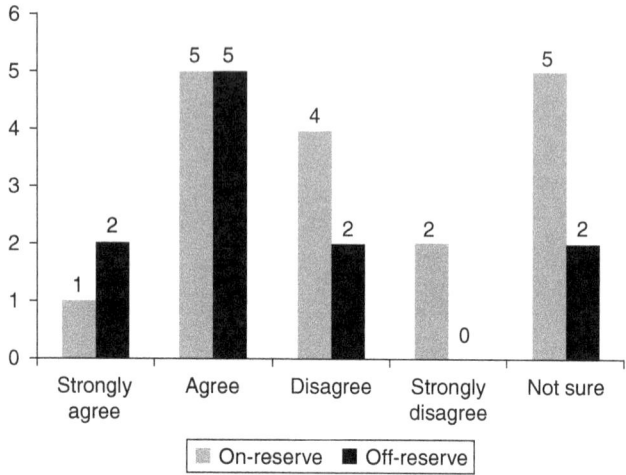

Figure 4.2 The RCAP report says that a minimum blood quantum as a general requirement for citizenship is unconstitutional under section 35. It is wrong in principle and it is perceived to be inconsistent with the evolution and traditions of the majority of Aboriginal Peoples. Do you agree with this statement?

be involved in Band membership voting. Although they are eligible to vote, I assume that members are more aware and involved with the code when decisions are made that will impact them and their families directly.

My question 8 addresses the blood quantum (figure 4.2).

Discussion

This is a complex question and the respondents needed time to dissect and interpret what was being asked. The intent was to find out if the respondents agreed that blood quantum should or should not influence Band membership because blood quantum is not specifically identified as a marker for membership. To determine whether there is a general agreement or disagreement about a blood quantum requirement, I have combined the percentage responses for strongly agreeing with agreeing as well as strongly disagreeing with disagreeing. The on-reserve members were almost split between agreement (35%) and disagreement (36%) in response to the blood quantum statement, while 29% were unsure. On the other hand, for off-reserve members, a total of 64 percent agreed overall while 18 percent disagreed and the remaining 18 percent were unsure. The main purpose

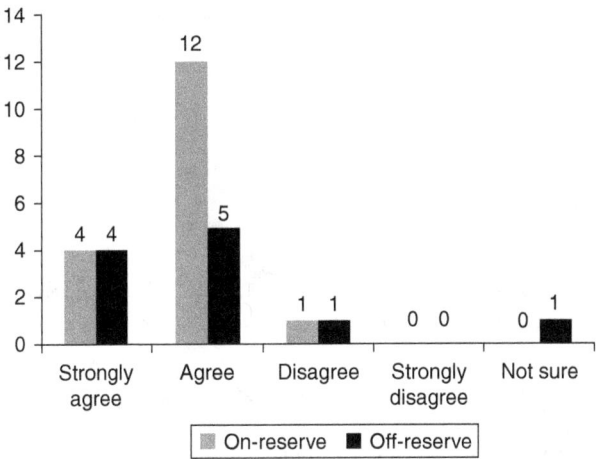

Figure 4.3 The RCAP report says that Aboriginal people in Canada should enjoy dual citizenship, that they can be citizens of an Aboriginal nation and citizens of Canada. Do you agree?

of this question was to get a sense of what members felt about blood quantum. For clarity to readers, the question states that according to RCAP, a minimum blood quantum as a general requirement for citizenship is unconstitutional, which means that requiring blood quantum proof goes against an individual's rights. In addition, it is wrong in principle and goes against Aboriginal traditions. I realize that the question was quite difficult to comprehend and should have been reworded to reduce the uncertainty in the respondents. This is shown in the percentage reflecting how many members were unsure in their responses.

The next question refers to dual citizenship between Canada and Aboriginal nations. Dual citizenship can become an issue should Indigenous communities gain the autonomy to declare the members of their nations as citizens (figure 4.3).

Discussion

When asked if dual citizenship should be permitted between Aboriginal nations and Canada, the results from both on-reserve and off-reserve members are overwhelmingly in favor of dual citizenship. These results are important because Aboriginal communities can only achieve political autonomy within the nation-state when they enjoy

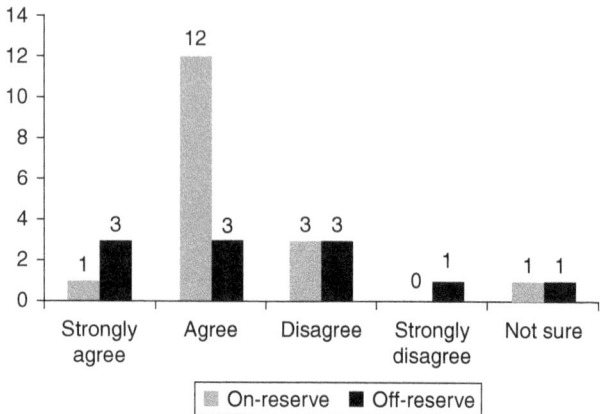

Figure 4.4 Do you think that dual citizenship should be permitted between Aboriginal nations?

important aspects of self-determining authority such as the right to determine members or citizens within their nations. Overall, the results of this question indicate that dual membership is preferred.

The final question refers to the portability of Band membership (figure 4.4).

I find the responses of this question quite interesting because I expected the outcome to reflect how individual Band member's situations could coincide with their personal circumstance. For example, I assumed that off-reserve members would resoundingly be in favor of this option because they live off-reserve due to various reasons, and in many situations both men and women relocate to another Band to join spouses or common-law partners. I anticipated that off-reserve members would find value in dual citizenship between nations. In this study, the on-reserve representation highly agreed with the notion of dual citizenship with 77 percent in agreement, while only 54 percent of off-reserve members prefer dual citizenship.

Analysis

The limitation of the analysis is that the sample size is too small to infer meaning for a test of statistical significance. The findings of the survey did produce some useful and interesting information, as well as it was exciting for both the researcher and the respondents to engage in very important topics regarding Band membership and citizenship at the community level. The findings of the survey indicate that the Canim Lake community members who participated in the study have some knowledge about Canim Lake Band membership code. The overall intent of the survey was to select a random sample of Canim Lake Band members who live on and off the reserve and interview them in respect to Band membership determination and authority. Since Canim Lake opted to administer their own membership, it demonstrates that they are moving toward self-control by including their Band members in Band member determination.

Conclusion and Recommendations

Prior to the Bill-C31 amendment to the *Indian Act* in 1985, there was no departure from the historical legislated influence of the Canadian government regarding Indigenous self-determination. Although this change to the *Indian Act* offered a process for Indigenous communities to determine who the members of their Band are, it was still aligned with the original philosophy of the *Indian Act* and no new arrangements reflected the traditional laws. As a matter of fact, Band membership started with the Indian registry that contained all Indian status Band members up to 1975, as defined in 1876.

It is important to understand that Indigenous communities can only achieve political autonomy within the nation-state when they enjoy important aspects of self-determining authority. The legislated authority of the *Indian Act* denies this because the current legislated instrument retains the federal government's legal authority to decide who is an Indian in Canada.

The major recipients of the colonized mentality regarding loss of legislated identity are the people who became disenfranchised, women in particular. Linda Sutherland in *Citizen Minus* concluded that colonial subjugation of Indigenous people has been internalized. All too often the mentality of the colonizers has been accepted by the Indigenous ruling elite. Sutherland (1995) explains how the elite class has taken on the Euro-Canadian characteristics and approaches and turned these ideals and methods on their own people by maintaining the colonizing mandate to exploit, oppress, and dominate their communities.

I believe that, rather than blaming the leaders in Indigenous communities, it is imperative to peel back the layers and investigate the root causes for the ruined Indigenous lives. Without exposing the problems instigated by the loss of self-identity, both rulers and community members will continue to accept the status quo. In addition to community healing, developing awareness of the colonizing behavior and attitude is necessary. Therefore, an objective of this chapter is to bring attention to the paternalistic relationships between Indigenous people and the state, which support the continued oppression of Indigenous identities. Band membership is a vehicle to lead the discussion in search for solutions to revolutionize the current oppressed mentality. If Band membership determination can be returned in some form to traditional/cultural practices applied before colonization, it is hoped that Bands can move into a state of self-determination rather than one of imposition. The incorporation of traditional and cultural practices into Band membership codes marks a return to a community's tradition of validating identity and kinship, thus moving away from colonization. It is necessary for communities to tell the government that they will decide who their members are as a first step toward self-determination and autonomy.

I conclude that imposed legislation eroded the rights of Indigenous people to self-determine their identity, and this modification caused many Indigenous people to lose their connection with the community and cultural roots. As demonstrated by the Canim Lake community survey results, the members' knowledge of their code varied. Given that 50 percent of the off-reserve members were not aware that a membership code existed is a strong indicator that more education and awareness is needed to ensure that Band members are fully informed about membership codes especially when they participate in Band member determination.

I feel that Indigenous communities will only regain their position within the Canadian state by moving away from a subordinate position to one of self-control. The transformation will diminish the federal government's realm of control and transfer key decision making to Indigenous authority. This will take reversing the colonial mind-set to support the transfer of authority; only with the locus of authority transfer will self-determination exist.

In order to invigorate serious shifts, I believe it is crucial for Indigenous communities to place greater emphasis on what membership meant in their communities prior to colonization as well as exercising manageable Band membership changes. For example, some considerations could be to embrace traditional identity and conceptualize what Band membership could be if a community began with a clean slate. Pilot projects for self-determination of membership may be a viable option to test several possibilities suggested by various sources such as the RCAP report. In order to remain inclusive, establishing mechanisms to include off-reserve members to reconnect with the community is important. I suggest further community-based research to develop communication strategies to ensure community members fully understand their roles in Band member determination along with treaty-making processes. Finally, further research is needed to consider the consequences and outcomes surrounding the impacts of the removal of the *Indian Act* on traditional Indigenous identity. How can this be achieved? Ultimately, it was important to extend voice and agency for the people of Canim Lake and show their views about how they prefer to be identified rather than compartmentalizing externally imposed identity. Band members will recognize their role regarding Band member determination and decision-making processes while negotiating treaties. It is imperative that Band members realize their role in the development of their communities. More work needs to be done to ensure off-reserve members remain part of the community. I recommended instituting a mechanism to include off-reserve members to remain connected with the community by way of newsletters, hosting special events like feasts/potlucks for homecoming, or offering accessible language training. In this way, members would remain connected from wherever they are.

Note

1. I prefer to use Indigenous as my identity marker; it expresses my affinity with people globally who have similar backgrounds. The use of this term is supported by the United Nations. I use other labels such as Aboriginal, Indian, Native, and First Nations when citing authors or referring to policy.

II

Knowledges and Epistemologies

5

"Being at Home in the World":
Philosophical Reflections with
Aboriginal Teachers

Marjorie O'Loughlin

The possibility of building an interface between indigenous concepts, ways of thinking, and practices with mainstream or culturally "dominant" traditions presents a challenge to many societies. In the Australian context, the proposed project shares with other nations a number of historically common features, including a history of the dispossession of the original inhabitants, a lengthy period of colonial control, and massive cultural disruption. As a philosopher working with students of Aboriginal background in a teacher education program over many years, I have been concerned with questions about what constitutes knowledge, being, reality, and other themes, which while familiar to the Western philosophical tradition are now critically assessed by a different paradigm. A useful conceptual peg is that of "being at home in the world" a cluster of ideas generated over many years in class discussions and student journal writing, providing opportunities to articulate crucial conceptions of "country" and "place" central to Aboriginal thinking. Utilizing philosophical and social sciences literature from the mainstream that foreground notions of place and belonging, opportunities are thus afforded for exploration of differences in worldview. Recalling some earlier attempts to explore a possible indigenous/nonindigenous interface, I am reminded of the pitfalls encountered in trying to explain one culture in terms of another. But while my concerns on that score remain, I have been heartened by intellectual developments on both sides of the divide in recent years.

The Contemporary Intellectual and Social Context in Australia

Over the past four decades, the most influential discussions of Aboriginal culture, experience, and contemporary life have been anchored firmly within a framework of a hegemonic postcolonial/poststructuralist orthodoxy, which, among other things, focuses heavily (and in many cases exclusively) on identity politics. Linked closely with these are the most influential versions of sociology of knowledge of recent decades. These emphasize the political and social conditions in which knowledge arises and the manner in which power infuses that deemed-to-be-legitimate knowledge, including, specifically, knowledge of those cast as "other," that is, the former colonized, socially marginalized, and the powerless. Compelling critiques of cultural domination have supplied the building blocks upon which stand analyses that are heavily reliant upon an uncritical assumption of a variety of social constructivist theory. These can frequently be bound up with complex and sometimes virulent forms of politics. One therefore needs to be aware of the sensitivities that surround the contemporary scene regarding the coming together of indigenous and nonindigenous perspectives on knowledge and culture. Many pitfalls await the naive and unwary, not least of which is the tendency to generalize about Aboriginal cultural practices across the entire country. As anthropologists and many Aboriginal people themselves have demonstrated, perhaps more clearly than any other group, indigenous Australians with their various histories can have very different forms of experience in different parts of the continent. Moreover there is at the present time an enormous variability of Aboriginal opinion, much of which arises out of differences in collective living in very specific places. Differentiations in cultural development and diversity of Aboriginal knowledge over a very long time, in remarkably varied physical conditions, mean that there will be differences in the knowledge that various groups may bring to discussion. Fortunately, participants in our classroom discussions appear to be mindful of this in ways that some non-Aboriginal students might not be.

Since people of Aboriginal ancestry identifying as such make up approximately 2.6 percent of the current Australian population, there are also social realities that must be acknowledged when addressing the question of differing worldviews in interaction. Given the diversity of those now living in the country and the avowedly multicultural nature of the society at large, the variety of customs, beliefs, and social organization, not to mention specific brands of identity politics (including those anchored in religious ideologies), mean that the issue is much more complex than a simple indigenous/nonindigenous formulation of its dimensions might suggest. From my own perspective as a certain kind of philosopher of education, acknowledging an overriding interest in matters environmental and ecological, I ask the following questions: Do the discursive frameworks of the cultures we encounter in contemporary Australia render the materially existing world inconsequential in light of the characteristic belief systems of some of those cultures? Are there means by which we might need to critique those belief systems purporting to make that world meaningful to us, but which in comparison with others actually damage the materially existing world in significant ways, perhaps in some instances, by simply ignoring it? If so, what form might such critique take and how might it be generated in a collegial manner? I take these questions to have significant ethical as well as unavoidable social and political dimensions.

Working with students of Aboriginal background to create a space for the meeting of indigenous and nonindigenous philosophical perspectives carries its own risks, even for those nonindigenous individuals approaching the enterprise in good faith. It may be viewed as patronizingly *Western ethnocentric*, thus compounding existing problems. Some may wonder if the process is yet another attempt to steep them in mainstream "Western" norms of thinking, thereby further marginalizing their culture. Is the process of assisting students to identify difficulties that can arise through, say, inappropriate appeals to authority, insistence on tradition and belief over evidence, reliance on false assumptions and untrue propositions, appeals to common practice, hasty generalizations, unrepresentative samples, as well as misunderstandings of key notions such as causality and prediction simply another means of indoctrination? Further, what are we to make of the differences in what is "valued" across cultures, for example, inculcating characteristics such as curiosity and knowledge-seeking in individuals, truth-seeking as a goal in knowledge construction, acceptance or repudiation of sorcery beliefs and practices, questions of ownership of knowledge related to land, and the primacy of loyalty to kin in circumstances of social conflict and so on. A systematic account of these themes is well beyond the scope of this chapter; so I focus here on those deemed most significant by students and myself in our many classroom discussions.

Aboriginal Knowledge

Indigenous knowledge is the generally understood term referring to the beliefs and practices of peoples of non-Western origin which, following the example of the United Nations Organization, some nations have recognized as a fundamental dimension in the lives of indigenous peoples around the world. Australian Aboriginals are an identifiable group having had a very long association with places across the continent. Their knowledge is said to be social, physical, and spiritual in character and was inextricably interwoven historically with the peoples' survival as hunter-gatherers, their sense of being at home in their place or *country*. At the very centre of their worldview is undoubtedly the knowledge of the land, country, environment—that is, in nonindigenous terms, environmental and ecological knowledge. Discursively, Aboriginal knowledge of the land and ecological awareness tends to be situated at present within varieties of discourse, some quite well developed and disseminated but others much less so. In terms of institutional curricula (in schools, colleges, and universities), it may be fragmented across a number of subject areas or disciplines, few of which provide any useful account of their own prior development and epistemological assumptions, let alone that of the more recently incorporated or added-on Aboriginal knowledge. Or, as "Aboriginal Studies," they may constitute stand-alone programs consisting of a core curriculum situated within a specialist unit in a larger University setting or in state school systems. In some circles, the term "indigenous science" is now used to cover a multitude of ideas and more especially practices of bushcraft and/or land management. Because of the focus upon the land or country, questions about the nature of Aboriginal knowledge in relation to science have been foregrounded in different ways with different emphases.

Prior to European contact, Aboriginal people worked *with* their country sometimes emphasizing, at other times mitigating, its characteristic features. As Gammage (2012) points out, mountains, rocks, and rivers were permanent features of the landscape and so had to be accommodated in some way or other. Yet despite this, the damming of rivers or swamps and the cutting of water channels through watersheds could still effect change. Fire was used to replace one plant community with another. The flourishing or not of particular plants and animals was intimately related to the manner in which they had been "managed" and this had to be done at a local level. For this reason, local knowledge was absolutely essential. Each group nurtured its own ground and recognized not only which specific species firing might or might not impact upon but also which individual plant and animal and their totem and Dreaming (Narrative) links were involved. Every meter of ground was deeply familiar and that of neighbors as well. In this way, any requirement for larger-scale care responsibility was grasped and dealt with in an appropriate manner.

Country was in the first instance managed for its characteristic vegetation, and the need to tend or even transplant was a clear requirement. Then there were the animals associated with a particular area. Their preferences for certain kinds of plant life were understood and utilized by Aboriginal people. As Flannery (2012) notes, Aboriginal fire management has been an act of environmental stewardship that encompassed the efforts over thousands of years on the part of particular Aboriginal guardians of country who bequeathed in a long stream of knowing and action that became the very heart of knowledge in the Australian dryer ecosystems. Flannery attributes the survival of those species of animals and plants that survive today to the remarkable care the previous generations have given to those who have come after—Aboriginal and non-Aboriginal. The knowledge Aboriginal groups may have of environment may truly be described as encyclopedic depending on their continued occupancy of a specific place and the nature of their links to it. Their bushcraft includes an understanding of the life cycles of animals, insects, and, in the case of a coastal region or around a river, of the creatures therein, notably fish. This encompasses not only those harvested as food but crucially those animals that are totemic, being integral to beliefs and practices.

A Sense of Place: Country and Kin as "Home"

Personal memory and identity is for many individuals in a variety of societies around the world linked directly to place and to a sense of home. But cultural memory and therefore cultural identity can also be anchored, so to speak, in landscape and physical environment. Probably the most striking aspect of this in relation to Australian Aboriginal people is the age-old manner in which landscape is marked out with narratives—with "songs"—by means of which that landscape itself is "sung" (and danced) into being. Thus the landscape comes to be what it is by the stories told and the lives lived there. Every cultural landscape is established through the "singing" of the land and the enactment of the stories through dance and ritual. Embedded within a particular physical landscape is a landscape of simultaneously personal and collective history, of social ordering and symbolism. In this manner, the stories involving geology and geography cannot be separated from those of the humanizing and enculturation of the very same. As so many scholars have insisted, the European tradition of narrative is most notably connected to time (though not in every instance), and Aboriginal narratives are connected to space/place such that the land comes to be what it is through the stories told and the lives lived there. The narratives of the country as it is humanized or enculturated cannot be separated from its geological features and physical structure (Austin-Broos, 2009; Sutton, 2009; Stanner, 2009; Swain, 1993). Historically, cutting through this were the brutal realities of colonial dispossession of land and the cultural destruction left in its wake.

Some older mainstream versions of Aboriginal cultures have depicted the people as drifting above the landscape in a realm of pure spirituality, separated from the physical world but in an original innocent state of harmony with nature. In my view, this renders absurd the beliefs and ways of Aboriginal people, inscribing them in what is an essentially Western dualistic discourse based in a spirit/matter distinction. Subject/object distinctions and a Western style man/nature separation do not seem to me to have been part of traditional Aboriginal thinking. Stanner (2009) has confirmed this. On the contrary; nonhuman and human seem to have been indivisible for the purpose of practical living. In making this statement, I am not suggesting a simplistic animist underpinning to Aboriginal belief and practice. If I have understood correctly, the material world provides the individual with images of himself or herself, *but that world is not "outside" the person*. Rather it is experienced as inextricably bound up in a quite concrete sense with the embodied individual. It is so because the subject is always "land-construed," as Swain (1993) reminds us, in the same way that all knowledge and everything in the world are so construed. All existence arises from the being of place and all things have people who are related to them. These will include crucially human kin, but also other kinds of being. Life for Aboriginal people has been represented as a billowing of the awareness of place, connecting in interesting ways with some sort of conception of a primordial generality in which self, others, and world are together constituted (O'Loughlin, 1996). And it may be that it is this complex cluster of ideas that can generate what Deborah Bird Rose (2000) refers to as a "Land Ethic" or what I would call an Ethic of Country in which the environment in all of its complexity is treated as a moral community. Of course just how this Ethic of Country might function across an entire nation, especially one of the kind Australia is, would need to be very carefully articulated with much goodwill on both sides and in a critical philosophical frame of mind.

An integral part of the cluster of ideas surrounding the concept of a country is that of kin. Being "at home in the world," that is, having a fundamental attachment to the country, means being in possession of the knowledge allowing one always to be aware of the multiplicity of kin relationships and to know what are the appropriate behaviors required in a given social situation. It has frequently been remarked that for Australian Aboriginal people there is an entire world of kinship or, as a friend has affirmed, "kinship is everything." Thus, the devastation wrought by separation from kin under past governmental policies cannot be underestimated. Kinship obligations are a central feature of an Aboriginal person's life, and it is imperative they be attended to irrespective of where that individual resides even today. Biological relatedness is the basis for all social relationships, and there is nothing beyond this complex web of relationships, though wider friendships and other sorts of connection certainly exist. Thus, kinship underlies practically all social interaction and kinship knowledge. As my Aboriginal students insist, it is therefore indispensible for feeling "at home."

Tjukurrpa—the Dreaming

In conveying the richness of the concept of Tjukurrpa (the Dreaming), the great anthropologist, W. E. H. (Bill) Stanner, said that it could not be understood except as a complex of meanings. Among these, the most important is that of a sacred era very long ago when the natural world and humans came to be as they are, when, for example, specific trees, streams, and other features of the landscape acquired Dreaming status purely by virtue of being located in a place where a Dreaming was active in the past. But though '"past" there is no notion of time elapsing in the Western sense, nor is there a sense of history, as non-Aboriginal culture might understand it. In the example of the Anangu culture, Tjukurrpa is said to be the foundational, furnishing rules of behavior and all of social life. It is referred to as Law—that which will guide the groups' relations of care with one another as well as that of country. It is simultaneously the relationship between people, animals, and plants interacting within the physical features of the land. Tjukurrpa encompasses all the meanings that explain how the relationships will be sustained. But it is also existence itself in past, present, and future, and as such is ontological. Specifically it is an ontology of a place or "country."

Tjukurrpa is omnipresent in the landscape, so that when Aboriginal people gaze upon the land and all life that exists within it, there is for them visual evidence that the ancestral beings are in a crucial sense still existent within that landscape. An example well known across the country and beyond is that of Uluru, the great rock formation with its multiplicity of features and the nearby mountain range Kata Tjuta (the Olgas). These monumental landscape features are replete with stories of the Tjukurrpa and, Aboriginal people believe, will continue to be so into the future. Out of a void and across a world, which in the beginning was unformed and without features, ancestral beings emerged and traversed the landscape in a process of creation. This creation brought into being all of the living species and the features of the country, which song, story, dance, and ritual have ever since described. The activities of ancestral beings are inextricably centered in those songs, which will at the same time include knowledge of how land is to be cared for, including animals, plant life, and people. Such knowledge has been passed down from one generation to the next over thousands of years in the form of Law and under the guardianship of elders. Needless to say, of course, such systems of belief or indigenous knowledge have felt the disruptive impact over time of a colonizing power and the dispersal of people to places not originally their own country.

Anthropologists such as Stanner accord the Dreaming centrality in Aboriginal societies. Along with the idea of kin, it is seen as the most complex yet most elusive key aspects of Aboriginal life. Stanner referred to it as a "subtle conception" and of being many things in one. Deborah Bird Rose writes of the cosmology of the Yarralin people of Victoria River Downs station in the Northern Territory as only being understood by reference to the Dreaming. Approaching her study of the Yarralin communities by way of an examination of her version of the Christian religion (a somewhat simplistic one in my view), she focuses upon Dreaming Law, which according to her informants is manifested as a set of unchanged moral principles established in Dreaming Time—that heroic time that existed in the past and which still exists at present as a kind of charter of events that will continue to occur. Rose's interpretation of Yarralin belief centers on the earth as a living female being who gave birth out of caves to all other living things and who remains in the present the ultimate source of life. The origins of life thus spring from the one mother, the earth. As such *all life forms can be seen as kin*—a deeply significant aspect of Aboriginal belief. As Rose encapsulates it, the essence of Dreaming Law is expressed through myth, song cycles, ceremonies, all of which reinforce the core idea that the cosmos itself constitutes a living system that was so in Dreaming Time and remains so today.

In philosophical mode, Stanner designated the Dreaming "a kind of *logos* or principle of order transcending everything significant for Aboriginal man" (Stanner 2009, p. 58) However, he noted that a philosophy of life is a system of mental attitudes toward the conduct of life, which may or may not be consistent with an actual way of life. Whether or not it *is* depends on how great is the gap or break between what life actually *is* in a given social group and what they believe it *ought* to be. If, as he argued, the *real* and the *ideal* move increasingly in opposite directions as they have done historically in Europe or other places, the choices can be stark. Reality and ideal must then be somehow reconciled or the gulf simply be unhappily acknowledged. But Stanner believed this was not something that troubled Aboriginal people living prior to white settlement. (In the twenty-first century, we of course cannot know whether it did or not!) In his monumental work *The Biggest Estate on Earth: How Aborigines Made Australia*, Gammage claims the profound truth about the Dreaming is that it is above all ecological in its character. As noted above, Deborah Bird Rose supports this view, positing the Land Ethic as arising from traditional Aboriginal practices, which appear to demand that the world be left "as found" (Gammage, 2012, p. 133). The saturation of land and sea with totem responsibilities is undeniably ecological as the responses of my students in classroom discussion tend to confirm. They often refer to local stories about the "letting-be" way of managing fish or other sea creatures or the various land animals, vegetation, and so on, and the knowledge passed on regarding this philosophy as practiced by parents, senior kin, or local elders. Gammage and others see Aboriginal landscape awareness as steeped in religious sensibility while simultaneously being full with environmental consciousness. But all acknowledge that is Tjukurrpa, as ancestral past, which continues to bestow meaning in the land at the present time.

Discussing "the Dreaming" with Students

The problem of very uneven knowledge among students themselves about the notion of "the Dreaming" and associated concepts can be a significant one. The long history of physical displacement of Aboriginal people, the submersion of cultural discourses over many decades, whether by design or neglect, the suppression of local knowledge, language, and other factors have impacted severely upon individuals and their kin to rendering their knowledge piecemeal at best (I am not referring here to Aboriginal peoples who did not suffer displacement and whose culture remains relatively intact). Yet it is always a cause for rejoicing when some can relate knowledge obviously preserved within families and seen by students as an integral part of their lives. Examples include local bushcraft knowledge of fishing spots, reading the seasons for signs of plant growth, and a myriad of other instances of practical wisdom attending daily life. But there remains an absence of a language in which to talk about what are very complex philosophical concepts. By this I do not mean the absence of an Aboriginal language (*that* is a problem for the nation, but not to be discussed here), but rather a large intellectual/linguistic deficit unfortunately encountered in many students—indigenous and nonindigenous—who have never encountered philosophical ideas fundamental to discussions of being and knowing.

One of the key conceptual hurdles to be faced in the attempt at a viable interface of indigenous/nonindigenous philosophies is how to deal with differing conceptions of the past and present, in other words with conceptions of history. Swain (1993) believes that the interpretative tradition of Aboriginal peoples has been cast in spatial and not temporal terms. What we understand of history, as a reconstruction of the past, is entirely alien to Aboriginal thought he and others believe. So Swain advances a hermeneutics of space and not time, as the essence of the long tradition of the life-world of Australian Aboriginal people. In encountering Aboriginal thought, no doubt many in the past have declared the impossibility of engaging in a genuine exchange between a culture for which time and history was the conceptual anchor and that in which the concept of history was merely absent. But that the notion of Being was in some complex form present in ancient Aboriginal culture is I think indisputable. Indeed I follow Swain and others in acknowledging that Australia can perhaps boast the oldest directly dated "hint" of ontological reflection in the world, though we cannot of course know today what those reflections might have been.

Contemporary Nonindigenous Resources for Contributing to the Interface

To assist students in avoiding a bifurcation into Western/non-Western in a conventional history of ideas, it is necessary to think outside of that philosophical tradition so much reliant on a Kantian consciousness illuminating a world full of that which serve as *objects for it*. So in discussion we attempt to focus on the idea of *being* per se as it may appear in Aboriginal and non-Aboriginal thinking. We ask the question not about *how we know* objects (Descartes' and Kant's questions) but what objects *are* or *what is their being* because what an object is cannot simply be reduced to a question of how we have access to it. Therefore, we may need to conceptualize other categories of being. Perhaps we can begin to accustom ourselves to thinking that each "mode" of being can only be addressed in its own terms. And this may require that we take seriously the proposition that nonhumans are to be regarded as actors. All collectives of objects are actors, in that they have a kind of agency, having the power to act. This idea I argue is by no means entirely foreign to Western thinking. On the contrary, we are continuing a discussion about a *subjectless object*, an object-orientated philosophy and onticology, and those interested in what is now referred to by Levi R. Bryant in his groundbreaking work *The Democracy of Objects* as simply a *single plane of being* populated by a great diversity of different kinds of objects including animals of all kinds with humans as just one kind.

Jane Bennett in her work *Vibrant Matter: A Political Ecology of Things* brilliantly articulates a world that is neither fully vitalistic nor wholly mechanistic, characterized by an ontological field that is without any differentiation between human animal, vegetable and mineral! Much earlier, Whitehead had insisted that the kinds of autonomous modes of existence we so often refer to have been poorly depicted as *nature*. Far from being merely a world of *human subject*, he argued, it is one also of the *nonhuman*. Indeed, *agency* is both *human (as animal) and nonhuman*. Whitehead refers to "beings left to themselves" and such that we do not automatically privilege of the human, depicting it as *the* exceptional mode of existence. The most significant issue here for Whitehead and others is that as a result of this privileging of the human, the vital (perhaps, *sacred?*) connection between persons and things has been lost and the latter becomes a mere thing, lacking its own *vital materiality*. Bennett sees all materialities—forces and flows—as having the capacity to become "lively, affective and signaling" (2010, p. 117). The field she has in mind lacks all primordial divisions but is by no means a uniform or flat topography. Her depiction is one of an "onto-tale" in which as in the Aboriginal narratives everything existing can be thought of as alive! I think that such ideas can be valuable in helping to develop the interface between the indigenous and nonindigenous understandings of being. But there is an enormous amount of work to be done if this kind of direction is to be followed.

Conclusion: Prospects for the Development of an Indigenous/Nonindigenous Interface?

Indigenous knowledge is obviously most significant to those for whom it is a part of their lives. But the question of whether or not it should be seen as science is another I matter I think, especially when certain kinds of traditional knowledge can be clearly demonstrated to have a scientific basis, for example, the huge variety of medicinally valuable plants and the many environmental preservation measures practiced by traditional owners in parts of the continent. It is undeniably the case that many of the things Aboriginal people know through their traditional forms of knowledge have indeed been shown to coincide with that of contemporary science examples. But there are others which do not. This means that traditional forms of knowledge per se can never be classified as wholly coterminus with science. Scientific knowledge carries a distinctive status for a variety of complex reasons, including its distinctive methodologies, and because it offers control over the material world in which all of us live. This control has not always been an unalloyed good, and in recent times there has been much criticism of past scientific thinking and practice with considerable justification. But as Flannery notes, any society in the modern world that rejects what science does and how it works is in grave danger. Indeed, science has arguably created modern society, and society cannot be maintained without it.

Science education needs to be more greatly valued by the Australian population at large so that all members of the society may be able to distinguish between genuine science and that of various kinds of pseudoscience.

So the solution is not to simply label traditional knowledge as "science." It is rather to carve out a space for the inclusion of Aboriginal knowledge such that it has legitimate status (as is already the case in some educational institutions and education systems across the nation), is presented systematically and respectfully, yet can also be placed alongside other knowledge traditions with the aim of facilitating a genuine interface. This I hope is the basis for the current initiatives aimed at assisting Australians of whatever backgrounds to become "culturally competent" with regard to Aboriginal culture. Attempting to make indigenous knowledge "acceptable" by claiming for it the mantle of either science or religion as we know them will not result in their becoming more truly valued. Nor I suspect would the mere assertion of the ethical uniqueness of traditional indigenous beliefs do so. So the approach must be one in which such knowledge is shown to be valuable *in its own right*. Such an enterprise requires open-mindedness from all involved, genuine curiosity, and mutual respect.

6

Indigenous Relatedness within Educational Contexts

Frances Kay Holmes

In this chapter, I explore several, but not all, notions of Indigenous relatedness. Historically, notions of capitalism have expanded and pervasive attitudes associated with marketplace ideals have infiltrated mainstream education (Vallance, 1983). I argue that the current state of many US dominant systems is symptomatic of a lacking in relatedness, which is inherent in an evolving market economy. Not only is relatedness missing from colonial models of instruction, dominant forces of industrialization and corporatization have worked to extinguish relatedness from education to achieve homogeneity. Later in the chapter, I will explore excerpts from interviews I conducted with several professors who are Native[1] and have taught from within US postsecondary institutions. Their experiences convey relatedness and its impact within Indigenous settings. I conclude this chapter by considering the potential outcomes of adopting concepts of relatedness in mainstream classrooms.

To explore the notions of Indigenous epistemology, it is important to recognize that mainstream society from the time of invasion has dismissed, romanticized, and reduced Native philosophies leaving academia and Western society in general, with little understanding of the experiences, worldviews, and perspectives of Native Peoples today. My exploration is not the definitive of Indigenous experience, and I do not speak for Native Peoples, a mistake often made by "whitestream" researchers (Grande, 2004). Moreover, my work is not just about the research, it is about deeply considering Indigenous epistemologies, internalizing them, and examining preconceived notions, while recognizing that learning about Native philosophy cannot be a substitute for living it (Deloria & Wildcat, 2001).

Indigenous Epistemologies

Whitestream researchers have often diminished Indigenous philosophies referring to them as "worldviews," in contrast to designations such as "ontologies" and "epistemologies" frequently used to describe Western thought. Watson-Gegeo and Gegeo reference A. Goldman's explanation of epistemology as "the theory of knowledge and theorizing or constructing knowledge" (2004, p. 242). Therefore, scholars who recognize the validity of Indigenous philosophies, and the prejudice that whitestream research creates through reductive terminology, refer to both Indigenous and Western philosophies in terms of ontologies and epistemologies (Fixico, 2003; Kovach, 2010; Norton-Smith, 2010; Waters, 2004; Watson-Gegeo & Gegeo, 2004; Wilson, 2008). I also refer to Indigenous philosophies as "ways of knowing," "ways of being," "Indigenous knowledges," "worldview," and "epistemologies" interchangeably.

In the next section, I define several theoretical concepts related to Native perspectives. Through shared concepts of knowing, a people's sense of reality is acknowledged and reinforced (Moore, Peters, Jojola, & Lacy, 2007). Watson-Gegeo and Gegeo refer to shared concepts of knowing as "deep culture." They explain that "deep culture" is at the

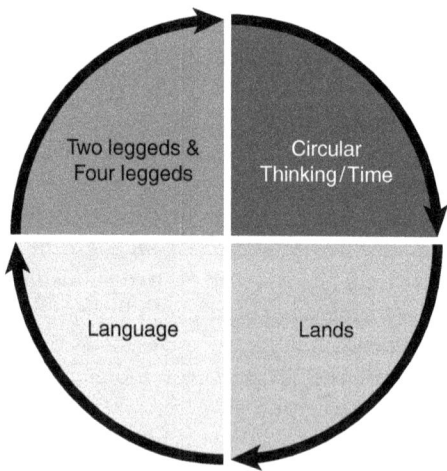

Figure 6.1 Indigenous epistemologies.

heart of cultural identity and "includes ontology, cultural models and epistemology" (2001, p. 241). While on many levels there are similarities across Native nations regarding the meanings inherent to Indigenous knowledges, meaning must be discussed cautiously when doing so in a generalized way (Semali & Kincheloe, 1999). Kovach (2010) stresses the importance of approaching Indigenous research through a tribally specific epistemology; she argues that tribally specific epistemology is the foundation of shared qualities in Indigenous epistemologies. Generalizations that overlook the precedence of local knowledge results in essentializing (Kovach, 2010). Langdon acknowledges that within each nation's definition of knowing, a synergistic and spoken "inter-textually to a similar set of meanings" (2009, p. 3) exists. In the following sections, I discuss four areas of Indigenous epistemologies (see figure 6.1) that reflect the beliefs of many Indigenous Peoples whose origin stories situate them in the currently occupied United States.

Time and Circular Thinking

Native Peoples and Euro-Americans have very different perspectives of time and the universe. Indigenous Peoples raised in a traditional Indigenous manner think and process their thoughts in a very distinctive way, as existence in the world is perceived through people and events. Concurrently, "the world is dynamic and change does occur. However, time is expressed as a cyclical aspect of Space, not separate or contradistinct dimension" (Makes Marks, 2007, p. 138). Native thinking is also visual as it is experienced through the living of it, as well as through observation (Fixico, 2003). Furthermore, Fixico asserts that time operates synchronistically with the rotation of the earth, the change of the seasons, animal migrations, birth, death and rebirth, new as it shifts to old, as well as through awareness of the ancestors who were once here and now exist in a different way (2003, pp. 44–47). The shape and characteristics of a circle is representative of Fixico's explanations, whereby the circle represents a continuity of thinking that spans time and life cycles.

Land

Another concept of Indigenous epistemologies includes relationship to the land. Sacred lands and places are the *basis* of religion for the Indigenous—not an extension of it (Makes Marks, 2007, p. 3). It is this deep reverence for relationship and respect for land and place that is at the core of Native consciousness (Jennings, 2004; Makes Marks, 2007).

Land is often a major element in Indigenous Peoples creation stories. Fixico (2003) explained that his people, the Muscogee Creek, "emerged from the Earth [...] the Muskogee Creeks learned to respect all of the elements for life and they celebrated the harvest of the green corn [...] Should the people fail in their respect for nature and forget the busk ceremonies, the people would disappear" (p. 1). Each creation story is specific to a group of people as well as to a time and place (Moore et al., 2007). There are many references stressing that Native Peoples are emergent from place (Basso, 1996; Cajete, 2004; Fixico, 2003; Wilson, 2008). As such, Native Peoples draw on the power or the "knowing" that they have from that place (Deloria, 2001b), so that relationship with the land is intrinsic to being Indigenous (Basso, 1996; Deloria & Wildcat, 2001).

As stated in the previous section, the circular way of thinking and approaching time for Native Peoples involves a discursive process that produces and reproduces historical knowledge (Basso, 1996; Deloria & Wildcat, 2001). Place is a symbol and placeholder of the past. Simply stated, "place-making is a way of constructing the past, [and it allows] a venerable means of doing human history" (Basso, 1996, p. 7). Place and time are not separate. Land is a container for social construction as well as for the construction of self (Basso, 1996). For Indigenous Peoples, place encapsulates the presence of their ancestors. There is also a sense of responsibility associated with people's homelands as the Creator entrusted them with its care.

Language

Indigenous Peoples interpret their surroundings through "a variety of semiotic materials (gestural, pictorial, musical), [but] few are more instructive than those which are wrought with words" (Basso, 1996, p. 73). However, language is not just a string of words; it has suggestive power well beyond the immediate and the apparent (Basso, 1996). "Language [i]s a sacred expression of breath" (Cajete, 2005, p. 70); it is the symbolic code by which people represent the world, and it is perceived through their experiences. Similar to Native concepts of time, "relationships between elements and knowledge bases [also] radiate in concentric rings of process and structure" (Cajete, 2005, p. 70).

Work in cognitive anthropology has shown through empirical research that "differences in languages do have a significant impact on differences in thinking" (Watson-Gegeo & Gegeo, 2004, p. 241). Indigenous language is not based solely on intellectual perception, but includes all of the senses, the soul, and the spirit. It is filled with meaning. Language is animate as well as animating and is an expression of spirit through sound. Verbalizing thought and awareness brings them to life—verbalization makes thought real. Native languages are associated with land and the nature of language expresses how Indigenous Peoples perceive the world. Native languages are of critical importance as they provide associations that connect today's Indigenous People to their ancestors, which maintains those relationships (Kawageley, 2001). Representing thoughts and notions actually calls into being the power and knowledge of the entity (Deloria, 1999).

Two Leggeds and the Four Leggeds[2] (Peoplehood)

It is often implied within Indigenous language frameworks that the speaker is part of "something bigger" than him/herself; this "something" includes family, clan, nation, and place. The underlying premise is that the individual is part of the larger whole (Jennings, 2004), which provides a sense of belonging and responsibility to those with whom the person shares a relation. The group or "something bigger" that the Native speaker identifies with includes countless members whom a Euro-American would not typically recognize as related to him/her. The difference between the Euro-American and Native perspectives of what constitutes life, personhood, self, and family reveals fundamental differences in approaches to how, who, or what can be known as essential to an Indigenous epistemology. For example, several Native nations treat the children of their siblings as their own children—teach them, provide for them, care for them, and refer to them as their own. Many nations have very deep and complex relations with a specific animal or animals. Some nations believe that in the era prior to the current one, animals walked the planet as a human would and lived among the people. One example of this belief is from the Salmon nations of the northwest coast. Many stories and teachings are built on relationships that occurred during this supernatural time frame and many individuals are able to trace their genealogy back to, for example, the Salmon people.

An important distinction between Native and non-Native beliefs concern how Native Peoples locate consciousness or peoplehood.

Deloria stressed that Native Peoples regard all things as alive, indicating all entities have within them their own power and wisdom (1999). Native Peoples assume consciousness is everywhere: that stones, water, trees, and animals, for example, all have some type and level of consciousness (Deloria, 2001b). Indigenous Peoples also assume that all conscious beings are moral and so must be alive. Furthermore, each living being has within it the possibility of choice (Deloria, 1999; Norton-Smith, 2010). For the Navajo, this concept is called "natoji." The Ojibway refer to "manitou," as that which recognizes the something that *drives*, *sustains*, and *is* the universe (Norton-Smith, 2010, p. 86). These Native concepts that extend consciousness, wisdom, and morality beyond the human to "all that is" can be difficult for non-Native people to grasp. Yet it is essential to recognize what Cordova explains as the force that creates diversity residing in and flourishing in the world (Moore et al., 2007). Knowing "all that is," with awareness of the sources that differ, explains the diversity that is the foundation for local, specific, or tribal knowledges.

The epistemological notions discussed in the previous sections are related and flow from one to another with little delineation; they comprise consistent themes that traverse broader topics. Time → Land → Language → Peoplehood and back again (see figure 6.2). This phenomenon, described as relatedness, is reflective of Native ways of thinking and being. This illustrates that Indigenous knowledges cannot be placed in fixed categories (Stocek & Mark, 2009). Analysis that delineates thought and experience, as often occurs with Western culture and modern science, is inconsistent with Indigenous Peoples' lived experience, as mind, body, and spirit are experienced as a totality (Deloria, 2001a).

Cosmology, ontology, epistemology, and axiology are interrelated in dominant culture definitions, but the foundational aspects of Indigenous relatedness makes these associations even more intertwined. The complexity of interrelatedness is similar to the orientation of Indigenous concepts of time in that relatedness takes on a circular pattern that folds in on itself and is concentric. Associations among time, land, language, and peoplehood are very conjoined. As a result of these linkages, Indigenous research and collaboration must incorporate relatedness so as to be accountable to Indigenous interests. Contemplating Indigenous epistemology supports efforts to understand lessons that mainstream society so desperately needs to learn from Native Peoples.

Indigenous Relatedness 93

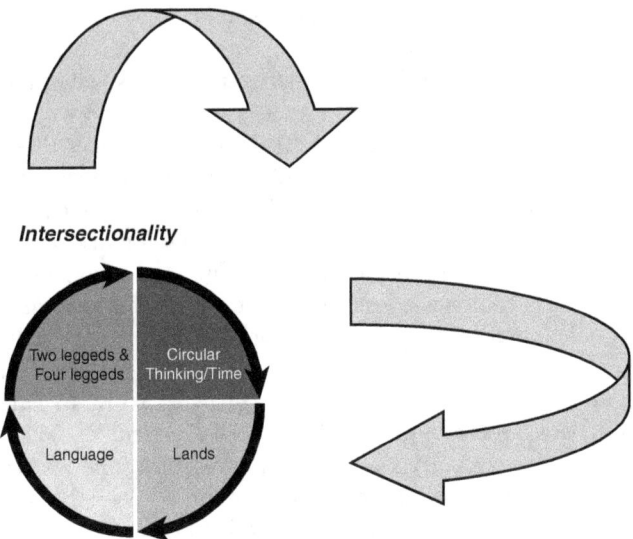

Figure 6.2   The intersectionality of Indigenous epistemological notions: relatedness.

Dominant Forces of Industrialization and Corporatization: Market Economy, Individualism, Dissatisfaction, and Education

When Indigenous notions of relatedness are juxtaposed with mainstream society's business ideals for a market economy, the ideology of American individualism comes into focus. Individualism is "shaped by capitalism, that generates competitive, egotistic and atomized social relations" (Cagan, 1978, p. 228). Recent circumstances associated with the US market economy have left many participants dissatisfied, while notions of corporatization have flowed into nonmarket settings.

For the past 30 years, the United States has watched as populist politics have been "instigated and instrumentalized by monied interests" (Brown, 2011). Society has been dominated by "the contingent faith in the market as the universal solution to all social problems" (Saltman, 2000, p. ix). As such, neoliberal deregulation resulted in a corporate-bought democracy. Recent government bailouts have benefited investment banks brought to the brink by their poorly schemed subprime lending practices. Yet many middle class to working class Americans who held those mortgages were unable to keep pace with the escalating payments that occurred from the resulting "Housing Bubble" crisis that began in 2005 (*The Economist*, 2005). Many workers lost jobs or were forced to return to work because of gutted retirement plans (Brown, 2011). Circumstances that benefit the few at the detriment of many would not occur in a society based on Indigenous notions of responsibility and community. Moreover, Deloria (1999) often argued that Western society has no sense of community as individuals placed themselves above everything and assumed that creation could be used in whatever manner they deemed appropriate.

The pooled predicaments of the working middle class paved the way for democratic uprising, similar to resistance movements that had begun in other parts of the world (Brown, 2011). In Fall 2011, protestors took Liberty Square in New York (Schneider, 2011), which became known as Occupy Wall Street. Representing the 99 percent— the middle class, the working class, and young adults—the protestors were angry, frustrated, and tired of capitalist power brokers corrupting the values and life ways of their country.

On November 18, 2011, Occupy came to the University of California (UC) at Davis. Simultaneous protests occurred at UC Berkeley and UC Los Angeles(UC Davis Fact Sheet, December 2011). Students angry over rising tuition costs, corporatization, privatization, and excessive administrative salaries were met with police clad in riot gear and armed with pepper spray. "Education becomes a matter of enforcement" (Saltman, 2000, p. x), and corporatization has become the new hidden curriculum, only it is not very hidden. Giroux (2012) commented that "higher education at all levels is being radically defunded while simultaneously being transformed into a credentializing factory restructured according to the values, social relations and governing practices of large corporations" (p. ix).

As mainstream universities changed, so too did K-12 education. During the 1980s, education was declared a national crisis. As a result, the Reagan/Bush eras ushered in state legislation that required standardization curricula, increased testing and measurement, while removing considerations of equity from coursework.

Relatedness within Indigenous Educational Settings

Ruth Wheeler Roessel once made this comment to Teresa McCarty regarding her philosophy of education: "Our book is the Mother Earth and the Father Sky." Education should be "based on experience," she continued, with the development of children's language embedded in Navajo culture—"like a weaving where everything is interwoven and forms a pattern" (McCarty, 2002, p. 75). Many scholars assert that the Western model of education is antithetical to the notions of relatedness within Indigenous education as described in the previous quote. Euro-American education was created to position students to compete in the market economy (Deloria & Wildcat, 2001). Indigenous education ensures spiritual growth and then professional expertise, affirming the principle that personhood comes from accepting the responsibility to be a contributing member of society (Deloria, 2001b). Within this paradigm, knowledge and "meaning (subjective) is integrated in the realm or reality of experience" (Wildcat, 2001, p. 15), and knowledge is derived by doing (Cajete, 2004).

Recognizing that it is "important to go beyond even seemingly informed but actually superficial notions of other people's cultures" (Watson-Gegeo & Gegeo, 2001, p. 236), I interviewed 23 professors who are Native, regarding their educational experiences. These professors were from 14 different Native nations and teach or have taught and conducted research from the perspective of ten different disciplines at some point during their career. The interviews occurred over a 12-month period. Individual interviews lasted anywhere from two to six hours. Several excerpts from the professors' interviews demonstrated how notions of relatedness occurred throughout their learning. I will discuss several of those interview excerpts here.

In this first example, Professor Marlon Sherman (Lakota) explained how his brother, Richard, taught him to hunt:

> *Professor Sherman*: He's in the middle and he's a great hunter, he always was. And so he'd take me out, and he taught me different things about patience, and stuff like that out there. When I was in grade school I was his spotter, I was his pointer? And [laughter] I'd scare up the birds and he'd shoot them.
> *Kay*: Wow.
> *Professor Sherman*: Anyhow,
> *Kay*: It's funny though, how I mean, so much of that is…it becomes life skill, it becomes part of who you are. Right? I mean, it's like, you probably don't go hunting so much out here in [laughter] Humboldt County. But, you probably use the patience!
> *Professor Sherman*: He taught me when you [are] hunting antelope they can see forever. Of course, it's how it's out there. It's a lot.…it's flat! He taught me how to sneak up on them on your belly, and of course it takes forever and ever to get there! And you're going

through cactus and stuff that you have to And so he taught me how to hear and not be heard and how to be patient in spite of the fact they are disappearing around you. You know, and so, yeah he taught me, I still use that stuff. (Interview, September 1, 2010)

In this passage, Professor Sherman describes how he was taught to relate and interact with his surroundings, how to be attentive to the situation that he was in. His brother, Richard, taught him patience and the determination to complete the task, the ability to tolerate discomfort, how to blend in, and how to listen. The respect Professor Sherman has for his brother is reflected by the number of times that he stated his brother "taught me." Professor Sherman also stipulated that his brother was a good hunter, another indication of Professor Sherman's respect. Professor Sherman clarified that the lessons were valuable because he "still use[s] that stuff," and most importantly, this experience allowed Professor Sherman to build on the relationship he had with his brother.

Listening and observing, which are important elements of relationship, are also traditional methods of learning. In the following passage, Dr. Donald Fixico (Muscogee/Seminole/Shawnee/Sac and Fox), a professor of Native American History, explained why observing is so important and determining when to observe is also a large part of the process:

> The kinds of learning experience that occurred in my family and the community was really among the Creeks and Seminoles, even though I'd learned something from Shawnee and Sac and Fox because I'm a quarter of each. And those learning experiences were really done by observations, kind of in the old ways. You watch things and how they're done. Then sometimes, at a later point, then you're asked to do those things. (Interview, September 20, 2010)

In this explanation, Dr. Fixico explained the importance of careful observation to learn the skills to complete the task. Similarly, Dr. Edward Valandra (Sicangu Titunwan), a professor of Native American Studies, learned a great deal by observing his parents operate the family's grocery store on the Rosebud Reservation:

> I was aware of the fact that we had this business. I think we all did [referring to his siblings]. And we had a small gas station too. Back then when people really had to like fix a flat, or actually change the oil with the distributors and all that stuff, but it seemed that [the] business

was more of a community service versus "I'm here to make a profit." Stories I hear about my parents when they would do business, my parents would actually...if you'd bread to sell, and people only needed 10 slices they'd actually open up a bag of bread and rather than sell them the whole bread, they'd just sell 10 slices of bread. And rather than say you know, here's a dozen eggs in a carton, I can only afford 4, they'd sell them 4 eggs. And there was a thing called egazu in Lakota means credit. It's a loose translation, egazu. (Interview, October 1, 2010)

At Valandra's Groceries, Dr. Valandra was able to witness the generosity his parents had for community members and the goodwill it engendered as the store took on the role of a "community service." While the store was there to sell goods to the community, it was not at the community's expense. The store was also a gathering place for the community. People would come by and share a cup of coffee, and the Valandra children would travel through and pick up a bite to eat and visit. The relatedness that was enacted at his family's business was just one of many opportunities that Dr. Valandra had to learn about his relationship to the community, to his family, and how to maintain a business that was not at the community's expense, but was instead a means of support.

Incorporating Indigenous Notions of Relatedness within Mainstream Educational Settings

Contrasting the previous examples of Indigenous relatedness to the market economy and its influence on education indicates that the philosophies associated with either mainstream or Indigenous education are markedly different. Given mainstream's current dissatisfaction with its corporate-bought democracy (evidenced by Occupy Wall Street, for example) and the competitive nature of Euro-American education, notions of relatedness need to be incorporated into all classroom settings. However, to be in relation, a person must know who they are. Klug and Whitefield (2003) suggest that teachers explore and recognize their own heritage. I argue that reflection needs to go further. Knowing does not entail labeling, describing, or aspiring to be a particular way. First a person must come to "know" by examining their belief system, contemplating the origins of those beliefs and the associated emotions. This process begins with absolute honesty, requiring that individuals consider and question their humility and generosity of spirit; it is about being truly human. Once engaged in introspection, *then* an individual has a higher capacity to consider other people's truths, contemplate them with curiosity and respect, instead of judgment and fear. Iterative reflection needs to occur regularly to incorporate new information into the process as it presents itself.

Will this in-depth reflection make a non-Native person Indigenous? Definitely not, as Indigenous "epistemologies...move in ways unimagined by most Western academics" (Semali & Kincheloe, 1999, p. 15). However, we will all be able to be more human. Moreover, "social development depends on our collective enlightenment" (Paci, 2006, p. 81). Students can gauge our openness to relate to them. Indeed, Klug and Whitefield (2003) found that teachers' dispositions are key to enhancing relationships with Native students. Therefore, incorporating relatedness into a way of being will allow educators (and individuals) to move beyond superficial notions of worldview, in a context that has a deeper understanding of culture, which will result in a richer, more educational experience for all participants, including both Native and non-Native.

Moving beyond the self and establishing relationships, coursework must be culturally relevant—this requires a "pedagogy recognizing the importance of including students' cultural references in all aspects of learning" (Fenelon & LeBeau, 2006, p. 26). This type of pedagogy would incorporate cultural knowledge, previous experiences, and the interaction styles of diverse students. To facilitate this "pedagogy of relatedness" as a basis for classroom operation, an instructor could include "learning through experience, or the discovery inherent in storytelling about the community, responsibilities to relatives, and [toward] the immediate environment" (Fenelon & LeBeau, 2006, p. 41).

To approach relatedness in the classroom in more concrete terms, the history of this country needs to be understood in relation to Native Peoples. As Grande (2004) indicates, the democracy of this country has been built on bloodshed. Classroom history must include Indigenous perspectives. Moving toward relatedness can only occur with truth as the rhetoric of colonization distances the teacher from the student. Teachers also need to acknowledge the heritage language of the student and understand its association to a student's sense of self. Enmeshed in an Indigenous student's language is their connection to ancestors, land, and relations (Fenelon & LeBeau, 2006). However, any lack of fluency does not indicate a non-Indigenous orientation to the world (Moore et al., 2007).

There must be a paradigm shift in mainstream classrooms whereby teachers become more engaged with their students and work toward a more relational orientation overall. The outcome of these efforts would result in richer and more culturally appropriate interactions with students (Klug & Whitefield, 2003). Once teachers more fully appreciate the cultures, values, and belief systems of their students, it will be easier to understand that schooling *enriches* an individual, and it is not the *foundation* of who their students are (Klug & Whitefield, 2003). Navigating the complexities of Native epistemologies and the ramifications of colonization for both Native and non-Natives is complicated and can be emotionally, intellectually, and socially risky for those who put their all into it; however, potential growth and improved educational circumstances for all students is more than worth the effort. It is in every way conceivable, an excavation of the soul.

Notes

1. In this chapter, I use Native Peoples, Native, and Indigenous to refer to the Peoples and their recognized descendants, whose origin stories place them as the first inhabitants of the land, prior to colonization or the establishment of a nation-state. (I am not referring to native, which can imply that an individual was born and raised in a particular location. Nor am I referring to indigenous, which can mean something that grows (i.e., a plant) in a certain area. The distinction regarding the plurality of Native Peoples refers to the United Nations–formalized acknowledgment of the diversity among Indigenous Peoples the world over and their legacy of nationhood. The terminology I use is similar to the intent behind First Nations (Canada) and Aboriginal. I capitalize these terms out of respect. I avoid using Indian or Native American, unless in a quote, as several Indigenous individuals have told me they found it offensive. Language referring to the original people of the land can be contentious. Some individuals are also insulted when "Native" is used. Therefore, it is always best, whenever possible, to refer to a person the way they prefer, which is typically by their specific nation.
2. This is in reference to Black-Elk's (2000) narrative where he shares a story that includes us two-leggeds and the four-leggeds and the wings of the air and all green things (T. M. Norton-Smith, *Dance of Person and Place* [New York: SUNY, 2010]).

7

Indigenous Knowledge, Muslim Education, and Cosmopolitanism: In Pursuit of Knowledge without Borders

Nuraan Davids and Yusef Waghid

Notwithstanding the flurry of pronouncements about Muslim education in recent years, in surveying some of the major philosophical ideas that constitute the concept, it appears as if three discernable epistemological and ethical practices frame a plausible understanding of Muslim education, namely *tarbiyyah* (socialization), *ta'līm* (critical engagement), and *ta'dīb* (social activism). These three practices have application in multiple areas of Muslim educational life for the purposes of both lifelong learning and social organization, thus contributing to its status as an indigenous knowledge system. Collectively, these three meanings serve not only to teach Muslims about the tenets of their faith, but offer the actual processes through which to socialize Muslims into an inherited knowledge system and how to flexibly use that knowledge in relation to, and in service of, humanity. It is our contention that these interrelated genres of Muslim education have as their morally worthwhile achievements the enhancement of people's sense of rational judgment, criticality, and deliberative engagement—all optimal pursuits in pedagogical settings that can engender moral and social responsibility toward others in humane modes of being and living. But, if the moral worth of Muslim education, as we contend, resides in the moral and social responsibility toward others in society and is not confined to its contribution to a community of Muslims, then what separates and defines the indigenous Muslim community (from which an indigenous knowledge system emerges) from the community or society, as constituted by others of non-Muslim descent in a society? In other words, does the claim to an indigenous knowledge system enhance or reduce its potential contribution to other communities? Alternatively, can we speak of nonindigenous communities at all, considering that their practices are inseparable from their own creativity as human beings? We would like to address the previous question by first exploring the notion of knowledge as understood in Muslim education. Second, by focusing on the purposes and goals of knowledge in Muslim education, we will examine whether the latter is reconcilable with what is commonly understood by an indigenous knowledge system. And third, by reflecting on the individual's moral and social responsibility toward others in society, what are, if any, the points of reconcilability between indigenous knowledge systems?

An Indigenous Knowledge System: Enhancing or Reductionist?

Indigenous knowledge, according to Semali and Kincheloe (1999, p. 3), reflects the dynamic way in which the residents of an area or community have come to understand themselves in relationship to their natural environment and how they have organized that knowledge to enhance their lives. Horsthemke (2004, pp. 32–33) explains that indigenous knowledge is generally taken to cover local, traditional, non-Western beliefs and practices, and frequently also to refer to alternative, informal forms of knowledge, and is unquestioningly employed as an umbrella concept to cover practices and worldviews, as well as theoretical and factual understandings. Although Horsthemke invites us to take critical issue with him vis-à-vis his stereotypically biased and somewhat skewed notion of indigenous knowledge, we consider his explication as a useful framework for our ensuing philosophical exposition of Muslim education as an indigenous knowledge system. The mere association of indigenous knowledge with what is non-Western and grounded in custom does not justify dismissing such forms of knowledge as indigenous as every and any form of knowledge has a commitment to critical consciousness forged through people's actions and dialogical relations with other human beings. Hence, the very notion of indigenous knowledge cannot be confined to a pseudodichotomous explication of Western versus other forms of knowledge. Every knowledge system, we argue, is inherently indigenous. By implication and far more cogent than Horsthemke's depiction, Odora-Hoppers's (2002, p. 8) view of indigenous knowledge is related to something natural, innate to a particular community, and therefore an integral part of culture. However, common to both views is the premise that because indigenous knowledge is innate to a particular community and culture, it is therefore a part of that community—which, to us, raises the question of whether it is the indigenous knowledge that gives shape and meaning to a specific community and particular culture, or whether it is the latter that defines what constitutes an indigenous form of knowledge?

We hold that the construction of knowledge in relation to culture is dyadically intertwined, that is, inasmuch as knowledge of a community is (re)constructed in relation to their ever-evolving culture, so their culture in turn remains open to the vicissitudes of itself and its knowledge system. There are two reasons the aforementioned question is important to us. First, in order to understand how Muslim education is reconcilable with other forms of knowledge, we have to have a clear sense of what is understood by indigenous knowledge. Stavenhagen (1996) says that through its language, a given group expresses its own cultural and societal identity—making language, in some cases, the only means through which to determine the existence of an indigenous people and identity. Second, if we follow Odora-Hoppers's assertion that indigenous knowledge is an integral part of culture, then we have to consider the dynamicity of a culture in relation to the dynamicity of indigenous knowledge. Odora-Hoppers's (2002, p. 8) argument that any dynamic knowledge system has to evolve through the continuance of traditional knowledge and contemporary innovations implies that inasmuch as indigenous knowledge is not immune to either the continuance of traditional knowledge and contemporary innovations, so, too, any conception of culture is by its nature a nonstatic one. In further elucidation of the dynamism of culture, we contend that culture can only be really understood as a phenomenon without end or completion that not only evolves through the continuance of traditional knowledge and contemporary innovations, but is indeed challenged, on the one hand, by contemporary innovations. And because of the unstoppable influences of other forms of knowledge and other forms of culture, the very notion of an unadulterated culture is indeed a contestable one.

In explaining how indigenous knowledge is constituted, Odora-Hoppers (2002) and Semali and Kincheloe (1999) explain that the purpose of indigenous knowledge is the preservation and reclamation of cultural and traditional heritage. Horsthemke (2004, p. 33) explains that what indigenous knowledge hopes to achieve is decolonization of mind, recognition of self-determining development, appropriation, legitimation of indigenous practices, and condemnation of, or at least caution against, the subjugation of nature and general oppressiveness of nonindigenous rationality, science, and technology. Again, Horsthemke raises a disconcerting issue in reference to the "oppressiveness of non-indigenous rationality." What concerns us is that Horsthemke seemingly ignores the fact that rationality cannot exist as a nonindigenous entity as pluralist forms of rationality are in abundance. So the MacIntyrean question would be: Whose rationality and hence whose justice is most tenable and ought to prevail? Surely for Horsthemke it seems as if anything—say reason—that is not platonically or ideally Western ought to be subverted as how can non-Western forms of reasoning be considered as tenable? Of course, we disagree. To dogmatically ignore the depth of interpretation and the receptivity of other than Western indigenous ideas to new reasons beyond mere novelty is to be dismissive of the humility, the ability to listen, showing care and respect for other forms of inquiry, and a recognition that an acquisition of knowledge should be open to take risks associated with most, if not all, indigenous forms of knowledge.

In mitigation, while acknowledging the subjugatory impact of Western knowledge, as well as the inferiorization of indigenous people's practices, Horsthemke (2004, p. 33) nevertheless remains in disagreement with the concept of indigenous knowledge, and its "legitimation," as a countermeasure to these forms of destruction and subjugation. Because he locates his disagreement in the application of the concept of knowledge, he distinguishes between three main kinds of knowledge: (1) *knowledge that* or factual knowledge, (2) *knowledge how* or practical knowledge, and (3) *knowledge of* persons, places, or knowledge by acquaintance. Horsthemke asserts that most indigenous forms of knowledge focus on *knowledge how* or practical knowledge—meaning that different individuals in different cultures possess skills or know-how not shared by others (2004, p. 34). If, as Horsthemke implies, in most instances indigenous knowledge does not focus on *knowledge that* or on *knowledge of*, does indigenous knowledge, then, meet the criteria of what constitutes knowledge, namely belief, justification, and truth? And for our purposes, if Muslim education is an indigenous form of knowledge, then how reconcilable is it with other indigenous forms of knowledge?

A Conception of Knowledge in Muslim Education

While it can be argued that all forms of knowledge are based on reason and experience, knowledge in our understanding of Islam also centrally and critically recognizes the authority of the Qur'an and the life experiences of the Prophet (known as his Sunnah) (Jah, 2010, p. 88). The second difference is that in Islam the acquisition of knowledge is a moral responsibility by virtue of the fact that all knowledge is of, and from, Allah (God) and that morality is attainable through happiness (*s`ādah*), practical wisdom (*hikmah*), and living a good life in service of Allah and humanity (*ibādah*). Consequently, the dichotomy of sacred and secular has no bearing on knowledge in terms of a Muslim's understanding. That is, Muslim education is constituted by two distinct but not necessarily mutually exclusive forms of knowledge, namely *'ulum al-aqli* (knowledge of the rational sciences) and *'ulum al-naqli* (knowledge of the revealed sciences)—that is, the nonrevealed or rational sciences are mostly associated with the construction of knowledge in the natural and biological sciences, human and social sciences, and technological sciences. Knowledge of the revealed sciences is encapsulated in the primary sources of the Qur'an and *Ahādīth* (Prophetic utterances and conduct) and interpretive exegeses of Muslim scholars, known as *tafāsīr*. The point is that inasmuch as revealed knowledge is rational, so nonrevealed knowledge should be considered as rational—there cannot be a dichotomous view of knowledge in Islam as that would create a subversive understanding of knowledge albeit of an indigenous kind. Our nonbifurcation view of knowledge in Islam is premised on the notion that any form of knowledge ought to have intellectual, judgmental, and ethical ramifications. Any pursuit of knowledge for worthwhile ends cannot be cultivated without impermeable convictions, that is, the recognition that things ought to be viewed with some closed-mindedness and that nothing new will ever unfold. Therefore, we contend that our intellectual thoughts ought to be constructed in terms of knowledge encountered through revelation (sacred knowledge) and deliberation (judgmental knowledge), which in turn would invariably make us responsive toward truthfulness (*haqīqah*), understanding (*fahm*), and patience (*sabr*)—all aspects of ethical conduct associated with Muslim education.

To have knowledge, explains Jah (2010, p. 87), is to have certainty (*al-yaqīn*) as opposed to doubt and conjecture. Jah distinguishes between three levels of certainty (*al-yaqīn*): (1) knowledge of certainty, corresponding to knowledge acquired through reason; (2) certainty itself, corresponding to knowledge arrived at by means of observation; and (3) true knowledge or true certainty, corresponding to intuitive knowledge, be it empirical or spiritual. In examining Jah's (2010) levels of certainty in relation to Horsthemke's (2004) three kinds of knowledge, the following linkages can be made: (1) knowledge of certainty, acquired through reason, can be linked to his conception of *knowledge that*; (2) certainty itself, acquired through observation, can be linked to *knowledge how*; and (3) true knowledge, acquired through direct experience, can be linked to *knowledge of*. Hence, while Jah's understanding of knowledge in Islam meets the three main kinds of knowledge as stipulated by Horsthemke, it does not, like other indigenous forms of knowledge in Horsthemke's view, focus mostly on *knowledge how* or practical knowledge—and, in terms of its inclusion of the Qur'an and the Sunnah, distinguishes it from other forms of knowledge. This means, however, that if knowledge in Islam, like any other knowledge system, is indigenous by virtue of its inherent connection to practices constitutive of that particular knowledge system, then knowledge, as Jah maintains, cannot be about certainty. Certainty about knowledge is simply not attainable as absolutism is always evasive in a world where the free flow of ideas is constantly escalating. What we can argue for is that the innate nature of Muslim education's indigenous stance is informed by the Qur'an's insistence on *fitrah*—that is, to see things from its ontological association.

What form of knowledge, then, is constituted by knowledge in Islam? Part of the answer is located in our conscious distinction between knowledge of Islam and Muslim education—in other words, we draw a distinction between *knowledge of* Islam and how this knowledge is enacted. To us, this is a crucial distinction, since, on the one hand, it draws attention to the heterogeneity of any community of Muslims and, on the other, recognizes that communities of Muslims are as susceptible to other types of communities and forms of knowledge, as any other community. Douglas and Shaikh (2004, p. 8) explain that because of the poorly nuanced use of the term "Islamic," which often fails to take into account that which pertains directly to Islam and its doctrines, as opposed to that which its adherents perform in the cultural or social realm, these efforts can more accurately be categorized as "Muslim education" (2004, p. 5). And yet, the diverse heterogeneity of communities of Muslims is not the biggest challenge confronting knowledge in Islam and which Alawi (2010, p. 61) describes as the process of diminishing and diminished Islam.

To Alawi, there are three related aspects, which have led to the reduction of knowledge in Islam: (1) the loss of meaning or nuance attached to key Arabic words, (2) the "modernization" of the Arabic language in reckless abandon of its purpose as both an interpretative tool for understanding the Islamic message and, to a considerable extent, the civilization of Islam, and (3) the drastic overhaul of both the scriptural basis and the contents of non-Arabic languages through which Islamic life is expressed in the non-Arab areas of Islam. It is for these reasons that Al-Attas (2005) maintains that the crisis facing Muslims today is a crisis of knowledge, which is exacerbated by a tension between remaining true to a form of knowledge, as shaped and revealed in the Qur'an and lived through the words and actions of the Prophet ("peace be upon him") (Sunnah), and in entering the global knowledge arena, which is increasingly being shaped by a dominant Western construction—one which Al-Attas describes as inherently secular. To this end, what makes knowledge in Islam unique is its basis of the Qur'an and Sunnah. This distinction, however, should not disqualify it from participating in the arena of knowledge, knowledge production, and dissemination. Even if knowledge of Islam were to be dichotomized (which it is not), this does not mean that knowledge is either secular or nonsecular. Communities do not live and function in isolation, which means that knowledge can never be pure and uninfluenced by other forms of knowledge. What this means is that knowledge of Islam can and might be inherently connected to other forms of knowledge and vice versa as the boundaries between all forms of knowledge cannot be impermeable and exclusive as if multiple forms of knowledge remain unrelated. Our view is that knowledge is permeable and cannot be compartmentalized as independent entities. Perhaps, then, our focus should be less on how and where knowledge is produced and more on what the potential contribution of knowledge can be. For us, any form of knowledge that can contribute toward the good of humanity cannot be considered as nonuseful, regardless of origin or community.

While knowledge of Islam reflects the dynamic way in which community members have come to understand themselves in relationship to their natural environment (Semali & Kincheloe, 1999), integrate traditional practices and worldviews (Horsthemke, 2004), and being particularist to a specific community, and therefore an integral part of culture (Odora-Hoppers, 2002), there are, however, two elements that problematize the location of knowledge of Islam as strictly indigenous. The first one pertains to the notion of an innate environment and whether indigenous communities are ever free from the influences of other communities. Both the sweeping effects of globalization and globalized knowledge have given rise to communities of Muslims across the world, who have little to no connection to a particular community.

Data released by the Pew Research Center show that there are more Muslims in the United Kingdom than in Lebanon, and more in China than in Syria. Of course, this does not mean that an aggregation of Muslims necessarily determines its culture or identity. Rather, an association of Muslims guided by its adherence to laws and traditions is often more influential in shaping the beliefs and experiences of people, which holds implications for knowledge of Islam. While migrant communities are not indigenous communities, it does not refute the claim to an indigenous knowledge. Because Alawi (2010, p. 62) views the integrity of the Qur'anic Arabic as a vital component in understanding the spiritual knowledge borne by the Qur'an, he criticizes what he calls the dissolution of the Arabic language to the point where original meanings have been lost. What he misses, though, is that meanings are flexible and their originality dissipates as contexts change. This means that we cannot ignore that linguistic conventions are determined also by the different contexts in which people happen to find themselves, and surely then the interpretation of the Qur'an and *Hadīth* in sixth-century Arabia will invariably be different than current interpretations. If not, we would be undermining the flexibility and transformation of language and culture itself. So, we do not expect Qur'anic discourses to be interpreted and lived out in exactly the same way, as that would not only mark the end of knowledge construction but also of (Muslim) civilization in particular. The Qur'an itself proclaims to be a text for all times and places, and its (con)textual manifestations will always be subjected to (re)interpretations as Muslims endeavor to live their lives in ethical conduct and obedience to the dictates of its primary sources. Failing to do so would not only render the primary sources superfluous but also undermine the constant possibilities to think anew and to enhance new rebeginnings so necessary for the advocacy of Muslim education.

Thus far, we have explored the conception of knowledge for Muslims as being indigenous to their culture and traditions. To understand how knowledge manifests or ought to do so in the practices of Muslims, we will now turn our attention to the three premises constitutive of Muslim education—namely *tarbiyyah* (socialization), *ta'līm* (critical engagement), and *ta'dīb* (social activism), considered as practices indigenous to knowledge construed by Muslims. We shall argue that such practices offer ways to socialize and initiate Muslims into an inherited knowledge system and how to use that knowledge in relation to, and in service of, humanity.

Muslim Education as Inherently Indigenous

By examining what is constituted by an indigenous form of knowledge, we have argued that any form of education that is constituted by cultural norms and other ethnic practices cannot escape being couched as an indigenous form of knowledge. Likewise, it would be difficult to consider a conception of knowledge of Islam without considering its indelible allegiances to cultural practices informed by both revealed and supposedly nonrevealed sources of education. Moreover, considering that it would be extremely challenging to divorce cultural norms from any form of knowledge albeit of a social, political, or ethical kind, it would invariably be equally difficult to speak about nonindigenous forms of knowledge, and indeed of nonindigenous forms of education.

According to Al-Attas, education for Muslims is the "recognition and acknowledgement, progressively instilled into man [woman], of the proper places of things, in the order of creation, such that it leads to the recognition and acknowledgement of God in the order of being and existence" (1977, p. 11). Stated differently, while education for Muslims is about recognizing God so that the individual might recognize herself, the purpose, ultimately, is to produce a good person, hence the focus is on ensuring that things are put in their "proper places"— that is, those places that can most appropriately represent the human understandings of justification in various contexts. Al-Attas cautions that unless the acquisition of knowledge includes moral purpose and just action, it cannot be called education (2005, p. 23). Education for Muslims, by virtue of its context of cultural practices, can be couched as an indigenous form of education leading to our consideration of Muslim education as that form of education that transcends the indigenous/nonindigenous dichotomous divide. However, and more significantly, our emphasis would now turn to an elucidation of the notions of *tarbiyyah* (socialization), *ta'līm* (critical engagement), and *ta'dīb* (social activism) as ways of how Muslim education is internally intertwined with socialization, deliberation, and just action, as well as its external manifestation in responsible action.

First, when Muslims are socialized into the tenets and traditions in and about Islam, they are taught individually and socially to be attentive to pedagogical authority. That is, one is nurtured through memorization and reasoned thinking to contemplate about the texts one is exposed to and simultaneously become attentive to the diligent implementation of what one has learnt. In a way, memorization for Muslims is a premise toward understanding critically the texts one is socialized in with the intention to serve Allah (God). Emanating from such a view is that *tarbiyyah* aims to produce persons who can think and act in accordance with knowledge as it is both transmitted and constructed vis-à-vis legitimate sources of knowledge. For example, a Muslim is often taught to memorize various portions of the Qur'an and *Ahādīth* (literally, sayings of Islam's Prophet) and then concurrently internalize its teachings that would then be reflected in her conduct in society—a conduct often associated with virtues of good character and morality, which demands acting respectfully and decently in society. Hence, *tarbiyyah* aims to engender a virtuous person—a person with profound morality and civility.

Second, *ta'līm* (deliberative engagement) for Muslims is associated with doing things in community, that is, engaging in deliberation about matters in society that interest them. Put differently, through deliberative engagement, Muslims are taught to be attentive to actions of deliberative kind. Through deliberation (*shūrā*), Muslims are encouraged to seek to nurture relation with others, respond to criticism, trust in the ability of others to act likewise, and be open to questioning and dissonance. Muslims embrace openness, adopt an investigative frame of mind, and become attentive to adaptations and a willingness to take risks. In a way, deliberation aims at engendering persons who act with humility, listen attentively to others, and show care and respect to especially those who are vulnerable in society—that is, Muslims learn to be truly human. Hence, Muslim education has a significant bias toward deliberative action. Yet, paradoxically, deliberation is not necessarily always harnessed in indigenous Muslim education. This seeming reluctance to advocate for deliberative engagement emanates from the unwillingness of several religious authorities to permit the cultivation of any activity that potentially reduces their often self-imposed hegemony. Yet, the prophetic legacy of consultation was extended to listening to the views of women who are often patriarchically considered as religiously unworthy of pedagogical authority. By implication, *ta'līm* (deliberative engagement) aims to bring the ethical person in conversational justice with other persons from all spheres of society who of course transcend the cultural, ethnic, class, and racial divide.

Third, through *ta'dīb* (social activism), which underscores the basis of Muslim education, Muslims are taught through belief, prayer, charity, fasting, pilgrimage, and the exercise of morality that their actions ought to be responsive to societal demands. In advancement of our argument for cosmopolitanism is the notion that the aspirations of a Muslim social activist ought to be endeared toward the cultivation of a virtuous society—one that recognizes the plurality of views of others albeit against one's own as well as connecting hospitably toward those whom we might not always consider as favorable to build a just and peaceful society. Thus, the constant striving of people toward doing acts of justice in service of humanity, including changing unfavorable situations, makes Muslims not only moral in their convictions as they endeavor to connect dialogically with others, but also instills in them a wide-awakeness that will make them attentive to the vulnerabilities of others.

Toward Cosmopolitanism as a Means to Transcend the Indigenous/Nonindigenous Divide

In emphasizing the inextricable connection between the individual and society, Wan Daud (2009) contends that an individual is meaningless in isolation, because as such he is no longer an individual, but everything. This individual, in being aware of his relationship with God and society, can deal successfully with a plural universe without losing his identity. Waghid (2011, p. 7) explains that the emphasis that the Qu'ran places is on achieving justice for all. Regardless of beliefs, it would be plausible to claim that the rationale for Muslim education is the achievement of 'adl (justice) in relations among people. Through its values, Muslims ought to view the achievement of human coexistence and peaceful activities as sacrosanct to their religious aspirations. Therefore, Muslim education cannot be separated from producing persons who enact their roles in every facet of society with dignity and hospitality. By implication as an indigenous system of education, Muslim education is inextricably interconnected with the establishment of human rights, justice, and peace—all aspects of a cosmopolitan education.

The greatest value of a cosmopolitan education, says Nussbaum (1996), is that in learning about ourselves we begin to recognize our moral obligations to ourselves and to the rest of humanity. A cosmopolitan education, through Muslim education, means more than the mere extension of hospitality to another. By looking at ourselves through the lens of the other, explains Nussbaum, we come to see what in our practices is local and nonnecessary, and what in our practices can be more broadly or deeply shared. The individual, therefore, cannot be inattentive to the state of others. Cosmopolitanism offers an open way of thinking about different cultures—which, to Benhabib (2011, p. 9), are not singular and pure but are formed and reshaped through dialogs with other cultures—not unlike the natural evolvement of knowledge and communities. Inasmuch, then, as communities and cultures are always open to the influences of other communities and cultures, we have to question not only the dichotomy of indigenous/nonindigenous forms of knowledge and education but also what purposes these suggested boundaries between knowledge and education forms actually serve. The purpose of education in Islam is to socialize Muslims into an inherited knowledge system, so that knowledge can be used in relation to, and in service of, humanity. It is within this conception of *service to others* that ought to serve the basis of any knowledge form—indigenous or not, and it is precisely this conception that offers reconcilability not only to all forms of knowledge but all forms of humanity. Approaching the forms of knowledge in terms of unnaturally constructed borders separates all of us from what ought to be our common ethical knowledge, which is that of humanity and how best to preserve that in its entirety, while simultaneously being cognizant of its particularities and peculiarities.

Finally, we have argued that Muslim education is uniquely indigenous in the sense that its aspirations are related to the cultivation of virtuous persons in society who can engender change of significant proportions ranging from creating conditions for ameliorating the plight of the vulnerable to conditions that make all human persons attentive to one another with the hope of enhancing mutual coexistence, social cohesion, and respect for dissonance. For Muslims, virtue is both intellectual (reasonable and emotional) and moral (ethical), which we acquire through action and experience. The acquisition of (indigenous) knowledge is identifiable with all pluralist communities with the aim to serve humanity. The corollary of such an understanding of indigenous knowledge (re)construction is associated with the cultivation of justice in society—that form of moral excellence that ought to characterize all forms of human engagement as communities endeavor to connect with themselves and others.

8

Curriculum Leadership Theorizing and Crafting: Regenerative Themes and Humble Togetherness

Vonzell Agosto, Omar Salaam, and Donna Elam

This chapter illustrates how indigenous concepts, philosophies, and traditions were introduced into a doctoral course on Curriculum Theory and undertaken by students to inform their development of cultural and curriculum leadership. A central activity in the course was clay-molding. Qualitative data in the form of personal reflections and student work samples (pottery, book review, essay) are accompanied by academic literature to provide insight into the question of how indigenous concepts support sensemaking in the development of curriculum leadership that is culturally emancipatory. Personal reflections on the course from the professor and the students are extended by a critical friend who contributes through the concept of culturally competent leadership.

Curriculum Leadership Creation: A Cultural Process and Product

Culture-based leadership (Agosto, Dias, Kaiza, McHatton, & Elam, 2013), understood as culturally emancipatory leadership, is concerned with the cultural hegemony of Western European and its contribution to cultural imperialism in education. Cultural imperialism "involves the universalization of a dominant group's experience and culture, and its establishment as the norm" that both marks the dominated group as remarkable (Other, deviant beings) and relatively invisible (Young, 1990, p. 59). Being treated as if invisible is echoed by Taliaferro-Baszile (2010) in her discussion of Curriculum Theory through the metaphor of sight (hypervisibility/invisibilty) (also read by students in the course) and works by Ralph Ellison (1952) and William Pinar (1975). In contrast to cultural imperialism is the term cultural emancipation, which has been associated with forms of critical multiculturalism (Vavrus, 2002). However, the term cultural emancipation may not include the analysis of Eurocentric hegemony over school and knowledge construction, leading some (e.g., McCarthy & Willis, 1995) to prefer the term critical emancipatory multiculturalism. Our term of choice, culturally emancipatory leadership, is grounded in critical and multicultural perspectives.

A critical theoretical framework linked to culture is TribalCrit Theory. Of its nine tenets, two are most relevant here: the recognition that colonization is endemic to society and the interrelationship between knowledge, culture, and change (the ability to recognize change, adapt, and move forward with the change) (Brayboy, 2005). Brayboy, focusing on American Indians in particular, describes three interrelational forms of knowledge addressed by TribalCrit: (1) cultural knowledge as (a) an understanding of what it means to be a member of a particular tribal nation with particular traditions, issues, and ways of being and (b) knowing what makes an individual a member of a community; (2) knowledge of survival or an understanding of how and in what ways change can be accomplished individually and collectively; and (3) academic knowledge that is acquired from educational institutions. He asserts that cultural and academic knowledge can be instrumental in building knowledge of survival. Brayboy's (2005) articulation of TribalCrit reminds us that culture, knowledge, and power are in a dialogical relationship and that education and government policies have tended to support assimilation rather than emancipation from cultural imperialism.

Leadership is a work in progress that "has the power to inspire, transform, heal and connect us to something larger than ourselves" (Klein & Diket, 1999, p. 25). However, as Boske (2011) notes, leaders are traditionally not prepared to transform schools but instead are taught to see themselves as system managers who are not expected to deepen their empathic responses and connections with school communities. The field of management outside of schools has given some attention to leadership as an artful experience rather than a technocratic process (Klein & Diket, 1999; Sutherland & Gosling, 2010). While literature at the nexus of culture and art is more prominent with regard to the K-12 students and teachers (e.g., Reif & Grant, 2010), it is less prominent for leadership preparation (e.g., Diamond &

Mullen, 1999). Approaches used thus far include poetic houses of dialog (Grisoni & Kirk, 2006), painting (Ridenour, 2004), and a combination of artistic forms (Boske, 2011). Taylor and Ladkin (2009) analyzed several accounts of arts-based approaches to leadership development and identified four distinct processes (skills transfer, projective technique, illustration of essence, and making) that promote reflection, inquiry, emotional intelligence, and meaning making. Meaning making was associated with fostering a deep experience of personal presence and connection (Taylor & Ladkin, 2009, p. 66). Social connections can foster situated learning through communities of practice (Lave & Wenger, 1991). A community of potters is a community of practice as pottery production is embedded within larger cultural systems (Huntley, 2008).

The Creation of Curriculum Theory

The Curriculum Theory course was developed during 2011–2012 and taught (by Agosto) in the summer of 2012 over six weeks on five Saturdays from 8am to 5pm. Fourteen of the students were in their first or second year of study toward a doctoral degree in educational leadership, and one was graduating at the end of the course with a degree in education measurement and evaluation. The 9 women and 6 men represented various racial and ethnic groups: African American (4), Latino (1), Asian (1), White, not of Latino descent (9). The contextually based Otherness of the assistant professor as a multiethnic, -racial, -sexual, -linguistic woman was diminished by the diversity within the class as the students' array of positionalities mirrored hers in several ways.

The central foci for the course were (1) curriculum theories (systematic, existentialist, pragmatic, radical, deliberative) as described by Null (2011), (2) concerns for practice including deliberation and sensemaking using aesthetic sensibilities, and (3) insights into the state of the field of curriculum studies (i.e., the call for its browning by Gaztambide-Fernández & Murad, 2011). The purpose of the course was to support students to serve as public intellectuals (Wraga, 2006) whose curriculum leadership (Ylimaki, 2012) would be informed by curriculum cultures (Joseph, 2011). In addition to clay-molding, students engaged in dialog with guest speakers, reflected on media (documentary, photographs), critically analyzed texts (i.e., academic research and scholarship, practical artifacts from the field), facilitated discussions, and wrote (i.e., curricular/pedagogical letters, book reviews, personal reflections, conceptual papers). Among the books approved for review, only one student (Salaam) chose the book about indigenous perspectives, titled *Integrating Aboriginal Perspectives into the School Curriculum: Purposes, Possibilities and Challenges* by Kanu (2011).

Indigenous Perspectives

Two of the curriculum cultures offered by Joseph (2011) helped to set the tone of the course: (1) developing self and spirit, and 2) sustaining indigenous traditions. This assigned course reading was completed for the first day of the course. The students received an orientation to the course that included the course goals, performance expectations, and indigenous concepts: Sankofa, Ourobouros, and the Ubuntu philosophy (Msila, 2009; Swanson, 2009).

Sankofa: Go Back and Get It

Among the Akan-speaking people of Ghana, Togo, and Cote d'Ivoire in Africa, Sankofa is a leadership practice represented by the Adinkra symbol: a bird looking back to its tail feathers. It communicates the idea that the best way to secure one's future is to spend time in the present learning from the past. This idea is captured by the phrase, go back and get it. According to Hotep (2010), Sankofa "is well-known in the national African centered community as a wisdom principle, Adinkra symbol, and rationale for studying Black history" (p. 15). Sankofa also carries the expectation that learners will seek the wisdom of teachers or elders. Hotep (2010) claims that as a leadership-followership principle, Sankofa is largely unknown in Black leadership circles. The Kwame Ture Leadership Institute is guided by the principle of Sankofa and the broader frame of the African-centered leadership-followership paradigm. When translated into leadership practice, Sankofa "means deliberately and methodically researching indigenous African societies and their diasporic expressions for leadership-followership precepts, principles, practices, theories, patterns, motifs, icons, institutions, rituals and ceremonies we can adapt for contemporary usage" (Hotep, 2010, p. 13).

Ourobouros: Regeneration

Similar to the image of Sankofa is the symbol Ourobouros, which is generally depicted by a serpent or dragon eating its tail. This cultural motif spans many cultures and reflects the achievement of psychic integration and the unification of opposites (Berman, 1981). Other meanings attributed to the Ourobouros include self-reflexivity and regeneration. Shaetti, Ramsey, and Watanabe (2008) argue that like the Ourobouros, personal leadership principles of mindfulness and creativity come together to nurture our capacity for presence and vice versa and thereby reflects intercultural leadership. Warner and Grint (2006) found that leadership among American Indians is more often discussed as a sphere of influence rather than a role. Also, the importance of the circle in the Tahdooahnippah/Warner American Indian Leadership Model is depicted by overlapping rings (circles) to represent interconnected forms of leadership (Elder, the Role Model, and the Social Scientist). At the center is the Tekwanipapv (the one who speaks for us at all times).

Ubuntu Philosophy: Humble Togetherness

Ubuntu philosophy reflects what Swanson (2009) calls a *humble togetherness* that is "centered on an accepted communal obligation to justice rather than 'individual rights'" (p. 11). According to Tutu (1999),

> A person with Ubuntu is open and available to others, affirming of others, does not feel threatened that others are able and good, for he or she belongs in a greater whole and is diminished when others are humiliated or diminished, when others are tortured or oppressed, or treated as if they were less than who they are. (p. 31)

Ubuntu philosophy has been described as an African worldview of humanism that can support the reduction of violence in schools (Msila, 2009) and heal wounds and scars (wa' Thiongo, 2009). These concepts were introduced at the beginning of the course but were not explicitly reintroduced.

Professor's Perspective: Clay-Molding

In the Curriculum Theory course, I introduced doctoral students to the complicated conversation of curriculum theory (Pinar, 2011) in connection to schooling and cultural imperialism (i.e., cultural representation, epistemic violence, linguistic genocide). I risked trusting that art making (clay-molding more specifically) would help students articulate their thoughts visually (Boske, 2012). Jacobs (2010) encourages educators to go out of their way to support learners in taking risks in artistic expression and when creating ideas and curriculum making. She claims that an intellectual, as a creative thinker, shapes ideas just as sculptors do when they throw clay on the table and experiment with forms and materials. I provided each student with a small block of clay and a few crafting utensils (dental picks, forks, wire). I asked them to mold the clay to reflect their thinking about the issue they were addressing in their curriculum leadership letters.

> Discussing the art object rather than discussing the issue directly provides a certain resistance and detachment from emotionally charged issues…The projective technique process then provides access to the multiplicity of meaning makings that exist within an organisation in a way that allows the non-logical, contradictory, and emotionality to be part of that knowing. (Taylor & Ladkin, 2009, p. 65)

I had no experience molding or sculpting clay, and only one student claimed to have minimum experience. To begin, I told the students that the campus potter said that people typically start by pinching clay to form a basic pinch pot. However, the exercise from the previous class session on thinking through an issue using theory using the metaphor of the problem tree's roots versus a rhizome (rhizomatic thinking) was coupled with an article by Tuck (2009) on how theories and indigenous worldviews can run counter to one another.

> I raise this not because I believe that the rhizome and Indigenous worldviews need to be reconciled (a futile task) but rather to make explicit the ways in which theory use is complicated. This is not a rare instance; it happens at every nexus of theory, experience, culture, and memory. In pottery, when bringing two pieces of formed clay together, the potter makes scratches, or "roughs the clay" on each piece at the locations they will be joined. In theory use too, we rough the clay in order to hinge unlike, unfired, textures and shapes. (pp. 118–119)

Pottery that was insufficiently "roughed" fell apart under the heat of the kiln. I salvaged most pieces and glued them back together. Though the students had only roughed the surface of their work as potters when the course ended. The following personal reflection (by Salaam) describes how indigenous perspectives found expression beyond the course.

Student Perspective: Culturally Emancipatory Curriculum Leadership

I attended a high school in the inner city environment of Flint, Michigan, an Historically Black College/University (HBCU) at Bethune-Cookman College, and am now a PhD student. I have taught music to severely cognitively disabled students, driven them to performances by school bus, been a high school band director, and served as an assistant principal before moving to Asia to teach music. I was blessed with a parent who taught me from aboriginal perspectives. My mother always reminded me of my ancestors and their importance in the making of my identity. However, the influence of traditional schooling was also powerful. It can be an overwhelming force upon those who do not have the constant reminders that my mother presented to me.

After years of schooling and through reading *Integrating Aboriginal Perspectives into the School Curriculum: Purposes, Possibilities and Challenges* by Kanu (2011), I have come to realize that what I have been missing and longing for in my schooling was the opportunity to learn from aboriginal perspectives: perspectives that are not solely Western European. Being formally educated from a strictly Western(ized) Eurocentric perspective has both directly and indirectly diminished my feeling of worth in who I am as well as who I could be. By what I have just stated I have partly answered the following questions presented by Dorothea Susag (2006) in the preface of the book by Kanu (2011).

> If the experiences in our public schools have the power to change the stories of children's lives, what happens to those who don't hear the stories of their own people? And if children do learn stories about their lives, what happens when their teachers and texts regard those stories as inferior, representing wrong values, and representing inadequate means for survival? What happens to children whose public education is rooted in an alien culture? What do they learn to value, what do they learn to reject, and what do they learn about survival when they don't ever hear or read about the suffering, loss, and endurance of their people? How do they establish positive identities about themselves when voices within their culture are ignored, twisted, and suppressed, and when voices outside their culture decide who these young people are and who they should become? What happens to the relationships among children from differing cultures within classrooms? (ix)

One perspective that stood out in my mind comes from an assigned reading by William Watkins (1993). In his discussion of Black curriculum orientations (functionalist, accommodationist, liberal, reconstructionist, Afrocentrist, and Black Nationalist), he explained that they "are the result of views evolving from within the Black experience, as well as from views that have been imposed from without" and related to the dynamics of colonialism, American apartheid, and discriminatory exclusion " (p. 322). The perspectives of Susag, Kanu, Watkins, and my mother remind me of the value of teaching children from multiple ethnic and cultural perspectives. In group discussions, it was inspirational to have supporting evidence for statements I would have made regardless of reading *Aboriginal Perspectives*, but the empirical evidence meant so much more to my Curriculum Theory classmates.

Months after the conclusion of our course, I came to realize how cultural perspectives such as those from the indigenous philosophy Ubuntu or traditions like Sankofa and Ourobouros (as well as Harambee, meaning all put together or working together for a common purpose) were entwined across our coursework. I will provide a few explicit examples of how I have experienced these indigenous philosophies and principles in the context of the course and beyond. First, we (as a class) went in search of the wisdom of our teachers/elders—as is in the leadership-followership principle of the Sankofa—when it came to asking questions of our assigned instructor we had to "go back and get it" and we took advantage of asking many questions of guest speakers who shared their experiences both nationally and internationally related to education and curriculum. Their visits had us digging deep for more answers, and their experience gave us all a better understanding of the functions of education and curriculum within local, national, and international systems of teaching and learning.

Second, I found myself mentioning "the snake eating its own tail" more than a couple of times when pointing out the connections between what we see occurring now in education and how it relates to, or is similar to what has occurred in the past. In such instances of referring to the symbol Ourobouros, I did not connect my thoughts with indigenous philosophies and traditions. I was simply making a connection between what had been introduced to us in the first class with what I was sharing. This is an example of how, even though the Ourobourus symbol was not reiterated in our class, the introduction and explanation of the philosophy of "regeneration" alone made it possible for me to connect, then later reconnect to it.

Third, "humble togetherness" as an interpretation of the Ubuntu philosophy is strongly exemplified in the group of doctoral students I became a part of since our first course (Curriculum Theory was the second). Even though we are not technically a cohort, we operate and function as a team in that we all work together, not only accepting each other's differences and varied views but also using these differences and varied views to benefit the growth, development, and support of each individual within our group. For example, when I was the only one from the group to enroll in the Thursday night section of a required course, I struggled. After the first half of the course, I sent an email to everyone from our group/cohort attending the Tuesday section inviting them to a study session. This outreach resulted in a large gathering on a Saturday morning spending hours working in concert on our individual assignments. "Humble togetherness" is not something that anyone in our "cohort" would likely connect to the Ubuntu philosophy, yet this translation of it was completely evident that morning.

Critical Friend Perspective: Culturally Emancipatory Curriculum Leadership

My (Elam) entrance into the world was one of hope, acceptance, and belonging into a cultural mixture of Caribbean, Irish, African American, and Cherokee descent. As the family story is told, I was embraced at birth by being placed in the arms of my Antiguan grandfather who held onto his last days on earth awaiting my arrival. It was the beginning of a foundational experience for later understanding the three guiding principles of Sankofa, Ourobouros, and Ubuntu philosophy. My acceptance into the education profession was also driven by a translation of the guiding concepts as seeking wisdom from the elders, regeneration, and humble togetherness. In general, building relationships as a leader becomes essential for the foundation of professional development and helps create a safe venue for expanding professional growth, competence, knowledge, skill building, and confidence. My reception into this team of authors as a critical friend relates closely to what was described about my arrival into the world and workforce.

Although there can be multiple aspects to the role of a critical friend, for the purpose of this chapter, I will focus my role on discussing the theoretical and practical matters in the reflections of the professor (Agosto), student (Salaam), as well as my research and professional experience. The collective reflections offer viewpoints with respect to the development of curriculum leadership that is culturally emancipatory regarding the delivery of content of the coursework, impact on the doctoral students, as well as strategies to inform research and the professional development of administrators. The Curriculum Theory course positioned leadership as a cultural process and product that could be understood and reflected through a visual representation. Salaam's reflections suggest that adult learning strategies allowed the learner to digest and dissect the elements of the theory introduced and put it into practice. It was evidenced in his reflection that he made personal meaning and operationalized the new concepts and terms. His reflection indicates how he is making connections between these concepts and the daily experiences he faces with his fellow students beyond the course.

The more I work in professional development, the more I realize that I need to be reminded to safeguard effective teaching for adults. This was an unanticipated, yet beneficial outcome for me as a critical friend in this project. Feeling safe to explore and respond to the thinking of Agosto and Salaam enabled me to reflect on my practice and urged me into the posture of learner. I am reminded that the roles of professional development provider and critical friend emphasize the responsibility of creating safe learning environments, encouraging future leaders to take risks, and shaping their personalized professional philosophies. It appears that regardless of one's position in this dynamic, all stakeholders involved in the exchange of these indigenous principles and philosophies found benefit in the context of their cultural leadership development.

Conclusion

The Declaration for the Rights of Indigenous Peoples (UN 2007) "emphasizes the rights of indigenous peoples to maintain and strengthen their own institutions, cultures and traditions, and to pursue their development in keeping with their own needs and aspirations." The course presented curriculum issues that limit the rights of indigenous peoples and other minority cultural groups across from experiencing culturally emancipatory education. To incite students to think about curriculum leadership as a force of transformation, they were asked to critique the movement to educate Pakistani girls, analyze the presence of multicultural literature in summer reading lists of local high schools, view a documentary on the global influence of American schooling on the divide between cultural backgrounds and aspirations, and read news about protests in Japan over the national curriculum. The course challenged the dominant discourse of neutrality in school leadership they had encountered in their schooling backgrounds and leadership practice. Resurfacing issues of cultural imperialism (i.e., linguistic genocide, assimilation) in schooling urged students to imagine curriculum leadership as culturally emancipatory.

Clay-molding served as a process for thinking through issues and an analogy for curriculum making and theorizing about curriculum leadership as a transformational/creative process that can support the decolonization of "colonial-blind" (and related color-blind) discourses (Calderón, 2011, p. 110), and the deterritorialization of educational institutions. O'Sullivan (2007) describes art as a creative deterritorialization into the realm of affects.

> Art then might be understood as the name for a function, a magical and aesthetic function of transformation, less involved in a making sense of the world and more involved in exploring the possibilities of being in—and becoming with—the world. (p. 51)

Creating pottery (conceptualizing, molding, roughing, glazing) required students to touch earth with their senses and sensibilities. The request to create an artifact reflecting the issues they were grappling with challenged them to (re)connect their thoughts and actions to a natural resource. Clay-molding was an opportunity to craft pottery while theorizing back (Tuck, 2009) on dominant narratives about the purposes to which we put education, curriculum, and leadership.

Indigenous concepts served as regenerative themes to inspire rather than as objectives to be acquired. Student A was inspired to craft a pyramid standing, a sculpture that reflected his interest in finding balance between types of leadership (pragmatic, existential) he would embrace and understandings of his cultural heritage. Of the pyramid he wrote, "This majestic figure also highlights the scientific, spiritual, and physical prowess of the African people. When I see a pyramid I am proud to be of the African diaspora." The infusion of indigenous knowledge helped to build community and creativity, and challenge seemingly objective (value free) notions of curriculum, pedagogy, leadership, and education. Student B submitted a paper on redemptive curriculum and discussed the possibilities and challenges of infusing the Ubuntu philosophy into school leadership practice. He and classmates commented that his cardholder took on the appearance of Buddha. Perhaps their ongoing study will continue to reflect the values presented in the indigenous concepts and support culturally emancipatory curriculum leadership.

Culturally emancipatory leadership begins by (1) recognizing the gaps between Western models of leadership and leadership models developed within or responsive to various cultures and cultural traditions and (2) relinquishing the singular use of traditional Western lenses for identifying and defining leadership characteristics (Warner & Grint, 2006). The indigenous concepts of Sankofa and Ourobouros, both depicted by images that are circular without final points of origin or destination, suggest renewal, unity, and regeneration. Such concepts, when roughed with concepts of leadership, can provide what Deleuze and Guattari (1987) call a *ritournelle*. The *ritournelle* is a "catalytic function" that "enables new things to emerge from existing ingredients." We might do, as Warner and Grint (2006) suggest: "Go back and reconsider what we mean by leadership and in doing so challenge the imperialist foundations of 'American' ways of leadership" (p. 226). The idea of culturally emancipatory (curriculum) leadership has been planted with these students and whether it propagates in them, as rhizomes or roots, remains to be seen.

9

Taking an Indigenist Approach to Research: Engaging Wise Ways of Knowing toward a Vision of Stl'atl'imicw Education

Joyce Schneider, Kicya7[1]

Beginning in a Good Way

Noninterference

She was only ten years old but she already knew much about the world. She knew she was loved, safe, that there was a place for her, and that she had much to contribute. All the wisdom of her ancestors was being passed on to her through stories, dreams, and traditions that engaged her mind, body, and spirit. She spent her winter days listening to the stories of her Ucwalmicw people, and with each telling she understood more of what they had to impart. Many hours of the day were spent watching her skícza7 and sta7 do the work she herself would practice through play, and she had responsibilities that were fitting for a ten-year-old, for example, returning to the river the buckets of zúmak insides collected by the women who so expertly cleaned this main source of life. She took pride in knowing what was expected of her and why it was important that she fulfill those responsibilities. She enjoyed the singing, drumming, and dancing that taught her about the connections between the clans—about honor, respect, and sharing, as well as the importance of laughter and enjoying the company of others. She participated in the rituals that built discipline and gratitude, routines like rising on each new day to give thanks to the four directions for another day of life and then proceeding to honor that gift through the entire day.

She was exposed from a very young age to the importance of the land, the plants, air, animals, and waters that gave and sustained her and her family's and community's health and well-being. She knew which plant life was to be picked and which would make her sick if touched or ingested. She had a sound understanding of what to harvest when and how, and she enjoyed digging roots with the sta7 in the early spring. She watched the animals for signs of impending danger or inclement weather and she valued the wisdom and strengths of each species as it informed how she and her community would live off the land and with each other. For this reason, she and her people gave thanks to each plant and animal that gave itself for the survival of her community, and they reciprocated by offering gifts, by using every part of the plant or animal, and by returning to the earth those small portions that could not be utilized. No part of any gift was ever wasted.

Her connections to the territory were woven into the story of their sacred sqwem—the story that told her where she came from, what her connections to ancestors, territory, and neighboring peoples was and it told how to walk a good path in harmony with all. She understood and honored the responsibilities and history that came with carrying the name the elders gave her not long ago and with speaking the language that carried the wisdom of ancestors from time immemorial.

Knowledge was a gift left at her feet to take up and carry with her and she knew that understandings would come to her when they were needed for she had experienced this several times already in her young life.

From the first stories she had ever heard she came to know the importance of valuing others regardless of their age, gender, or personality. She truly valued the little ones who looked up to her, the older youth from whom she learned much about what was to come, the adults who modeled the roles she would fill in her own adult life, and the elders whose soft, warm eyes lovingly welcomed her whenever they saw her. She learned that all beings and things had smáwal̓—and all had equal rights to be, none more important than the other. This teaching was the foundation of the respect that she held for herself, everyone, and everything.

And at this tender age she was also fully aware of the protocols around death and how to behave during feasts and ceremonies. She participated in the drumming and singing that carried the families through the grief of their great loss so that they would not trap their loved one here by getting stuck in this great pain. She further participated in the drumming, songs, and dances that gave thanks for and celebrated the many gifts of life.

She prepared for the fast approaching puberty ritual that would mark her transition into the next stage of her life in the community—where she would join the women and take on the same roles and responsibilities that they carried and fulfilled. Responsibilities that would one day require her, as an elder, to share her own experiences and life stories—like the story of the day she opened the shiny metal box she found on the riverside just last Fall.

I am Samahquamicw of the Stl'atl'imx, but in my academic work and studies I need to consistently check myself through spending as much time as possible with elders, leaders (Schnarch, 2005), and community members to ensure it is the dreams and needs of the community that are being addressed and not just what I think is needed or suited to academia. I have the added responsibility to also honor the ancestral name of my grandmother, Kicya7, which was given to me at a community ceremony on December 13, 2008. It is a very big name to carry, for Kicya7 means "mother to all" meaning that everything I think, say, and do must be done in a way that nurtures family, community, nation, and earth. I must ensure that any actions I consider and any steps I take contribute to the growth, health, and well-being of my community. Carrying this name frames how I proceed in all areas of my life, including my student, instructor, and researcher lives, and the responsibilities that come with it will guide me in addition to the criteria set out in university and Tri-Council Policy Statement research guidelines. Remaining cognizant of this responsibility will keep me humble throughout my PhD research program processes, so that I may genuinely put community first and listen with my heart as well as with my ears (Archibald, 2008) to respectfully take community direction from start to finish.

The purpose of this chapter is to outline/practice Indigenist knowledge-seeking/making processes in the dissemination of a research approach that engages with Stl'atl'imicw ways of coming to know toward a collective vision of Stl'atl'imicw-controlled education. Our Indigenous communities have important protocols that come with and prior to knowledge seeking and making. Taking the time to come together in good ways before the knowledge-seeking processes of visualizing, reflecting, and reaching consensus allows our hearts and spirits to join in the process effecting deeper understandings on levels with and beyond the intellectual. Providing the space to practice local protocols allows us to connect, in spirit, with each other, our ancestors, and the universe, and it is critical to the outcomes of what we are preparing to do. Our Stl'atl'imicw communities believe that everything must begin and proceed in a good way if it is to result in good outcomes. These knowledge-seeking/making protocols are little known let alone practiced in mainstream education and research. The purpose of this chapter is to disseminate an approach to authentically engage two Stl'atl'imx on-reserve communities—namely Skatin and Samahquam—in visualizing/defining what locally controlled education looks like/means to our membership. In taking up the Indigenist principles of self-determination, political integrity, and resistance, community members and I wisely approach knowledge seeking and making in a way that decenters decolonizing paradigms of knowledge seeking to alternatively engage with alive and well Stl'atl'imicw concepts of knowledge seeking and making.

What are Wise Approaches/Practices?

There is a recognized need to return to and invigorate ancestral "wise practices" and engage community members, from youth to elders, in a reassertion of fundamental belief structures, values, and ceremonial practices. Taking back and revitalizing our own ways will ensure that Aboriginal peoples will continue to reconnect with our respective traditions and practices and strengthen the sacred circle of life (Wesley-Esquimaux & Calliou, 2010, p. 3) that is evident in the noninterference story.

"Wise practices always are situated thoroughly in their context" (Davis, 1997, p. 93). The purpose of the study described herein is not to extract and engage the best practices from other communities and studies for those are the best practices for those communities. "When one explores the term 'best,' one question that arises is by whose standard...[the wise practice] approach integrates communal experience to qualify, or describe, the community's sense of well-being, socio-economic and cultural efficacy" (Wesley-Esquimaux & Calliou, 2010, p. 20). Davis submits that the "general quest for best practices has certain liabilities, especially in education" (1997, p. 92) because of its insistence on a singular, best path and its tendency to focus on concepts as opposed to practices. "The expectation is that 'best practices' in one situation can be replicated in a similar situation and have the same positive effects" (Thomas, 2007, p. 12). Thomas goes on to state that the Canadian Aboriginal Aids Network (CAAN) takes issue with the term best because it is viewed as a "hierarchical, non-Aboriginal construct" (p. 12) that attempts to fit Indigenous peoples and lives into mainstream processes that serve only to further marginalize Indigenous knowledges and practices. The study my communities and I are about to embark upon seeks to design with community a vision of locally controlled education based on local (wise) concepts of how to do that. So long as we continue to frame our research activities utilizing mainstream processes of knowledge production, we will consistently end up with ill-fitting results and outcomes that do not promote/perpetuate our communities' ways and/or values. "Since research is inextricably linked to European imperialism and colonialism... a thoughtless use of standard research techniques would run the risk of perpetuating European imperialism in a study that hopes to further, rather than diminish, Indigenous self-determination" (Wesley-Esquimaux & Calliou, 2010, p. 23). Approaching instead from a wise practices perspective we are better able to honor and protect the "culturally heterogeneous, socially diverse, and communally 'traditional' while at the same time ever-changing" uniqueness of the communities with whom we engage (Wesley-Esquimaux & Calliou, 2010, p. 19). Seeking to facilitate change in an Indigenous community requires that we do so utilizing Indigenous knowledge-seeking processes if we hope to attain wise outcomes that are of the utmost benefit to the participating community.

The study presented herein seeks not only to develop a vision of local education for the Stl'atl'imx, it further proposes to contribute to the virtually nonexistent collection of wise approaches so that "the steady increase in case studies of wise practices [can] add significantly to the understanding of education...[and] enable the profession to move, however gently, from the flawed concern for best practices to individual professionals' mindful consideration and use of improved, wiser practices" (Davis, 1997, p. 96).

Indigenist Research Frameworks Set in Motion Are Wise Practices

Few scholars have defined the term Indigenist and only one speaks to the variations of terms currently in use. De Costa (2005) states, "Indigenism (like Indigeneity) is a term without a standard meaning...several clear variations in use are apparent amongst scholars and activists" (p. 1). Those who use the term Indigenist do so with little or no articulation of the origins and/or meanings of the concepts used. It appears that the term Indigenous refers to the specific ways of being, doing, knowing, and valuing internal to individual communities of Original or First Peoples around the world (Ramos, 1998) while Indigenist speaks to the resisting and self-determining actions of those communities in the face of ongoing colonial processes and practices. While there is and always has been a great diversity of worldviews and ways of being between Indigenous peoples, these distinct groups can come together (physically, intellectually, spiritually, emotionally, and/or politically) in the "spirit of resistance" (de Costa, 2005, p. 1) under Indigenism to mobilize the Indigenist project, which is one of action and social justice grounded in practicing/living and making space for the values, philosophies, languages, and sacred traditions of Indigenous peoples.

The themes that most commonly surface in Indigenist discourse include self-determination, political integrity, and resistance. It is in reclaiming our rights and responsibilities to decide for ourselves how our children will be educated, how we will work together for the health and well-being of our communities, and through teaching future generations about the importance of resisting our assimilation into mainstream ways that our communities maintain ways of being, doing, knowing, and valuing unique to our nations. Much is at stake for as Charleston (1994) writes,

> Our tribes are at a very critical point in our history again. We can stand by and wait for our children and grandchildren to be assimilated into mainstream...society as proud ethnic descendants of extinct tribal peoples...or, we can protect our tribes, as our ancestors did, and ensure a future for our children and grandchildren as tribal people. (Grande, 2000, p. 488)

Indigenist Ward Churchill (2003) states that he is "one who not only takes the rights of Indigenous peoples as the highest priority of [his] political life, but who draws upon the traditions–the bodies of knowledge and corresponding codes of value—evolved over many thousands of years by native peoples the world over" (p. 275). This Cherokee scholar takes up the spirit of resistance from a space and outlook that "guided our great leaders of the past" (Churchill, 2003, p. 275). Inspired by what he considers "the only historical examples of proper attitude and comportment on this continent" (p. 276), Churchill embraces the values and traditions of his ancestors and is activated from that sacred place. Through acts of self-determination, political integrity, and resistance, the Indigenist scholar, researcher, student, instructor, leader, community member contributes to the building of wise approaches to knowledge seeking and making. De Costa concurs and indicates that to be Indigenist is to be an "indigenous activist," one who is inspired by tradition to "resist [the] invasive and deracinating forces" of imperialism, colonialism, and globalization (2005, p. 1). These Indigenous warriors are not like the typical soldier in a number of ways; whereas "soldiers serve the state; warriors serve their people…[and]…have a social responsibility…to create the geographical and political space for [their] people to practice their way of life" (Alfred, Couthard, & Simmons, 2006, p. 22). It is through Indigenist scholarship that we confront and counter the numerous illegitimate actions of state, corporate, and institutional power—and this is where the Indigenist turns away from the hegemony of colonial ideas and values through engaging with Indigenous tried-and-true frameworks that are grounded in the values, worldviews, and, most importantly, the practices of our Indigenous ancestors (Alfred, Couthard, & Simmons, 2006).

"Indigenous people now want research and its designs to contribute to the self-determination and liberation struggles as defined and controlled by their communities" (Rigney, 1999, p. 109). To further the discourse on wise, Indigenist practices, we need to support "Indigenous theorists and practitioners to determine what might be an appropriate response to de-legitimate racist oppression in research and shift to a more empowering and self-determining outcome" (Rigney, 1999, p. 110). Just as I conducted my Masters research in a manner that honored our oral traditions, I further Indigenous ways in the academy by taking up a research framework that engages our own knowledge-seeking/making processes in the visioning of Stl'atl'imicw-controlled education.

Stl'atl'imicw Research Processes

The first step toward communal development of a Stl'atl'imicw vision of locally controlled education is to ensure/facilitate authentic community engagement in the process. For this reason, this study will utilize processes that I have observed and/or practiced in/with my community toward seeking the knowledge, experiences, and understandings of the membership of the two communities that are local to the school built for the Lower Stl'atl'imicw. Through engaging such processes in our education and research, we can begin to "shift the construction of knowledge to one that does not compromise Indigenous identity" (Rigney, 1999, p. 119). To enact self-determination, political integrity, and resistance, we will activate the wise protocols and processes of local knowledge seeking and making, namely smudging, drumming, singing, sharing food together, and taking our thought processes to the land before enacting the visioning, reflecting, and consensus-making processes of Stl'atl'imcw knowledge making.

Stl'atl'imicw Knowledge-seeking Protocols

Before we even begin with the knowledge-seeking process, there are certain protocols that must be honored to ensure that our knowledge seeking begins and proceeds in a good way. This is critical if we want the outcomes of our time together to be of benefit to the community.

Smudging will be available at the beginning of each of the three knowledge-seeking/making days. We smudge to cleanse our hearts, bodies, and minds in preparation for the day. We smudge to cleanse the space around us from negative energies and we smudge to begin anew. After smudging we will proceed with an Opening Prayer. In our Stl'atl'imicw communities, prayer holds a different meaning/understanding than that which is typically understood in mainstream settings. When we open a Circle or event with a prayer, it is to bring all those participating together in one heart and one mind to do the work we are preparing to do. It is also to remind us to think of those who cannot be there, those who came before us, and those yet to come so that we are cognizant of the implications our visioning and decision making have on those who are not physically present. We pray for good hearts and minds, we pray for understanding and for the guidance of the Creator and our ancestors. After the prayer we will drum and sing together. This activity further serves to remind us of the importance of relationships and our connections to ways of being, knowing, and valuing that are rooted to the lands on which we live. Singing together, keeping on beat with the other drummers pulls us into the same sacred space and engages our spirits, inviting our ancestors to watch over us as we deliberate together. Beginning with prayers and drumming calls our spirits into the process that has much to do with beginning and enacting community work in a good way.

We will break for nutritious/traditional foods on each knowledge-gathering day for sharing meals together is a protocol that connects us in a good way to each other, to the teachings and understandings we are being exposed to, and to the process and its eventual outcomes.

We will walk the land together as part of our deliberations process to honor the significance that the earth holds in our thinking, feeling, and decision-making processes—reminding us of our true place in and responsibilities to this world—aligning us with the earth and cosmos so important to our surviving and thriving. These rituals/protocols are critical to ensuring that whatever we do is done in a good way—for that is the only way that the outcomes will also be good for the community.

Gifting is an important Stl'atl'imicw protocol that shows we honor the gifts of time and knowledge the contributors have given to the process, and offerings of respect and appreciation will be gifted to each contributor to this project. These are the protocols that prepare us to engage as a collective on knowledge-seeking/making matters that are important to our communities. These are the ways of the Stl'atl'imx that I am familiar with, that I have witnessed and participated in with both communities. These are the preparatory processes required to proceed with each of the following three knowledge-seeking/making processes that are local to Stl'atl'imicw territories. We will spend an entire day on each process with one-week reflection periods between each of the three engagement days.

Visualizing

Once we have completed the protocols/ceremonies described above, we will begin our knowledge seeking with a process of visualization. The process I refer to here is one that I first learned about in reading James Teit's (1906) compilations of the ways of the Lillooet peoples (English name for the Stl'atl'imx). Upon embarking on a new stage or phase of our lives, or when preparing to make decisions important to the community, the Stl'atl'imicw people would engage with a process of visualizing the outcomes of a decision or a new role in life. One example of this is the puberty ritual. Unlike today where most pubescent girls must figure out womanhood as they go along, our ancestors practiced a ritual that prepared the teenager for what was to come. Secluded for one to four years, the young woman began this ritual by fasting for up to four days inside a hut constructed specifically for this purpose. She spent much of her time praying that she would be well skilled in the activities that are expected of the women of the community. She visualized, enacted, and prayed for smooth birthing, strong root-digging, and nimble berry-picking hands, and she came away from this process fully understanding what was expected of her when she returned to her community. This process of visioning, praying, and enacting her role as a Stl'atl'imicw woman brought the teenager in sync with how she would be and what she would value when the puberty process was complete. This act of visualizing outcomes that benefit the collective is critically missing in much work that is being initiated in our communities today, and it is an approach to knowledge seeking and making that needs to be revitalized to a far greater degree.

By visualizing together what Stl'atl'imicw-controlled education looks like for our communities, we engage with a process of wisdom that was practiced by our ancestors toward the consistent creation and maintenance of strong, healthy, beautiful, and spiritually connected communities. Coming together in good ways through smudging, prayer, singing, drumming, and laughter we are better able to envision a system of education that can best engage our children and families in knowledge seeking and making that is relevant to and respectful of community-defined aspirations and goals. I will participate with participants/contributors in the visioning process for this study where we will consider, with our eyes closed and hearts and spirits open, a variety of Stl'atl'imicw knowledge-seeking/making scenarios. The group will then decide on and create a visual (drawing, collage, clay model) of what we came up with for each participant to take away with them for the upcoming reflection period.

Reflecting

Critical to Stl'atl'imicw knowledge-seeking/making processes is the time to reflect, pray, internalize, discuss with family and community the ideas put forth in the visioning process. This aspect of coming to know is not typically present in mainstream systems that prefer immediate and generalizable responses. In my Masters research project, my Aunty Laura stated that in today's world elders are expected to respond to questions right away—and that is not right. Elders need the time to think about the question, the person asking it, time to pray, fast, and/or dream on it before responding. This approach to visioning Stl'atl'imicw education provides the space needed to engage with this important process, which is why there are weeklong Reflection Periods between engagement sessions built into this project.

One week after the visualizing day, we will come together to share the processes and outcomes of our reflective processes. After the preparatory protocols have been honored, we will gather around the Circle to respond to a set of questions designed to draw out group understandings of and experiences with coming to know what Stl'atl'imicw education looks and feels like.

The changes and/or additions raised during our Reflections Circle rounds will be incorporated into our group vision of locally controlled education. A photo/copy of this new vision will be provided for each contributor to share with family and community members over the next weeklong Reflection Period.

Before leaving on this second knowledge-seeking day, contributors will be informed that we are going to come to a consensus on our next knowledge-seeking/making day on what our vision of Stl'atl'imicw-controlled education looks like. Over the next week we will reflect on the visual representation of our vision and share and discuss it with family and community members. These further thoughts and aspirations will then be considered/incorporated into our third and final vision of locally controlled knowledge seeking and making to be constructed on our third engagement day, Consensus-making Day.

Consensus-making

One of the most important decision-making processes for the Stl'atl'imx people is the process of consensus-making. Critical to initiating activities that will serve the community as a whole in optimal ways is our ability to come to an agreement as a group on how best to proceed.

Once we have honored the preparatory protocols outlined above, we will come together in a Circle to dialog about our understandings of and experiences with consensus making and the effects we have seen these have on the outcome of our decisions. After much thought and walking together on the land to consider the visions put forth, we will, as a group, discuss until we come to a consensus on what visions/aspirations/values consistently came up for us and others so that we can incorporate them into our third version of what it means to regain control over our knowledge systems. This final visual of our vision may be created with pictures/images/ symbols/paintings/ drawings, clay models, or a group weaving as preferred by the group. A photo of the completed representation will be provided for all contributors to share with their families and communities.

This day of consensus making will end with gifting, singing, and drumming to acknowledge the good work that we have done together. A closing prayer will signal the end of this first phase of our Stl'atl'imicw-controlled education process.

Summary

I began this chapter with a story about a more nurturing approach to knowledge seeking, making, and sharing; an approach that ensured that even the children were aware of their roles in family and community life, which facilitated a strong sense of purpose and belonging in community members from a very early age. I chose to begin with this story because it presents a wholistic picture of what the outcomes of education for our communities could and should look like. It reminds me that we need only turn to and practice our own wise ways of coming to know if we wish to effect change on how we proceed with community projects, educational or otherwise. I also began with a story to demonstrate the possibility of speaking to our histories in a manner that honors our own traditions of storytelling so that I am not just saying we need to practice our own ways—I am also practicing them. I chose to begin by reflecting on the beauty of Indigenous ways to demonstrate that there are other conceptions of education available to draw upon as we seek to transform mainstream systems in ways that move us to spaces where "new ways of thinking and being and new ways of being connected reshape all people" (Prakash & Esteva, 2008, p. xxi).

The approach to research presented in this chapter is innovative in that it will facilitate wise as opposed to best or academic practices of knowledge seeking in the processes of envisioning/defining Stl'atl'imicw-controlled education. Through engaging with Stl'atl'imicw knowledge-seeking processes; our coming together in a good way protocols, visioning, reflecting, and consensus making, this study will contribute greatly to expanding the parameters of authentically engaging collectives in relevant, respectful, and community-driven and desired research and educational processes. Presentations and publications of the outcomes of this approach to knowledge seeking and making will contribute to the broadening/deepening of mainstream concepts of knowledge production as commonly taken up by the academy and push the boundaries of current understandings of rigor in research and educational processes to the extent that both aspire to be of benefit to the community.

Note

1. The number 7 is used when recording the Ucwalmicw languages of the Stl'atl'imx people in written format. The 7 represents a catch in the pronunciation of the word—for example the catch one uses in saying the word "uh-oh."

10

The Politics of Loyalty and Dismantling Past-Present Knowing

Ingrid Tufvesson

Indigenous sovereignty would be the first Khoisan[1] concept to submit for South Africa to move toward education for humanity. Drawing on "outsider inside" experiences in two prominent South African universities, this chapter encourages the reader—whether academic, academic manager, university council member, local, regional and/or national politician, educators, students and parents of students who have the desire and ambition for their children to enter higher education—to pay attention to the metamorphosing of the old guard and to understand what this could mean to the throughput rates of students, the student experience, the lecturing staff's experience depending upon their stance toward the expectations of the entrenched politics of loyalty and how proponents of the latter impact on reviving the latent building blocks of historical forms of oppression as well as resistance. Of particular importance are practices of purposed erasures, self-serving denials, and transformation[2] rhetoric belied by verifiable realities.

The prominence of the universities that inform this chapter is that one, the University of Cape Town (UCT), is historically white, privileged, and at least rhetorically liberal (Hall, 2010). It is located in the largely affluent, predominantly white, English-speaking southern suburbs on the slopes of what colonialists named Table Mountain, but the Indigenous populace call *Hoerikwaggo*. The other is North-West University (NWU), an unlikely offspring of the "new South Africa" that remains problematically composed (Maake, 2011) with a persistent inability to establish an "institutional identity that will unify the three campuses and be shared by the university in its entirety" (Kamsteeg, 2008, p. 433).

While highly debated by many, UCT has a history of being "liberal." NWU, however, by virtue of the continued dominant role of the apartheid bastion of education, namely the Potchefstroom University for Christian Education (now called the NWU Potchefstroom Campus), and the location of its "head office" in the predominantly white, Afrikaans, Calvinist, affluent area of Potchefstroom, called "Die Bult," has never been and is still largely seen to not be "changed" or even close to being "liberal" or "progressive." Arguing the merits of this contention is best informed by comparing the public rhetoric of NWU to contrary and existing debates like that of the Higher Education Transformation Network (www.hetn.org.za). Furthermore, these two universities have played significant roles in the disputes between English- and Afrikaans-speaking national politics (van der Westhuizen, 2007), and today, they are the only of South Africa's 23 universities that have white, middle-aged, heterosexual men as their second-term-serving vice-chancellors.

Against this backdrop, how does one contribute Indigenous concepts to foster education for humanity, where the very notion of what and whom fitted into what constituted "humanity" was, and some would say still is, based upon systemized, institutionalized, legalized, and sermonized racism, sexism, and socioeconomic classism? Furthermore, how is this to be practically proposed to a community, a region, a country, an institution, indeed the world, where a racialized monocultural norm has been permitted to take root within the very fiber of what exists as education? Given the South African history, even today the very same seepages also saturate the very notions of what is authorized and acclaimed as "knowledge" and "success," completely ignoring Indigenous ways of being and defining, doing, living, sharing, imparting, and receiving education.

> The legacy of Terra Nullius sticks to our shoes with the dirt as we walk over Indigenous sovereignties everyday. (Nicoll, 2004, p. 1)[3]

This chapter locates itself in the South African higher education sector and aims to contribute modestly to understanding the challenging and complex factors that impact on the ambitious undertaking to establish workable educations for humanity. It also attempts to proffer possible methods by which to counter those factors that impede the establishment of such. In particular, this contribution wishes to counter the elisions that subsume and deny the Indigenous Khoisan, their sovereignty, and thereby the factors of learning, knowing, educating, and being, which identifies their humanity. These Aboriginal peoples of southern Africa, who unlike any other group, remain excluded from the university curriculum and its pedagogies, are no longer willing to remain in the shadows as though they were just relics of a time gone by. Having survived innumerable amounts of hardships and extermination attempts, the Khoisan are challenging myths and setting historical records straight. This chapter decries the denial of Indigenous sovereignty and its rightful place in the establishment of workable education for humanity that is continued through the subsumption of the geosocial, geopolitical, and geocultural knowledges, as well as ways of knowing and learning of the Indigenous Khoisan of South Africa.

The theoretical bases for the discussion below draws upon the concepts and methodologies of (Critical) Indigenous Studies, postcolonial feminist theory, intersectionality, native feminist theory, critical race theory, critical whiteness theory, narratology, critical legal theory, cultural studies, and woman-centric theories, which in turn variably annex a number of disciplines, including anthropology, sociology, gender studies, feminism, literary criticism, history, and psychoanalysis in order to elucidate the contextual dynamics of power that are at play in situations of oppression, marginalization, exclusion, and enforced deprivation. In the tradition of these theoretical perspectives, the subsequent discourse is imbued with real-lived and human elements that require a narrative upon which to illuminate interactive and intersecting factors. This choice of explicative tool can draw critique of subjectivity from disciplinary purists and die-hard positivists, but it fits in well with theoretical perspectives it purports to be aligned with, and as such it remains true to its chosen positionality, gives appropriate conceptualization for the emerging notion of *politics of loyalty* (Tufvesson, 2012), and adequately follows the analytical reasoning and action of *intersectionality* (Crenshaw, 1991; Young, 1997).

Dynamics of the Politics of Loyalty

Moreton-Robinson (2002, 2004, and 2007), van der Westhuizen (2007), Maake (2011), and Wilkins and Strydom (2012) provide some significant ideas on how *the politics of loyalty*[4] shapes, informs, and maintains historical status quo in taken-for-granted ways of doing and speaking in higher education institutions. From these performances and discourses, the manners in which the perpetuation, reification, as well as the nurturing of the erasure of Indigenous knowledges, ways of reasoning, understanding, and debating becomes "natural." Most often the final product is an assimilation of Indigenous thought through mainly misappropriation, but also via the succumbing of the subaltern (outsiders on the inside) to the tools that have existed from the moment the house of higher education was unduly occupied in the first place. Countering this historical travesty forms an intrinsic part of the so-called transformation agenda in South Africa today.

Du Preez (2008) shares stories of KhoiKhoi and Khoisan actions, variably swayed by either a loss of or commitment to group loyalty in the face of colonialist actions. As one reads Du Preez's accounts, one is taken on a journey of fluctuating anger, disappointment, pride, and respect for the Indigenous protagonists. Without launching into a full review of Du Preez's book, it is this author's politics of loyalty that is of interest here. In well-known "white person commenting," and not Moreton-Robinson's "native informant" manner, we find the author (Du Preez) skirting the issues of Indigenous dispossession, sovereignty theft, and denigrated identity through lighthearted, well-meaning sarcasm so reminiscent of *The Gods Must Be Crazy*. It seemed as though the reality of the pain, anger, and suffering of the Indigenous body and body politic is too much for Du Preez to bear and hence he reverts to the comic, which is so often utilized by those who have not actually experienced the pain, rage, and suffering. In it a misappropriation of Khoisan experience is exposed. And with it, hope, as fragile as it already is, evaporates.

One of the most debilitating suppositions made at the time of defeating the old political dispensation and enacting a transition to democracy in South Africa in the early 1990s was that *all* of the country's people were united in "doing the right thing." It is reasonable to argue that if this were indeed so, then clearly *what* was understood as doing the right thing was not a consensus notion. How else does one explain the continued degradation, exclusion, marginalization, and lack of recognition that continues to hound the majority populace, particularly the Khoisan? Some would argue statistics to measure those most hard done by in terms of ethnicity, but it is the totality of exclusion that places the Khoisan in the unwelcome position of being the most excluded.

Breaking the yoke of the masters and mistresses (the racialized historically privileged) of the unjustifiably occupied house (Southern

Africa and all its institutions, of which education is one) is not easily done and cannot readily be reclaimed just by coining new concepts or trying to reclaim old ones. Besides the nonnative occupant, there is also the collusion, purposed or not, of the postapartheid black elite, who have lost sight of the past in the present of those they have outgrown.

When attempting to introduce Indigenous concepts to shape education for humanity, those who would do so must remain ever cognoscente of the fact and the accuracy of the assertions of Lordé (1984) and Hall (2010) in order to try to effectively elucidate the subaltern voice in relation to conceptualizations of "success" and "quality" as commonly verbalized by those dominant voices that have set the merited and accredited knowledge agenda for *all* South Africans.

In the process of dismantling education, questions that could inform the formulation of Indigenous-sensitive concepts, which we should consider, are the following: Is there wisdom in placing the sensitive and unsettling agenda of transformation in the hands and under the power of those whose historical privileges led to the imperative of transformation in the first place? Given the role of universities in the specific oppressions of Indigenous South Africans, why has there not yet been a surge of investigation into the role of each university in the colonization of knowledge in order to test whether these higher education institutions are recolonizing and conditioning the minds of the recently liberated in ways that will further socioeconomic and psychosocial maladies that keep them occupied elsewhere instead of dismantling the house with self-forged tools? What, in the curriculum of each university, makes a meaningful contribution to the acknowledgement of Indigenous sovereignty and that which was done to dispossess it in the first place?

Indigeneity and Aboriginal Southern Africans (Khoisan)

In his *State of the Nation* address on January 9, 2012, President Jacob Gedleyihlekisa Zuma, stated:

> It is important to remember that the Khoisan people were the most brutalised by colonialists who tried to make them extinct, and undermined their language and identity. As a free and democratic South Africa today, we cannot ignore to correct the past.

President Zuma's statement was heralded as the first ever made on South African soil to formally acknowledge Khoisan communities and their history. The attempt rendering the Khoisan extinct was significantly driven by "education" in and through dominant disciplines like anthropology, ethnology, history, biology, and the like. It is therefore not strange that one expects that in the supposedly "pro-transformation" and "new South Africa," the inclusion of the country's "most brutalised by colonialists" would be vigorously and enthusiastically advocated for in education given its express role in the attempts to "make them extinct." Sadly, even the new world-renowned South African Constitution, when speaking about redress in relation to the dispossession enacted by the Land Act of 1913, implicitly denies the reality that by *that* time the Khoisan had *already* had their land declared *terra nullius*, forcibly stolen, and occupied.

The absence of inclusive transformative development has given momentum to Indigenous Khoisan engagement with historical factors, practices, and processes of oppression that continue to sustain the past in the present. It is from that *positionality*, to quote a long-standing women-centered conceptualization, that this chapter is shared.

Warnings about the harsh punishment that would follow the graciousness with which Khoisan peoples met the marauding character of European imperialist and colonialist agents have been recorded in documents kept hidden purposefully in the hope that by so doing the Aboriginal populaces of southern Africa would vanish "naturally." Hendrik Witbooi, a nineteenth-century Nama chief, wrote a letter to a Herero chief, who had just conceded to German colonialist "protection." Witbooi, in Hallett (1974, p. 622), stated:

> You will have bitter eternal remorse for this handing of your land and the sovereignty over to the hands of the White people. This giving of yourself into the hands of the Whites will become to you a burden as if you were carrying the sun on your back.

Witbooi's reference to sovereignty and the burden of settler-colonialist pervasion is the cornerstone of all voices who decry the usurping of Indigenous sovereignties across the globe. Moreton-Robinson, an Aboriginal Geonpul professor, warrior-woman, and activist from Minjerribah in Australia, explains the importance of sovereignty and ontological knowing as follows:

In postcolonizing settler societies Indigenous people cannot forget the nature of migrancy and we position all non-Indigenous people as migrants and diasporic. Our ontological relation to land, the ways that country is constitutive of us, and therefore the inalienable nature of our relation to land, marks a radical, indeed incommensurable, difference between us and the non-Indigenous. (2003, p. 31)

Reclaiming stolen territory and Indigenous sovereignty, according to Moreton-Robinson and many other native feminists and Indigenous theorists, requires differentiating between those who have intimate knowledge of settler-colonizing institutions, which includes education, and "native informants."

The colonizing settler cannot be a native (Mamdani, 1997, 1998; Tufvesson, 2012) and in fact settler-colonists have historically made painstaking efforts to make this distinction clear in "unquestionable" ways. For example, until the late 1970s, Aboriginal peoples in Australia were categorized as part of the country's flora and fauna by the White Australia Policy (Tufvesson, 2005), and forced removals of "mixed race" children in keeping with the tenets of this policy led to what is today known as the *Stolen Generation*, which continues to plague the sense of belonging and identity of many Aboriginal Australians today.

In South Africa, until the late 1990s, laws like the Natives Land Act 27 of 1913, the Bantu Trust and Land Act 18 of 1936, the Prohibition of Mixed Marriages Act 55 of 1949, the Immorality Amendment Act 21 of 1950 (amended by Act 23 of 1957), the Population Registration Act 30 of 1950, the Group Areas Act 30 of 1950, the Group Areas Act 41 of 1950, the Bantu Building Workers Act 27 of 1951, the Separate Representation of Voters Act 46 of 1951, the Prevention of Illegal Squatting Act 52 of 1951, Bantu Authorities Act 68 of 1951, the Natives Laws Amendment Act of 1952, the Natives (Abolition of Passes and Co-ordination Documents) Act 67m of 1952, the Native Labour (Settlement of Disputes) Act of 1953, the Bantu Education Act 47 of 1953, the Reservation of Separate Amenities Act 49 of 1953, the Natives Resettlement Act 19 of 1954, the Group Areas Development Act 69 of 1955, the Natives (Prohibition of Interdicts) Act 64 of 1956, the Bantu Investment Corporation Act 34 of 1959, the Extension of University Act 45 of 1959, the Promotion of Bantu Self-Government Act 46 of 1959, the Coloured Persons Communal Reserves Act 3 of 1961, the Preservation of Coloured Areas Act 31 of 1961, the Urban Bantu Councils Act 79 of 1961, and the Bantu Homelands Citizens

Act of 1970, *all* existed to draw a clear chasm between the "native" and the colonizer. Today, ironically, vigorous argument is presented by those apartheid architects, supporters, beneficiaries, and foot soldiers who were protected from eviction from all institutions and parastatals by the so-called *Sunset Clauses*, taking umbrage at not being considered to be Indigenous and native.

Central to the collusive oppressive agenda between all colonizing settlers are two significant factors among many, namely the eradication of Indigenous peoples' sense of self (identity) and sovereignty (Mamdani, 1998; Nicoll, 2004). The Khoisan, as an ethnolinguistic group, is also a recognized identity albeit one that is very rarely spoken of or included in educational debates and has only recently been acknowledged as being absent from the Land Restitution Act of 1994 by the new democratically elected government. Should this oversight not be remedied without reservation and expressly, it would be quite feasible to argue that the "new South Africa" is guilty of continuing a heinous dispossession that dates back ages prior to the Native Land Act of 1913. This would be no different to colonialist theft.

The defragmentation of identity, as well as land and sovereignty confiscation, occurred in tandem with the emaciation of the Khoisan populace by wars, the introduction of alcohol, and European settler-colonist diseases like smallpox against which they (the Khoisan) had not previously needed any immunity because it never existed in Southern Africa. Khoisan identity/ies and its propensity for being inclusive, driven by collective thinking, being heritage conscious, and largely peaceful, have been argued to be the main reasons why the inhumane methods of colonialists were tolerated as just being confusing but curable. This willingness to be tolerant in the face of clearly different behaviors and attitudes ensued for a considerably long time until it became unmistakably clear that the non-Indigenous peoples had no intention of respecting Khoisan ways of being, doing, thinking, understanding, communicating, and/or educating.

By the time the Khoisan were forced to register themselves as "Coloured," the systematic defragmentation of their identity and the usurpment of their sovereignty necessitated their incorporation or assimilation into the newly established racialized categorization in order to "belong." Resentment, which had remained simmering over centuries, about the denigration of the fundamental elements of Khoisan ontology, rocketed in the 1980s. Subsumed for too long under the fluid racialized identification of "Coloured," which lacked the ethnolingual singularity of Khoisan identities, has led to a steadily emerging action to reclaim their sovereignty, and in this quest, identity politics has been considered as a possible tool of agency, to cite a postcolonial feminist terminology.

Afrikaans, one of the languages of the historical oppressors of Indigenous peoples in the Southern African region, developed out of the original Dutch through the incorporation and bastardization of key nomenclatures of the Indigenous languages, as well as the Anglicization of Dutch words (Barnard, 2004). The yoke of colonization in all its forms and persistence over centuries, and as lives on in the settler colony, South Africa, is identifiable today through the "adoption" of Afrikaans by the Khoi as a means by which to survive the contrariness of these foisting modes of being, knowing, and learning.

From the age of 11 years, I remembered Ant'Bea each time the Khoi-debasing word was used in my presence, whether directly at me, descriptively, and/or toward someone else. Many times my physical attributes drew, still draw, comments informed by internalized notions of "the Hotnot," and depictions related to Saartjie "Sarah" Baartman, and the movie sequels of the debasing *The Gods Must Be Crazy* range. Unlike a commonly made statement, the word "Hottentot" did not *become* derogatory; it *was* offensive from the moment it was first conjured up by the colonialist mind and then used with impunity. The lasting injury of this word is often evident in the utilization thereof by people when they wish to belittle and denude individuals of their sense of self. Ironically though, the utilization also confirms the Indigenous sovereignty of the Khoi, in my mind. There is, however, nothing to validate the speculation that it would be empowering to appropriate this label in the same manner as has been done with the word "queer." The latter speaks about and to the issue of sexuality without immediately acknowledging racism, ethnocentrism, and/or whiteness as the operative criminal discrimination, while the former does.

As one of the oldest Indigenous populaces, the Khoisan have, in conjunction with other forcibly colonized Indigenous populations, weathered multitudinous, mercurial, and rapid changes, none more so than in knowing, learning, and educating. For example, white colonist notions of property relations have identified itself over centuries as being premised particularly on stringent individualism, possession, exclusivity, territorialism, and protectionism. Contrarily, Khoisan property relations are based upon complementary relations predicated upon the directive of sharing.

Selfishness, as it is commonly known, was not a governing element in Khoisan society in the seventeenth century. Barnard (2004) explains that sharing "implies not simply equality, but rights to dispose of property, and indeed requirements to dispose of it" (p. 3). Barnard has been led to the same conclusion since his early 1970s studies, namely that for Khoisan people, social aspects outweigh and operate way beyond economic necessity (ibid.). Education, in Khoisan tradition, had to and has to be based upon a number of fundamental values, namely cooperation, sharing, reasonable consumption, limited procreation, consensual decision making, and above all respect for humanity, the land, animals, and ancestors (Lévi-Strauss, 1966; Mostert, 1993).

It was this way of selfless collective sharing, thinking, understanding, teaching, interacting, and being that was and is in conflict with colonist-settler thinking. After all, despite the "primitive" nature of Khoisan communities and living, as is most commonly depicted by white colonist-settler records, Khoisan kinship (in a broad sense) probably enjoyed "a more real happiness in life than the destitute class of any European city" (Theal, 1910, p. 25). Theal, a conservative nineteenth-century South African historian, whose intellectual notions and educational framework were embedded in immovable notions of white superiority, would have written that phrase very grudgingly so it would be quizzical to question its veracity.

The significance of Theal's way of thinking and educating is that his studies and explications were and continue to be considered "definitive" on the "indigenous races and ethnic groups of sub-continental Africa" (Mostert, 1993). It is imperative, therefore, that sensitized understandings of the facets of knowing, learning, and educating under circumstances of marginalization and repression are forged in order to stem the tide of prescriptive and assumptive education regimes that continue to purport the extinction of the Aboriginal peoples of Southern Africa. The interactive and intersecting factors of education that give rise to definitive ways of knowing, educating, and measuring acumen must be tempered by a more humanized formation and point of departure. In this, identity politics fails because of its inability to escape the erasure of difference when applying its reasoning.

Concurring with Crenshaw (1991) that identity politics lends itself to collusion with oppressive ways of knowing, educating, and understanding because it decries the veracity of difference, another analytical perspective is requisite.

None of the factors, elements, and/or realities mentioned in the earlier discussion exists or occurs in isolation however. Rather, all context-specific dynamics, all immediate identity-related attributes, and all systemic, structural, and institutional power factors are in active intra- and/or interaction, intersecting at multiple levels and at multiple points that result in specific manifestations of inclusions, exclusions, privileged centrality, and marginalized periphery. The intersectional mosaics, once located, provide points of clarity about the diverging and converging conceptualities that foster or resist the establishment of humane inclusive education for humanity.

Crenshaw's (1991) conceptualization of *intersectionality* is by now an established liberating analytical tool by which to explicate the actualities of marginalization, exclusion, and oppression as it relates to the conflating dynamics of racism, whiteness, sexism, religion, and socioeconomic classism. It would be pointless to argue that the aforementioned factors were not, indeed are not, pivotal in today's Khoisan-erased South African education. It is this Indigenous populace that has distinguished itself to be fundamentally different to all others who usurped their land, sovereignty, education, and community, as well as denigrating their methods of communication, spirituality, identification, governance, and being (Mostert, 1993).

Among those that have utilized this investigative perspective to elucidate economic, legal, and ideological intersections of hegemony are Young (1997) and de los Reyes and Mulinari (2005), who favor postcolonial and black feminist emanations and resist the tendency to "flatten out" identity markers that result in the rendering of specific experiences of oppression to a hinterland that is then never mentioned and hence totally forgotten in "objective" reasoning. A case in point would be the manner in which the history of oppression in South Africa tends to be glossed over by even the most respected educating and researching entities. Ironically, many of these also have Khoisan ancestry. Central to applying an intersectional analytical framework is the acknowledgment of the importance of *difference* in order to aptly locate subjugation. The notion of "basic human needs" ought not to be opportunistically deployed to justify the erasure of Indigenous sovereignty and its related facets.

Much about the ways of knowing, acting, and performing in circumstances of continued suppression or containment has been formulated and explicated by women-focused theorists. Unfortunately, *the politics of loyalty* (Tufvesson, 2012), which is intrinsic to the settler-colonist knowledge agenda, is very rarely examined for the androcentricity and ethnocentric principles that underpin it. This chapter does not propose to engage with the issue of masculinity[5] (inherent to androcentricity) but instead emanates from the posits that feminists have individually and collectively illustrated and which maintains that academia and higher education, per se, are domains that are inherently white, Western, male, Christian, able-bodied, of a certain age, and heterosexual.

Education for Humanity, Historically Tainted Educating

In recent years, there has been a flurry of increasing interest in the matter of education and its role in human prosperity and posterity. Available discussions that claim to be engaged with expounding what education for humanity is and/or should be tend to conflate this discussion with education and human rights, or education as a human right. Multiple forms of conflicts, recalcitrant and/or absent national and international leadership, corrupt governmental systems, and religion-based abuse are expected to bring about the expansive malfunction of education (Trevors & Saier, 2009).

Others argue that the problem with education today is that it is no longer purposed for educating human beings but rather for the creation and sustaining of economically centered beings (Abbott, 2010). Yet others argue that a problem-centered pluralistic approach to teacher training or the inculcation of the philosophy of education would be the answer to educating humanity in South Africa (Venter, 2008/9).

The often recurring gap in the reasoning of accessible, authorized, and often prominent academics and community commentators about education for humanity is the repeated failure to engage with the presumptive preeminence or foreordained supremacy of education as we have been made to participate in and know in the South African context. The bedding ground, character, composition, and structures of education is taken as a given. It is this gap that at worst suppresses into oblivion, or at best tolerates as addition, the diversity of Indigenous knowledges while advantaging and entrenching racialized, gendered, classed, religio-biased, Indigenous lingual intolerant education. The links of hegemonic notions of education with its foundations in the occupation and denial of Indigenous sovereignty remain a polemic that requires rigorous exposure. In South Africa, we live in a time where the historical minority oppressors are permitted constitutional protection to speak freely, even when it pertains to denying the heinousness of the past. Claiming "freedom of speech" and/or "academic freedom" are among the new tools being wielded in the quest for regaining yesteryear.

Education was made inhuman and inhumane in South Africa through cleverly crafted legislative tenets. The Bantu Education Act 47 of 1953, for example, racialized the right to freedom in and of education, as well as what could/could not be taught to black students. While academics from the old Potchefstroom University for Christian Higher Education presented "objective" pro-arguments, UCT academics implicitly accepted the ideology and purpose of the Act and chose to only amend some of its content (Tufvesson, 2012). The same passion enacted in making education inhumane became entrenched in the "educated" arguments made before, during, and after the promulgation of this Act; today, the past in the present is protected through the politics of loyalty in new ways—for example, resistance to national transformation imperatives through creative arguments about culture, demonizing, and punishing of Indigenous academics and academic managers who cry foul (see Maake, 2011),[6] refusal to or minimal change of curriculums, "stacking" of university councils with like-minded members of powerful community leaders, the enactment of punitive measures that ensure silence, suppression of Indigenous languages, accommodating reactions to white students who vilify Indigenous university staff[7] or perpetrate racist acts,[8] to name a few.

If a South African university is known to be steeped in apartheid traditions and thinking; is known to be a place and educational space where silence, fear, and the punitive measures of the Afrikaner Broederbond[9] are still whispered about; and where the pervasiveness of promises of reprisals continues to make cowards of the otherwise bravest of people, how can we justify *not* examining each and every feature of its institutionalized policies, practices, and processes? How can we *not* examine its curriculums and the people who educate? After all, the further up the academic management or tenure ladder people are, the power dimensions of gendered, racial, status, institutional, historical, educational, geopolitical, and educating are considerable. Here we need to apply the Khoisan concept of straight-talk and be collective in our approach to dealing with the repercussions. So too, universities known to fence-sit for the ultimate reason of ensuring survival and economic gain ought to be subjected to the same scrutiny. In neither case should "academic autonomy" be permitted to serve as a shield and buffer.

The objection to raise is not about "opinion" but rather about past knowing and present power in the formation and dissemination of "knowing," as well as the impact this has on furthering a possible re-establishing, of the "ultra secretorganization" through our students into the future. We need to be as alert as the Khoisan hunter, who though small in stature is able to bring down enormous beasts with a tiny well-informed and aimed arrow that is housed within a confident quiver of knowing.

History shows, in the end, that the Afrikaner Broederbond emerged from a minimal colonizing population group, which was nonetheless able to convince the Indigenous majority populaces, those deemed to be incalcitrant and devious, as well as their archrivals, namely English-speaking whites, of their dominance and power. As a result, this settler-colonist group became all-powerful and all-encompassing through insidious infiltration into every nook and cranny of social, political, economic, legislative, religious, and educational structure institution, systematizing and perpetuating self-serving understandings and knowing (Wilkins & Strydom, 2012).

A contemporary South African irony is that it remains the settler-colonial minority's understanding of education that pervades and persists. Not surprising, according to Terrance (2011), since colonization continues to instill and reinscribe heteropatriarchy, to naturalize historical social hierarchies, entrench heteronormativity, and impart new ways of reintroducing racialized marginalization through covert processes and collusive partnerships.

Many would argue that it is this continuance that ensures sustained oppressions and forms the bedrock of low throughputs, low rates of retention, attrition, and setback rates among the black majority in basic and higher education in South Africa today. This line of thinking is found even in Jansen's (2010) reasoning as he writes about push-in and push-out factors that temper access to and success in higher education in South Africa.

> The first of these push-out factors is the weak preparation of high school graduations for higher education, resulting in very high dropout rates, especially among black students. After the initial triumph of gaining access to the educational system, these students find themselves struggling with academic failure and its consequences, whether institutional exclusion or individual dropping-out. Either way, the personal and social costs are very high. (p. 131)

Jansen is one of many bemoaning this legacy of apartheid, and like many, he chooses to level blame narrowly at the doors of policy, national government, acceptance procedures, and the chasm that divides high school and university education. The given of failing basic education and high school education can only be used as a shield by higher education institutions for so long as protection from "doing the right thing." After all, one cannot help but wonder, if the entrance of students from "previously disadvantaged" communities is "naturally" accompanied by the ravishes of being fundamentally unprepared for university, then why are *widespread* empowering and remedial entrance initiatives still not endemic at historically white and privileged universities in particular, and at *all* universities generally in order to counter the challenge? Ironically, Jansen holds accountability high in relation to macrolevel entities but fails to do so at the microlevel (speaking of the horrendous so-called *Reitz* incidence) where immediate interaction and intersection have immediate effects.

A significant progressive step was recently taken by the vice-chancellor of the University of KwaZulu Natal (UKZN), Professor Malegapuru Makgoba. This vice-chancellor announced that Zulu, the Indigenous language of the KwaZulu Natal province, would be compulsory for any and all students, who chose to undertake studies at UKZN.[10] Professor Makgoba has remained resolute in the face of tumultuous objections.

Educational transformation for humanity, transformation for the education of humanity, and an education for humanity for the transformation of historical disadvantages all require unapologetic engagements with the key elements of the historical South African failure to educate humanely for humanity. For such an activity to be effective, the role of identity and the application of intersectionality analytical tools are viable options to consider as we forge concepts that are Indigenous-sensitive in our institutional structures and modus operandi employed in educating and learning.

Conclusion

This chapter started out by declaring that it was not aimed to provide definitive or exhaustive answers. It has, hopefully, contributed to an awakening of what needs to be considered before the journey toward an education for humanity can even be blueprinted as an endeavor. Across the globe, Indigenous nations are committed to the reclamation of their sovereignty, which they *never* ceded even in the face of adversity and loss of numbers.

Khoisan peoples are not extinct and hence any venture toward an education for humanity must reflect a move away from colonialist thinking and doing within each facet of what is deemed valid and valued knowledge and education. From the incorporation of languages, to pedagogy, to understandings of education as a collective activity for collective well-being, to inclusion in national agendas, Khoisan sovereignty in all its forms must be evident for South Africa to not remain an extension of colonial practice in real terms.

Sustainable peace and true reconciliation for a collectively advantageous South African future will remain elusive as the inclusion of Indigenous educational methods and knowledge remain in a place of elision.

Notes

1. Explicating the complexities of the Aboriginal peoples of Southern Africa is the subject for other discussions and is not entered into elaborately in this chapter. In fact the collective nomenclature "KhoiSan" was first introduced by Leonard Schultze in 1928 and is heavily debated often.
2. The notion of transformation, its project, directive, and national agenda is highly debated in South Africa with increasing arguments that resemble those in the United States, which decry affirmative action and instead label it as "reverse racism."
3. The colonialist and settler-colonist practice of determining all things Indigenous "no man's land" and hence free to be occupied with impunity.
4. For a broader conceptualization of a politics of loyalty, see Tufvesson (2012).
5. The notion of masculinity is not used without a keen awareness of the polemics that accompany the concept and its heteronormative tropes, as well as social constructs.
6. Also see http://mg.co.za/article/2013-02-27-a-monster-of-racism-at-potch.
7. See http://www.citypress.co.za/news/reitz-four-incident-forgiven-and-cleansed-20110226/. No meaningful legal action was taken against these students and they have been permitted to go on with their lives.

8. http://www.news24.com/SouthAfrica/News/Racist-Facebook-group-hijacked-20081006.
9. "A dominant force is an ultra-secret organization, the most exclusive and influential underground movement in the Western world. It is called the *Afrikaner Broederbond* (Brotherhood) (Wilkins & Strydom, 2012).
10. http://www.timeslive.co.za/local/2013/05/16/zulu-to-be-compulsory-for-ukzn-students.

11

Seal Meat in the Classroom: Indigenous Knowledge and School Mathematics

Melissa Kagle

Nancy Sharp, a Yup'ik educator from Manokotak, Alaska, describes herself as an *elitnauristet maklagtutulit* (Sharp, 1994, p. 8), meaning "a teacher who eats seal meat." Unfortunately, she is an exception; most teachers of native students, the majority of whom are white, do not have the knowledge or cultural connections to live on traditional foods such as seal. Likewise, those who do subsist on seal most often do not teach in schools. However, such bridges are needed to bring together the world of indigenous culture with that of the classroom, creating new cultural spaces where both the mandated curriculum of schools and traditional cultural practices such as eating seal can thrive. While we may have left behind the era of education as simply a vehicle for the assimilation of native students, schools still have not found consistently meaningful ways to incorporate indigenous knowledge in the classroom (Kanu, 2006). In this chapter, I describe a successful approach to this task that gives teachers of indigenous students the understandings they need to become an *elitnauristet maklagtutulit*.

Math in a Cultural Context: Lessons Learned from Yup'ik Eskimo Elders, or MCC, is a long-term collaboration between principal investigator Jerry Lipka at the University of Alaska Fairbanks and Yup'ik Eskimo elders and teachers to develop mathematics curriculum units that incorporate mathematical and pedagogical ideas intrinsic to Yup'ik knowledge. MCC has had notable success in bringing indigenous knowledge into the classroom in culturally meaningful and educationally effective ways. The MCC curriculum has shown statistically significant positive results in multiple quasiexperimental design studies as well as in a large-scale random control trial comparing the MCC curriculum with other elementary math curricula in place (Lipka, Kisker, Adam, & Millard, 2007).

In this chapter, I trace the development and implementation of one of the MCC curriculum units, *Designing Patterns: Exploring Shapes and Area* (Watt, Lipka, Parker Webster, Yanez, Andrew-Ihrke, & Adam, 2006), from its inception to its use in the classroom. This case demonstrates the complexity, challenges, and potential rewards of bringing indigenous knowledge into the classroom.

Creating a Place for Indigenous Knowledge: Development of a Third Space in the Classroom

Given the history of exclusion of indigenous knowledge from the classroom, bringing cultural knowledge and pedagogies into the classroom necessitates creating new ways of being for both students and teacher—a "third space" that occupies the borderland between indigenous culture and mainstream school (Dunlop, 1999). Such a space "brings academic content into dialogue with indigenous cultural knowledge that has historically been left outside the schoolroom door" (Webster, Wiles, & Clark, 2005, p. 35), implying both a pedagogical shift toward indigenous knowledge as well as a challenge to historic and current asymmetric power relations between indigenous communities and schools. The MCC curriculum facilitates the opening of a third space by making indigenous knowledge and pedagogies the basis of the mathematics curriculum.

Indigenous Content Knowledge: Listening to Elders

The development of the curriculum specific to the *Designing Patterns* unit described in this chapter began when eight Yup'ik elders traveled from their villages in western Alaska to Fairbanks in May 2004 to demonstrate how they made the shapes seen in the border patterns of Eskimo parkas that use geometric shapes, such as squares, triangles, and circles. Because Yup'ik families each have their own distinctive parka border patterns, there was a wide range of shapes used. The *Designing Patterns* unit was developed from the rhombus shape used in the border pattern design of the family of Winifred Beans of St. Marys, Alaska.

A challenge in creating culturally based curricula such as MCC is to keep the primacy of the indigenous ways of knowing, given the tendency of such knowledge to become subsumed by Western constructs within school curricula (Pinxten, 1997). In the next section, I describe the *Designing Patterns* unit in more detail, paying particular attention to the ways in which the MCC curriculum is grounded in indigenous conceptions of mathematics.

Translating Indigenous Knowledge: Content of the *Designing Patterns* Unit

Winifred Beans' method for cutting a rhombus from a rectangle with one cut, at the same time creating four symmetrical right triangles with an area equal to the rhombus, involves folding the paper twice in opposite directions and then cutting along the diagonal of the resulting rectangle.

Elders have developed methods for cutting out these shapes in ways that conserve as much of the animal skins used in parkas, traditionally seal, as possible. This approach is evident in Winifred Beans' method of cutting the rhombus where all parts of the original rectangle are used to make the rhombus and triangles as explained above. The elders made use of midpoints and diagonals to create the shapes they wanted through folding; in this way, their approach illustrates the mathematical properties of the shapes. Further, this method for constructing geometric shapes incorporates the concept of conservation of area, a major topic of the *Designing Patterns* unit.

The unit also includes an associated literature text telling the story of Iluvaktuq, a legendary Yup'ik warrior. Descendants of Iluvaktuq have a distinctive border pattern on their parkas honoring their ancestor's feats, connecting the story with the mathematical content. Including this story gives students a context to understand the border patterns they are studying.

Finally, the curriculum describes pedagogical approaches that are aligned with approaches to teaching and learning in the Yup'ik Eskimo context, leading classrooms to become more culturally congruent, two of which are described below.

Expert-Apprentice Modeling

In indigenous cultures, children traditionally learned through a process of observing skilled adults and then trying to accomplish small parts of what the adult demonstrated; learners were expected to be keen observers of the adults (Rogoff, 1990, p. 27). Expert-apprentice modeling is aligned with the theory of a cognitive apprenticeship where "the goal is to make visible and explicit thinking strategies that experts use in particular domains" (Lee, quoted in Lipka, Brenner, & Sharp, 2005).

Joint Productive Activity

Once a skill has been modeled, teachers engage in joint productive activity with students to practice the skill together. Joint productive activity involves "experts [teacher] and novices [students] work[ing] together for a common product or goal" (Tharp, Estrada, Dalton, & Yamauchi, 2000, p. 21). In the classroom, this strategy means the teacher works on the same problem or activity as the students. Should students encounter difficulties working independently, they can return to observing the expert (teacher).

Joint productive activity works against the prevailing paradigm of learning as a transfer of knowledge from teacher to students (Putnam & Borko, 2000) and is an equalizing force between the teacher and the students (Tharp et al., 2000); the teacher has less opportunity to directly manage student learning, and the student, who can decide whether and how long to observe the expert, gains autonomy as a learner.

Learning to Teach Indigenous Knowledge: MCC Professional Development

In the center of the room, Theresa Mike, a Yup'ik elder from St. Marys, Alaska, sits on the floor. Theresa carefully folds the paper she holds in half, checking to make sure the edges line up exactly. After a few adjustments, she folds the paper in half again and makes a single diagonal cut through the middle of the paper with her scissors. She unfolds the paper revealing the shape of a rhombus along with four right triangles that comprise the other half of the cut paper. She covers her rhombus with the triangles, proving that the area of the rhombus is one half the area of the original rectangle.

"No waste," she explains, emphasizing the Yup'ik value of conserving resources.

A teacher holds up the rhombus she has cut, "Look at this! Theresa didn't have to say a word and I learned how to do it!"

"Yeah," agrees another, "you know, my students always tell me I talk too much, but I never listened."

This scene was part of the Summer Math Institute, the two-week professional development workshop provided by the MCC project to Alaska teachers intending to teach the Designing Patterns unit. In the Institute, participants learned about the mathematical properties of shapes from a math educator as well as traditional ways of cutting out those shapes from Yup'ik elders through the culturally appropriate strategies of expert-apprentice modeling and joint activity, as described in the vignette above. On the cultural side, participants also learned about both traditional uses and the cultural significance of various shapes in parka border patterns. This infusion of Yup'ik cultural knowledge and indigenous pedagogy allowed participants to experience the MCC curriculum in its sociocultural context and pushed the Institute into a third space.

The next section recounts the experience of one of the Summer Institute participants, a white novice teacher.

Creating Space for Eskimo Culture: Sarah's Classroom

Sarah teaches in White River,[1] a small village near Kotzebue, Alaska. White River is home to approximately 400 people, almost all of whom are Inupiaq Eskimo. The school in White River enrolls about 170 students in grades K to 12. Sarah teaches a fourth/sixth-grade multiage classroom with 18 students.

Village teaching in Alaska holds unique challenges. Villages are small and isolated and school achievement levels consistently lag behind those of urban schools. In White River, only 23 percent of the sixth-grade White River students received proficient scores on the state mathematics assessment compared to 67 percent statewide (Alaska Department of Education and Early Development, 2006). In Sarah's classroom, three of her 16 students were functionally illiterate and eight were identified as needing special education services. Despite these challenges, Sarah's students had some of the highest test score gains in the study.

The use of the MCC curriculum had a profound impact on Sarah's teaching. Despite being a novice teacher, Sarah was able to effectively incorporate many of the culturally aligned pedagogical strategies, increasing student engagement in the mathematics content. Below I show how

Sarah's use of the MCC curriculum opened a third space in her classroom, reflecting the third space she experienced at the Institute.

The lesson consisted of three distinct components, following the trajectory of typical reform-oriented mathematics lessons (Lappan, Fey, Fitzgerald, Friel, & Phillips, 2002). First, Sarah introduced the lesson by demonstrating what she wanted students to accomplish during the class period. The bulk of the class time was then spent with students working on the task independently. Finally, Sarah reviewed the lesson to help students synthesize their learning. Sarah's use of a third space was limited to the first two parts of the lesson; in the final part of the lesson, Sarah reverted to a typical Western approach of the teacher initiating the discussion, calling on students and the students responding when called upon. This was a departure from the more fluid structure of the first two parts of the class and had the effect of diminishing students' ability to learn and function.

The mathematical content of the lesson focused on conservation of area through the construction and deconstruction of shapes. For example, students could use diagonals to divide a rhombus into four right triangles and then recompose these shapes to form their design. The lesson also introduced design principles of Yup'ik parka border patterns, which follow particular cultural forms. An example of the expected product is shown in figure 11.1.

Part One: Lesson Introduction

Sarah introduced the lesson by having students gather around her while she sat in a student's desk. The students watched intently as

Figure 11.1 Example of a design from Sarah's lesson.

she carefully cut out a rhombus using the method demonstrated by Winifred Beans. Next, Sarah made a cut about a quarter inch below the edge of the folded rhombus, producing the outline of a rhombus. This made the students gasp in amazement. "It's a boat!" said one. "It's a rhombus," corrected another.

Sarah then arranged the shapes on her own piece of paper to model the product she was looking for from students. She changed the configuration of her shapes once before looking up. Two students made suggestions about how to place the shapes and one then held Sarah's pieces down on the paper for her so that she could work more easily.

This demonstration was done in complete silence by Sarah. When Sarah found a design she liked, a student asked her, "You happy now?" and Sarah broke her silence to answer "I don't know, but that's what I want you to do. I want you to see what kinds of shapes." At this point, a student completed her sentence, "We can make." With a few instructions about where to find supplies, Sarah released the students to work on their own pattern pieces.

This introduction differs markedly from the typical patterns found in classrooms. A beginning of the lesson demonstration such as this one is typically done by the teacher alone, who narrates what she is doing. If students are asked to contribute at all, it is at the invitation of the teacher, usually through questioning. Sarah's decision to be silent gave students the space to co-construct knowledge with her: they described what was going on mathematically, as when students identified the shapes that Sarah made; they gave input into the execution of the project, as when they made suggestions to Sarah about her design and physically helped her to accomplish it; and they took ownership of the project itself, as when the student finished Sarah's description of what needed to be done.

Part Two: Individual Exploration

In the second part of the lesson, students worked independently to construct their own pattern pieces. Prior to attending the Institute, Sarah reported that she was worried about her ability to support students' independent work on mathematical tasks and consequently did not have students do much independent work. After attending the Institute, Sarah was motivated to include more independent work in her pedagogy and even made a structural change in her classroom to facilitate this type of learning: she rearranged the furniture to have a big table near the front of the room and used it to engage in the pedagogical strategy of joint productive activity with her students. In this lesson, Sarah spent approximately 75 percent of the independent work period at this table; there were students at the table 100 percent of this period with a few spending the majority of the time there and 80 percent of the students in the class approaching the table at least once.

An important aspect of the table was that students took responsibility for approaching Sarah when they wanted to interact with her. In the typical classroom where students generally stay at their desks, most discourse about the task is initiated by the teacher as she circulates. Another common pattern in classrooms where students work independently is for the teacher only to engage with the student when he or she has called on the teacher for help; this leads to interactions based on a problem the student is having. Sarah's class departed from both these norms because students could come to the table if they wanted to show something they had done successfully, watch others work, or get help with a problem. Below I discuss several interactions that occurred at the table over the course of the second part of the lesson.

In the first interaction, a student, Josh, was having trouble cutting out a rhombus using Winifred Beans' method. Coming to the table allowed him to ultimately complete the task on his own by first working jointly with the teacher and other students at the table.

> Josh approaches the table where there are three students. He waves a white paper rectangle in the air.
> *Josh*: Make this into a rhombus?
> *Sarah [to Josh, but still looking down at her paper]*: Okay, how did I cut?
> Sarah cuts out a rhombus. Josh watches, his own paper still untouched.
> *Margaret*: Make the rhombus this way. Make it this way.
> Margaret demonstrates to Josh how to make the first fold on his paper.
> Carl approaches the table and shows Sarah his rhombus without saying anything.
> *Sarah [to Carl]*: That's a good one.
> Carl shows Sarah the folds on his rhombus. Josh watches Carl fold and unfold his paper.
> *Sarah*: You did two folds? There's the first one, and the other is in the other direction. Good!
> Carl demonstrates his correctly done folds. After watching Carl go through the steps, Josh folds his piece correctly.

This example shows the power of joint activity. Josh was able to get help from the teacher, who demonstrated the technique without narration, as well as a student, Margaret, who provided more direct instruction, doing the first fold for Josh. When Carl came to the table to show his successful effort, Sarah had the chance to reinforce the procedure to Josh by narrating with Carl's shape. Although Sarah ensured that Josh had some experience with cutting out the rhombus, Josh and other students maintained an active role in the process.

This interaction demonstrates how discourse patterns within the third space are better aligned with indigenous discourse patterns than with those found in the typical classroom. In Eskimo culture, traditionally learners were expected to rely on observation rather than questioning (Lipka, 1998), a norm that Josh is able to follow because of the structure of Sarah's classroom. When Josh approaches the table, he is able to get Sarah's attention and signal that he cannot complete the task independently ("Make this into a rhombus?"), without ever specifically asking for help. Similarly, Sarah never gave him step-by-step instructions but rather arranged for Josh to get the modeling he needed. Her one bit of narration ("You did two folds?") was aimed at a successful student, thereby avoiding the direct teaching that would have prevented the modeling and joint activity to occur. This interaction is also aligned with indigenous norms of de-emphasizing individual achievement in favor of working for the good of the community (de Haan, 2002).

In another interaction, Wassily, a nonliterate student, had attempted to cut an outline of his rhombus as Sarah modeled during the introduction to the lesson, but instead ended up with two large triangles, which he brought to Sarah's table.

Wassily [holding triangles]: Miss Sarah, I messed up.
Jaylene, another student also at table, to Wassily: Yeah, but you could still...
Sarah: You could still use those shapes though. [looks at Wassily's paper] Oh, did you mess up?
Wassily: Yes.
Sarah: You think?
Wassily: Yeah.
Sarah: Could you turn...?
Just then another student with the same triangles as Wassily's comes up to the table.
Sarah: Look at that! Did you mess up?

Wassily: Awww...
Sarah: You just came up with a different way, what could you do? [takes his papers and puts the triangles back on] What could you do with this Wassily? Wassily? [touches his hand to get his attention] What could you do with this?
Jaylene, pointing to Wassily's paper: Cut that right here.
Sarah: So can you cut it out?
Wassily: Cut it out like what? Like this?
Wassily cuts his piece and gets an outline. Jaylene and Sarah watch as Wassily cuts but do not provide any more assistance.
Wassily: Sweet!

In this exchange, it took Sarah some time to diagnose Wassily's challenge with the assignment because she was unsure of what Wassily was trying to do or even if there was a problem. Bringing Wassily's attention to the other student with the same result served as a way to reinforce that he was not the only one making mistakes. The help from Jaylene allowed Wassily to both get assistance and to see other students in the role of expert. The result of Sarah's interventions is that Wassily went from being frustrated and unengaged with the task to being focused and involved. The joy he derived from cutting out the shape he wanted successfully was palpable.

This example shows the power of the third space that Sarah has created in her classroom. First, the hands-on nature of the assignment allowed Wassily to identify that there was a problem. Thanks to the work table Sarah established at the front of the room, Wassily had a place to receive feedback and work jointly with the teacher and more expert students. And the fact that Jaylene easily jumped in as an expert is a testament to the fluidity of Sarah's classroom.

Wassily's performance on the project assessments also reflected the positive learning environment he experienced in Sarah's class. Despite not being able to read, his pre- and post-test scores showed a 9-point gain, not too far from the average 13-point gain for the class overall (much of the assessment consisted of math problems requiring minimal reading). Sarah commented on Wassily's experience in an interview:

> Last night was parent-teacher conferences. [Wassily] has never had a positive conference, but this time he was taking his mother around the class and showing her everything. He asked his mom if she could cut a rhombus. She kept cutting the hourglass and he pointed to the directions, which he can't read. But she can read them. He leaves the class every day and gives me a kiss. This has been almost like a religious

experience. How different it is teaching these kids! Once we started doing [the MCC unit], they're doing it because they're interested in it.

Part Three: Review/Debrief

In the third part of the lesson, review and debrief, Sarah attempted to elicit an analysis of the lesson from students. However, she was uniformly unsuccessful in getting students to respond in the way she wanted; I argue this disappointing result was the outcome of the loss of the third space operating in the first two parts of the lesson.

Sarah transitioned to this part of the class by having students return to their seats and be quiet. After the constant hum of student talk during the individual exploration and with the students seated in rows for the first time during the period, the classroom felt very different. Once the classroom was quiet, which took a threat of lost recess time, Sarah asked questions to probe students' learning during the lesson.

Here is an exchange typical of the ten minutes spent on this section of the lesson.

Sarah: Okay, talk to me about this, James. About this, what you just did.
Kristin: It was cool!
James: It was fun.
Larissa: It was fun because we made pretty stuff.
Sarah: Pretty stuff, okay. Did you learn anything? Lucinda?
Lucinda: We made designs and we could see everything colored. At the end I think they were pretty.
Sarah: Alright. Anyone else?
Lily: I think it was cool.
Sarah: You think it was cool, what was cool about it?
Lily: They were like repeating patterns.
Sarah: And we said what when we created repeating patterns? What was something that happened again and again and again?
Lily: It's a pattern.
Sarah: It's a pattern? Um, what was the definition of a design? [silence] Cause that's what this is going to end up being, this is going to end up being your design.

What explains the lack of success in eliciting student explanations of what they had done and learned during the exploration phase of the lesson? One could argue that Sarah, as a novice teacher with the added pressure of a researcher and video camera in her classroom, simply lacked the necessary skill in using questioning strategies to promote a rich discussion of students' thinking. For example, she asks a leading question looking for a specific answer when she says "And we said what when we created repeating patterns?" However, I believe the students' lack of engagement with the review section was not the result of poor questioning, but rather due to this use of questioning itself.

In this exchange, unlike those in the first two sections of the lesson, it is Sarah who controls the flow of the conversation using what Cazden (1988) describes as the Initiate-Respond-Evaluate (IRE) structure; that is, Sarah *initiates* the questioning, then a student *responds* to the question at which point Sarah *evaluates* the response. Naming a specific student to respond to a prompt is called "spotlighting" and has been shown to be an ineffective technique for indigenous students in particular (Lipka et al., 2005).

These elements of typical IRE classroom discourse are easily identified:

> *Sarah*: Okay, talk to me about this, James. About this, what you just did. [*Initiation with spotlighting*]
> *Larissa*: It was fun because we made pretty stuff. [*Response*]
> *Sarah*: Pretty stuff, okay. [*Evaluation*] Did you learn anything? Lucinda? [*Not getting what she wanted, the teacher re-Initiates with spotlighting.*]
> *Lucinda*: We made designs and we could see everything colored. At the end I think they were pretty. [*Response*]
> *Sarah*: Alright. [*Evaluation*] Anyone else? [*Initiation without spotlighting.*]
> *Lily*: I think it was cool.
> *Sarah*: You think it was cool, what was cool about it? [*Teacher probes, incorporating student's word use. Re-Initiation.*]
> *Lily*: They were like repeating patterns. [*Response*]
> *Sarah*: And we said what when we created repeating patterns? What was something that happened again and again and again? [*Initiation. Sarah is looking for the fact that parka border designs contain a core repeating pattern.*]
> *Lily*: It's a pattern. [*Response*]
> *Sarah*: It's a pattern? Um, what was the definition of a design? [*Teacher negatively Evaluates by changing student's word (pattern) to the one she is looking for (design).*]
> Silence for 15 seconds. [*This is the first time the teacher gets no response due to the fact that she is looking for a specific response from students who realize that if they do not know exactly what she is asking for they will receive a negative Evaluation as above.*]

Sarah: Cause that's what this is going to end up being, this is going to end up being your design. [*Sarah gives her own Response, tying her answer to the project overall rather than answering the question she posed.*]

The change to the IRE structure negatively impacted student participation. In the first two sections of the class, students displayed signs of high engagement in the material. While the beginning appeared somewhat chaotic with students wandering around the classroom looking for friends and supplies, by the end of this period every student had a completed project and, further, they were eager to show their pattern pieces to me and have them recorded on videotape, reflecting pride in their work.

By contrast, in the final part of the lesson, students' affect changed to be closer to that I have seen in less successful indigenous classrooms: not meeting the teacher's eye and speaking under their breath when forced to respond. The change from using strategies such as joint activity and expert-apprentice modeling to a typical Western classroom structure drawing primarily on IRE interchanges resulted in the disappearance of the third space in Sarah's classroom, diminishing their ability to express what they knew. The juxtaposition of these two teaching styles within one lesson underscores the importance of the third space in the implementation of culturally based content and pedagogies.

Conclusion

The successful inclusion of indigenous knowledge in the classroom holds extraordinary promise, as demonstrated by the positive outcomes for the students in Sarah's class; at the same time, the enormity of the undertaking must be respected as superficial inclusion of cultural elements will not lead to the fundamental shifts in classroom dynamics needed to promote the implementation of indigenous pedagogies and the authentic inclusion of indigenous knowledge. The MCC curriculum series serves as a useful model of what is possible in terms of shifting classroom dynamics toward the incorporation of indigenous pedagogies and knowledge, as well as demonstrating the positive impact these approaches can have on student achievement. Curricula like MCC that is firmly grounded in indigenous knowledge and provides guidance on implementing culturally congruent pedagogies has the possibility to promote and nurture a third space where indigenous knowledge can finally take root in schools, ultimately bringing more *elitnauristet maklagtutulit* into the classroom.

Note

1. The names of the teacher, the village, and students have been changed for anonymity.

III

Culture, Histories, and Language

12

I Will Chant Homage to the Orisa: Oriki (Praise Poetry) and the Yoruba Worldview

Dolapo Adeniji-Neill

This chapter explores the role of "oriki," praise poem/songs and folklore of the Yoruba culture in which I was born and raised. The Yoruba territory lies in southwestern Nigeria, West Africa, commonly known as "Yorubaland." However, the influence of the Yoruba culture, its music, and its indigenous religion extends into the Caribbean, the United States, and South America, especially Brazil and everywhere black people reside around the world. There are an estimated 20 million Yorubas in Nigeria and millions of expatriates worldwide. Yoruba culture is largely oral. From praise songs and folklore, people have learned basically how to live, what to value, and how to organize a life in a particular time and place. The word "Yoruba" in our culture refers to the people, the land, the language, and the culture. It is in the context of a sentence that a reader understands how the word is being used.

I have selected examples of oriki, folklore, and folktales that have been translated from Yoruba into English by myself, and in some instances by others (duly referenced), to explain how they can affect one's conception of oneself and one's role in society. Those oriki and folktales that are not cited have come from my childhood memories of evenings listening to my elders in Ilesha (my homeland in Nigeria). I have written these in two languages, starting with the Yoruba as I recollected it and then translating them into English. The poems are presented in the original Yoruba as well as their translated English versions, for the original language of oriki and the folklore is Yoruba, and Yoruba is their soul. The value of the original voice is incalculable for so much meaning lies in every breath and inflection. Audible qualities of oriki provide great emotional resonance. The Yoruba language is tonal; the meaning is often dependent on the rising and falling inflection of the voice. Because this document is written and not oral, in the interest of simplicity I have omitted accents and marks to indicate inflections. However, I have included respondents' comments on the effect of hearing oriki.

The part that oriki plays in Yoruba tradition defies categorization in the Western mode. As pointed out by Olatunji, "since a poem employs the patterns of its language of composition for its literary effects, any meaningful discussion of the poem must take the structural patterns of that language into consideration. Categories ought, therefore, to be derived from the material in question and are only true for that material" (1984, pp. 3–4). Therefore, the subject materials of this chapter being based in the Yoruba language can only be measured according to Yoruba oral tradition and vocal arts. Olatunji continues, "It is meaningless to talk of rhyme or meter in Yoruba poetry as one does in English poetry; it is the structural and tonal configurations, for example, that can be useful in a discussion of Yoruba poetic structure" (1984, p. 4).

Oriki and folklore are important Yoruba traditions that have endured the test of time, especially in the modern-day mass-mediated world. Many of my interviews from Nigeria were done on the Internet, and Yoruba, especially the younger generation, have been fully assimilated into today's world. Still the tradition of oriki endures in their souls.

There is an adage, "If you want to know about water don't ask a fish." Swimming is natural to a fish; therefore, it may never think about its mechanics. Yet, as a result of researching for and writing this chapter, this native-born Nigerian has been able to examine the waters in which she spent her formative years and discover how the power of the spoken word has such great impact on the individual and the community of her native land.

To the Yoruba, oriki is a point of honor and pride. The effect of oriki on the subject is enormous, for it infuses the recipient with a sense of self and connects the past with the present. During the writing and translation of oriki I recollect my childhood. I dream about a time when I was encircled in poetry, songs, and stories. I am a child of oral tradition. I have heard every oriki, epic, and folktale referred to in this chapter sung at appropriate times; I have sung many of them myself as a child; I have watched every ceremony as I grew up in Ilesha and Lagos. This is why I love words; I adore poetry; and I live for stories of ancestors and stories to come.

Praise Poetry and the Griot

Oriki or praise poetry is not limited to Yorubaland; the role of the oral poets in Yoruba is akin to the role of the griot in Mali and other African countries. The word "griot" is controversial among Africans; some consider it an insult.[1] However, the roots of the word can be found in the Mende, Bariba, Songhay, Wolof, Hausa, and Fulani languages, to name a few. The word "griot" means oral historian, praise poet/singer, and the keeper of our collective memories. The griots are professional historians trained through years of study to remember all the important happenings in the life of their people. The information is handed down from generation to generation. Traditionally these professional historians, poets, and troubadours are assigned to important families, mostly those of kings. They serve as masters of ceremony at important events, advisors to kings and chiefs, and official spokesmen.[2]

For many centuries the griots have been close to the seats of power. They have served as the voices of the ruler and the "go-between" from the ruled to the ruler. As court historians, part of their responsibility is to remind kings of the traditions they must uphold so that there will be a harmonious reign. Modern historians are beginning to listen to these ancient bearers of tradition as well. Djeli Mamoudou Kouyate, a griot whose family has been in the service of the Keita princes of Mali from time immemorial, said of the family career as griots: ".We are vessels of speech, we are the repositories which harbor secrets many centuries old. The art of eloquence has no secrets for us; without us the names of kings will vanish into oblivion; we are the memory of mankind; by the spoken word we bring to life the deeds and exploits of kings for younger generations...I teach kings the history of their ancestors so that the lives of the ancient might serve them as an example, for the world is old, but the future springs from the past" (Clark and Brennan, 1991, p. 48).

Oriki is now performed on television, radio, and various media; the performers can be grandiose, showy, and flowery. Praise poetry is adaptive, and it is necessarily so in order to engage new audiences and prevent potential loss of traditional values. Some older generations bemoan the loss of authenticity, as people now sing traditional poems accompanied by synthesized kora, traditional guitar, and digitized drum sounds. Some are professionals who sing on television and radio, make compact discs, and perform in large concert halls. A well-known Malian griot, Tiemoko Cissoko, supports the approach taken by many contemporary oral poets in order to keep the traditions alive by saying, "Show business has three things: no faith, no law, and no religion." Elaborating further, he claims that the American contribution to show business, via Michael Jackson, was "a look, a character, and a style." He adds that to protect all the above in himself, he no longer plays at naming ceremonies and events of that kind, to protect his "look and character" (Hale, 1998, p. 315). In the past the same griot who sang at naming ceremonies would have had no qualms in singing and uttering the stories and histories of families and nation before kings and queens. This statement is not meant to demean professional griots or oral history performers but to bring to the fore the changing role of the performer.

A griot is not limited to one task. His job description is extensive; he is a teacher, historian, adviser, diplomat, genealogist, spokesperson, mediator, interpreter, translator, musician, composer, exhorter, witness, and praise singer. As a genealogist, the griot recounts the genealogy of families at ceremonies bringing alive their past deeds and misdeeds and transforming them to a living, breathing product. This is helpful to the audience, for example, in the case of a marriage or an engagement ceremony; it tells the audience how well matched the prospective bride and groom are not only in the context of who they are today but also who they are in terms of their ancestors. As historians, griots recount social facts. They recount great events of the past, stories of great men and women. "If one places the notion of history and literature into one category broadly defined as interpretation of the past, the griot as historian emerges as a 'time binder,' a person who links past to present and serves as witness to events" (Hale, 1998, p. 23).

The griots can serve as advisors to monarchs, members of communities, and patrons. As a repository of the past, they can help with how similar issues were resolved in antiquity. At times their advice may be imposing and critical and the listener has no recourse but to obey. Advice can be given publicly.

The griot can serve as a spokesperson or mouthpiece for rulers, for it is unusual for many African monarchs to address their subjects directly. The griots may also convey the community's wishes to the ruler, thus also serving as an ambassador. The griots can also mediate cases in which people involved feel they cannot speak directly to each other. The griots are usually fluent in several languages, becoming interpreters. The griot is a wordsmith and can put words in special forms that allow people to be receptive. The griot can be a musician and composer like King Sunny Ade, who sings and composes poetry and music about people and events and also plays many instruments. The griot as a teacher is as ancient as history. In the Epic of Sundiata, Balla Fasseke was Sundiata's griot and teacher. "Balla Fasseke gave the child education and instruction according to Mandingo rules of conduct. Whether in town or at the hunt, he missed no opportunity of instructing his pupil" (Hale, 1998, p. 38).

Oriki and Oral Culture

Yoruba griots are part of this tradition; their medium is praise poetry or oriki. Oriki is musical art. Musical art to the Yoruba encompasses singing, dancing, and audience participation. In the absence of audio visual aids, it is impossible to register all the vocal, visual, and dramatic aspects of oriki. When oriki is transcribed we are only left with texts, "bereft even of the voice of the artist/performer. What the student of Yoruba oral poetry presents is a mere shadow of the substantial living art of the Yoruba people" (Olatunji, 1984, p. 6).

Although this verbal art in many other African countries like in the Sahel and Savannah regions of West Africa appears to have only been practiced by hereditary griots, among the Yorubas, this complex poetic genre is sung by all who wish, by family members and groups as well as by hereditary griots who sing in Obas' or Kings' palaces across Yorubaland.

Some oriki performers are specialists like hunters who perform "Ijala" chants, which occur especially after group hunts. They also perform Ijala chants on special occasions such as when they celebrate the festival of the God of hunters and iron, known as Ogun. Others such as masqueraders perform oriki during festivals, going from place to place. Many make names for themselves by becoming professional performers of this most celebrated genre of Yoruba oral literature. Both men and women perform oriki. Oriki is composed for all types of occasions, from naming ceremonies, to the description and praise of animals, and Gods and Goddesses. Oriki is performed during funerals to link the world of the living with the world of the dead, especially at a time when those left behind find it difficult to let go of the departed loved one.

> Oriki remains the vital link between the living and the dead. Throughout the funeral, the deceased is continually and intensely addressed, with

exhortations, farewells, regrets, reproaches and warnings. After the funeral is over, communication becomes less concentrated, but it continues, and the idiom hardly changes. He or she is addressed in oriki in the same tone, the same terms as living subjects. The dead remain, in oriki, perpetually and potentially present. (Barber, 1991, p. 134)

The importance of oriki to the Yoruba has not diminished from ancient days. It is a means of honoring a person being addressed. It can stand on its own or tell a family history or person's history; it can also tell the truth about someone's personality and describe physical appearance. In fact, it can be used to describe just about anything. Often, it is used as an introduction to an epic.

The role of the oriki poet in Yoruba society is as an encyclopedist; their function continues to be important to the psyche of the Yoruba even with the onrush of modernization. The poet informs us of things about society that can only be gleaned through the spoken word. The oral knowledge of the Yoruba is neither authoritarian nor static; it is creative, adaptive, and can be highly personal. Many aspects of oriki poetry evokes playfulness, sexiness, seriousness, "play on words," repetitions, simplicity, complexity, and creativity. And like the ancient orikis, these newly adapted versions possess the power to evoke all human emotions.

Incantation for Self-protection
Ibi won ri o kan ki igbe mi lo
Ori ki fo ahun
Edo ki rin igbin
Otutu ki mu eja ni ale odo
A ki ki odidimode ki o ku iroju
Bi igi ba roro onila ti ba igbo gbe
Iwaju, iwaju ni opa ebiti nre si
Ategbe lese te na...

(Yoruba Traditional)

English Translation
Wherever they know they can broadcast my name
A tortoise does not suffer from a headache
A snail does not suffer from liver damage
A fish does not suffer from hypothermia
We do not say to the deaf and dumb, sorry
If a tree is terrible it still has to be in the forest
A weighted walking stick will always fall forward
A footprint on the road is final...

The above incantations or oriki for "self-protection" serve the following functions: (1) They show the Yoruba worldview in the belief that the innocent cannot be harmed and are protected by the Orishas (manifestations of the divine, commonly referred to as God), and that the person asking for help need only to cite cases in nature that support this worldview; (2) they cite myths about the Orishas that have a historical and "legal" nature that show the Orisha to be on the side of right; (3) they serve as a prayer and supplication to the ancestors and the "Orishas"; and (4) nearly all modern Yoruba troubadours like Sunny Ade use traditional oriki in their music and they enhance them by adding at the end or the beginning of the poems the names of their clients, as well as additional lines constructed by them to personalize the oriki. The oriki cited in this case, like most poems in this genre, does appear serious; the theme is folkloric, and it also has elements of a play on words such as "A fish does not suffer from hypothermia and a footprint on the road is final" and has elaborate language that is evident throughout the oriki.

Repetition—A Hallmark of Oriki

One distinct feature of praise poetry is repetition.

The Yoruba use repetition to emphasize and bring clarity to the incantations by the speaker or singer. It is also used to gain the audience's attention. For many believers in the folk religion, repetition ensures that the divinities are aware of the needs of the supplicants.

"Repetition is also a re-representation.... It represents an earlier period of time, which itself may have been a repetition. As a representation of time, repetition embodies creativity, for representation itself is a form of creativity" (Drewal, 1992, p. 1). In other words, when a sentence is uttered it only functions at that time and space; it cannot be recovered. It has gone into its own universe and taken a shape of its own. "A gesture, once made, can never be made the same way" (Drewal, 1992, p. 1). Even as the words above are essentially the same, the performance of the poem each time takes a new meaning, a new inflection and attitude. "This is because time does not repeat itself: rather, repetition operates within time to represent it, to mark it off, to measure it, to imbue it with a feeling of regularity and permanency, or even to substantiate its existence" (Drewal, 1992, p. 1). Repetition within incantations to Orishas (Gods and Goddesses) provides the chanter a common point of reference, a unifying feeling. Repetition may induce a sense of permanence and predictability.

Repetition that is ritualistic allows the worshipers an illusion that time has stood still. They can recall and reuse time and space endlessly by repeating phrases in their prayer, for in the spiritual world there is no time or space, there is only "knowing" and "knowledge," which is sometimes called faith.

Oriki as a Reflection of Oral Culture

Although obviously creative and visionary, many praise poems appear formulaic and patterned because Yoruba culture remains oral. "In an oral culture, to think through something in non-formulaic, non-patterned, non-mnemonic terms, even if it were possible, would be a waste of time, for such thought, once worked through could never be recovered with any effectiveness" (Ong, 1982, p. 35). The repetition ensures that the performer of the praise song gathers his or her thoughts so that no beat will be missed during the performance. "Oral cultures encourage fluency, fulsomeness and volubility. Rhetoricians called this *copi*" (Ong, 1982, p. 40). It is important that the materials be repeated as often as possible to solidify and ensure their survival in the minds of the listeners. The following interviewee, Adefunke Mustapha, a Yoruba now living in the United States, was asked about her views on Oriki:

> Oriki is used by the Yoruba in all aspects of life, such as during naming ceremonies, weddings, burials, parties, and by wives to make their husbands feel important. In ancient times it inspired warriors preparing for battle. Parents use it, especially mothers who want to encourage their children. It is also chanted daily in palaces across Yorubaland; for instance, in the Ile-Ife palace the praise song of the king is chanted every half hour. The chanters come from special families and only they can assume this role in the palace of Olu of Ife. The position of the praise poet/singer is hereditary. Praise song is also used for religious rituals and liturgy. In Ondo, Ilesha, Ibadan and Ile Ife, to name a few Yoruba cities, during the new yam festival or harvest festival, the people chant praise songs to the gods asking that the land be fertile, and to appropriate divinities of farms and farmers, and to Ogun, the Divinity of Iron.

Oriki as a Preservation of Culture

All those interviewed referred to oriki chants as bordering on the spiritual, especially at family ceremonies:

"It gives me joy." "It shows the family status." "It gives me happiness;" "It gives me a sense of belonging." "It encourages me to be a better person;" "It encourages me when faced with life's challenges." "It provides a soothing mood." "It reminds me of my origins and family background." "It promotes self-esteem." "It reminds me of my roots."

In addition to creating a feeling of joy, happiness, and pride, oriki establishes the historical tales, stories of origin, and genealogies of families. These stories describe and often explain family genealogy by weaving elements of "truth" and "myth" throughout the fabric of the oriki. Clearly, oriki resonates powerfully among contemporary Yorubas. It serves to associate the Yoruba with their past and instill in them a sense of pride in their ancestry.

The Family Oriki

Each Yoruba family has a distinct oriki, chanted on family occasions such as births, weddings, and funerals. The family oriki refers to the family name derived from the history of the family and then expands on that history. My interviewees all mentioned their family names: Omo Oni Wo, "The owner of Iwo village"; Odenla, "The Big Hunters"; Lafija, "The Great Warriors"; Aladirelaba, "The one who dyes cloth"; Aji bo oba re, "The King's friend"; Abengunde, "The Masqueraders"; Ile Ologun, "The House of Warriors". Below is the family oriki of the author.

English Translation

I am the daughter of Eki, the king of the forest, a brave warrior. The one whose scarification is so bold and brave it is six lines tattoo in the stomach! The great elephant that opens doors. The one we asked not to buy, not to buy, who buys a thousand slaves a day. The owner of the river that you have to drink quickly from in the forest of Eshu (the devil). The one who does extraordinary feat. Loro does not steal, Loro does not take anything that does not belong to him; but when Loro visits, the most beautiful woman is sure to disappear. Loro is the slayer of the six lions that terrified our people. From then on, Loro used the lions' skins for loincloths. Warrior, Loro! Do not be afraid, your subjects are afraid! Do not be afraid, your subjects are afraid! Do not be afraid, your subjects are afraid!

Oriki is passed down through the family, and in some cases through the village community. Individuals are singled out and praised.

Yorubas say, "a ki pe oruko eni ki a ba ni wi, akii pe oruko odo ki odo gbe ni lo, be ni a ki so oruko omo ki inu re ma you si ni" [One does not get annoyed because his name was called; a river does not drown an individual because he calls the river's name] (Daramola and Jeje, 1995, p. 67). So it is, when we say oriki in praise of a child or children, they are glad. Oriki always evokes a sense of well-being and joy for the individual being praised.

Praise Poems of Chiefs and Kings

"Praise poems of chiefs invite entrepreneurship, as old formulas and themes have to be made to interact with new and often complicated political situations. But formulas and themes are reshuffled rather than supplanted with new materials" (Ong, 1982, p. 42).

In Yoruba oriki, new materials are supplanted and inserted all the time. Modern Yoruba troubadours make use of poetry of the past and then weave new works into them to make them attractive to younger generation. The kingship system among the Ijesha people is hereditary as it is in all of Yorubaland. However, there are ways of impeaching a terrible and tyrannical king, and it has been done in antiquity. An example is the mythical story: "Obakoso," translation: "the King Did Not Hang," is a story of how King Shango was impeached and driven out of Ile-Ife and he subsequently committed suicide outside the city walls.

Oriki as a Chronicler of Heroic Deeds

Oriki is akin to heroic poems spoken throughout Africa. It is not so much about telling stories as it is about touching upon incidents of heroic deeds and qualities of the subject as in this oriki of this writer's family:

> There were six lions that terrified our village
> Loro bravely slew all six lions
> From then on he used the lion skins for loincloths

"Oriki is not necessarily panegyric" (Olatunji, 1984, p. 194). While the genre is full of terms of endearment of the subject, the poet inevitably touches on the shortcomings as well. This is done euphemistically, pleasantly, and diplomatically, as in the continuation of the above poem: "Omo mora mora ti ra igba eru lorijo!" [He was told, don't buy, don't buy, he buys a thousand slaves daily!]. No matter how it is couched, the not-so-complimentary side of the subject being praised always surfaces. Oriki praises the subject, but it also brings out the inconsistencies of the subject's life with love, humor, and respect.

Is Oriki Being Lost to Urbanization and Immigration?

Oriki is the most used of all Yoruba poetic genres, a fact attested to in that no wedding, naming ceremony, or celebration of life after death is complete without copious use of oriki. In November 2003, I attended a nephew's wedding in London, England, where the oriki of the bride's family was sung intermittently for what seemed like hours. Perplexed that the bride's family was the only one receiving the honor, I asked my sister, "What about our oriki? Have things changed so much that only the bride's family is praised?" She answered me regrettably, "You weren't here last week when the oral poet asked for it so he could learn it for the wedding and no one here knew it!" My extended families are expatriates in England, and among them and their children have lost the knowledge of our family oriki or may have not had the occasion to learn because they have been away from the sources. Other than functional uses of the Yoruba language, the deeper ceremonial language is lost to many who have long left Yorubaland.[3] My assumption is this also would have probably been the case if they lived in non-Yoruba big cities in Nigeria, like Jos or Kano. In the villages, every Yoruba oral poet strives to know the oriki of important people as well as their lineage. If this had been the case, my "European" family would not have had to forgo it due to their lack of knowledge.

So as the wedding celebration went on, the oriki singer nonetheless delighted us with "oriki orile," the origin oriki of Ilesha, our home town, by artistically weaving our family name into the songs: "Ijesha re, aro'kun yo, ye se gbodo fowo kan omo obokun" [This is Ijesha, the lover of the Atlantic Ocean, no one can harm the sons and daughters of this mighty ocean]. And, "Adeniji ni Oye yi kan, Oniyan ni oye" [This chieftaincy belongs to Adeniji; yes, his character already made him the chief]. Every time these praises of our ancestors were chanted throughout the evening, we "sprayed"[4] the oral poets with crisp American dollars as well as on other relations who may have been dancing to the songs, especially young women married into the family and older women, our mothers. It is customary that all relations get up from their seats and dance whenever their praise song is sung. This creates a sense of community, solidarity, intimacy, and pride. Time and again this proved the power of the sounded words in evoking memory and calling the listener to action. Also the adaptation made by the poets at the wedding is constant in oral culture. Every time someone tells a story, it is unique to the situation and to the audience.

Oriki is the poetry of the people. The continued celebration of this literary genre attests to the power of the people to carry tradition forward.

Notes

1. Although the root of the word "griot" can be traced to many African languages, some people think that it is derived from the French language and, therefore, is viewed as related to colonialism in the francophone West African nations.
2. Alex Haley, the author of *Roots*, found his place of origin in West Africa after three hundred or more years of absence by listening to the recitation of a griot. This is but one example of the life-affirming and life-changing function of this type of histo-literature.
3. Brazilian Yorubas, however, have long held on to the ceremonial Yoruba language; over 300 years of forced physical disconnection have not dampened the spirit of worship and awe they hold for their ancestors and traditions. However, the new self-imposed diaspora may not have the same urgency to know or preserve the "language" of oriki. They can always find it if needed in written form or can send "home" for it if the need arises.
4. To proffer money, usually done by moistening a paper bill with the lips and pressing it onto the forehead of the performer.

13

Containing Interwoven Histories: Indigenous Basket Weaving in Art Education

Courtney Lee Weida

Introduction

In college and graduate school, I worked as the director of summer arts programs at sleep-away and day camps near the ocean. A paint shortage halfway through one summer led me to sort through seemingly ancient art materials boxed and forgotten from a predecessor's supply stash. I located several dusty half-made baskets and unwoven reeds. One of my staff members expressed great joy at this finding. Obliging her interest and initiative, our students trailed out of the art cabin later that afternoon, wading into the cool and shallow water along the shore, equipped with reeds and her helpful guidance on basket weaving. That day, a calm washed over us as we wove water-softened reeds into baskets and discussed the history, use, and look of them along the beach. Weaving in beads, shells, and scraps of colorful paper over subsequent sessions, we were spellbound by the process Meilach (1974) described as "revising creative methods used centuries ago" (p. 1).

Although a potter at heart, I have often sensed that there is something incredibly valuable in basketry and basket weaving to be explored within art and craft education. In fact, it is commonly believed that baskets preceded and gave birth to the art of pottery, as clay was discovered within the dirt used to plug holes in the baskets. Further, both pots and baskets are vessels and can have lids and feet. I have become particularly intrigued by the deeper commonalities and cross-influences of the origins of pottery and basketry (also called basket weaving). Theorizing basket weaving as an art form that is romanticized, misunderstood, and/

or neglected in manners similar to the treatment of indigenous studies, this chapter will explore relationships between basket craft and indigenous cultures. Writing from an outsider, Western perspective, I will also problematize my own positionality as an artist and educator and the troubled/troubling roles of colonial influences on basket traditions. This chapter explores basket weaving in the context of Native American histories and craft traditions (especially Cherokee and Pomo tribes) in the Americas and basketry traditions from Southern Africa, including topics of family relationships, gender issues, traditional mythology, and the related development of pottery. This chapter also seeks to examine the "metaphor for history" (note by Sarah Hill, 1997) found within baskets in contemporary art education as a relevant, if neglected, thread of art and craft. By reclaiming the aspects of gender, myth, and connections to other crafts, we can make a case for baskets as part of an inclusive, culturally rich, and socially just art curriculum.

Historical Roles of Family and Education in Basketry

Baskets have been what Sandy Heslop (2011) describes as "a Cinderella subject, a poor relation with no profile as an artistic activity and relatively little as a contemporary craft" (p. 11). Despite some Renaissance of Native American baskets recently, basket weaving is in many cases as likely to be heard as a joke as an artistic endeavor (e.g., underwater basket weaving as a jest). Yet we may overlook how many of the most common colloquial phrases make reference to baskets. For example, darker phrases like "hell in a handbasket," "basketcase," or more neutral ideas like "putting all your eggs in one basket," or how the "glass half empty/glass half full" analogy was once used to reference a basket in lieu of a glass. Poet Olympia Morata (1526–1555) has identified the key symbols of the female sex as "yarn, shuttle, basket, and thread." Baskets are frequently filled with food as gifts of celebration or markers of consolation. Meanwhile, although people may not use traditional baskets in all parts of everyday life, we do find a great many altered or adapted forms of baskets in present-day shopping baskets, wastebaskets, fruit baskets, and basketball.

Many educators overlook baskets as I had initially done; early childhood educator Cantu (2004) even suggests parents purchase "craft baskets" to store supplies for crafting, where children could have created and personalized these functional objects themselves with help from adults.

In many ways, baskets contain a great deal of context that is similarly invisible, yet in plain sight. Basket weaving, although neglected in the mainstream, has been incredibly eclectic, extending into craft programs for children and adults, within community centers, college courses, and enrichment programs. Beyond these educational communities, families and familial relationships are commonly at the heart of craft education, especially in basket weaving. Specifically, indigenous traditions of baskets and baskets themselves are generally passed down through families (often apart from formal studio art and art history). Historically, families served extensive educative roles, once as the primary sources as education, and even now as the original educators that young children encounter before entering schools. As noted by Stankiewicz, Amburgy, and Bolin (2004), "the family was the first teacher, elders transmitting eye and hand skills along with beliefs and rituals" (p. 34). A great deal of the literature on basket weaving addresses the family learning traditions in the baskets of North American Indians during the twentieth and twenty-first centuries (Sullivan, Schwartz, Weiss, & Zaffran, 1996; Wroth, 1994; and Hill, 1997).

The book by Brooklyn Museum educators Sullivan et al. (1996) provides an interesting parallel for family learning components of basketry, for the book itself is intended as a curriculum resource for adults and children to share basket making at home. Sullivan et al. document autobiographical comments of Susan Billy (born 1951), a Pomo basket weaver from California. Billy's comments in the text focus upon the 16-year education she received in basketry from her great-aunt Elsie Comanche Allen. Billy writes, "On my first day of weaving, as I walked into the room, my great aunt held out her hand and gave me an old awl and knife. She said, 'These were your grandmother's and I want you to have them'" (p. 41). Like techniques, tools can be an integral part of traditions passed down by relatives.

Pomo researcher Wroth (1994) also records the history and traditions of the Allen family, focusing on the narratives of Elsie Allen and her mother, Annie Burke. Burke both wove baskets and taught basket weaving for her family during the American Craft Revival. When Burke's mother passed away and was buried with both her baskets and her basketry tools, Burke and her daughter, Elsie Allen, felt a "deep sense of loss" emotionally and artistically for her lost relative and lost tools (p. 83). For this reason, Allen's mother decided not to be buried with her baskets and tools upon death, but rather to bequeath them to her daughter. This artistic shift in an artistic tool's function from memorial and funerary relic to keepsake and heirloom went against both family and cultural tradition and serves to demonstrate the powerful experiences of family education and sensibilities of inherited tools for these individual women. Traditions can be fluid and constructed in this adaptive manner.

Adapting her teaching beyond the domestic sphere, Burke also participated in fairs where she taught basket weaving to nonnatives "to instill in them a sense of the skill and genius of Pomo cultural traditions" (p. 83). In several cases, schools and/or teachers from outside the Native American family could also provide basket weaving instruction. Elsie Allen also went on to author books on basket weaving and her experiences of crafts with others. Sarah Hill (1997) details another compelling educational history of Arizona or Zona' Nick Swayney, a Cherokee basket weaving instructor of the Indian schools during the early 1900s. Swayney learned basketmaking not from her mother, but from various male and female teachers outside her family home (p. 219). Still others would be self-taught. For example, another Cherokee weaver, Lucy (Nola) George, remembers, "There were no teachers available and...I realized...that I would have to learn on my own" (qtd. in Hill, 1997, p. 191). Hill argues that the absence of home basketry instruction for George is but one case of a widespread decline in "traditional systems of learning" in the twentieth century among the Cherokee (p. 192). The basket serves as a symbol of lost ways of indigenous learning from the past.

Cherokee basket weaver Rowena Bradley also mentions the lack of a mother-teacher figure. As Hill (1997) writes, "Rowena speaks often of her mother" and expresses the wish to "see a picture of one of her baskets" (p. xvi). George and Bradley both lament the loss of family figures to provide the dual and often interrelated role of caregiver and craft teacher. This longing aptly raises the issue that for some the mythologized or remembered parent-teacher may be as compelling a motivation to learn a craft tradition as the actual presence of a parental figure as one's teacher. All of these memories and longings weave into the stories of the baskets and their meanings and can provide interesting connections to home and family in the classroom. Similarly, they may inspire us to reconsider those objects and traditions of home that might not currently seem relevant to curriculum. For example, several of my Latin American students revealed that they have relatives that create beautiful crafts, cakes, dolls, and objects that are not seen as "art" by relatives, and yet can be valued and shared in the art classroom. What crafts might be reclaimed from today's homes and brought into art curricula? Linda Tuhiwai Smith's

(2012) frameworks of indigenous research includes influential practices and frameworks teachers can explore of writing, representing, gendering, envisioning, reframing, protecting, creating, negotiating, discovering, and sharing that can be particularly suitable to the art, craft, mythologies, and histories of basket traditions. The following sections are inspired and informed by these frameworks.

Women Weavers: Gender in Basketry

Within homes, baskets may represent traditional gender relationships and daily activities. The design, function, and education associated with baskets reveal a great deal about the lives of their female makers, from where they lived to what they ate. Along these lines, students can examine ways in which craft may have been linked to past gender roles and ways of life. So too, baskets marked shifts in community. Writing of Southern Africa, Patricia Davison (2006) emphasizes that "communities of techniques and plant uses speak to the value of indigenous knowledge passed down from one generation to the next...and traditional basketry was never static, but constantly adapting to changing social and environmental conditions" (p. 2). Socially, Hill notes that Cherokee family relationships were matriarchal, with "clan identity" drawn from the mother (p. 27). Basketry as an art form coexisted well with the domestic expectations of Cherokee women, for, as Hill writes, "weaving baskets did not interfere with other responsibilities that shaped the days of women [because] weavers could prepare material and make baskets in their homes, day or night" (p. 192). It was for this reason that women were the primary basket weavers. Art educator Patrick (2011) has also observed another gendered connection in how plaiting baskets can feel very similar to braiding processes (e.g., braiding hair). Meanwhile, artists can even create baskets from hair, highlighting the delicateness and luminosity of the material and its connection to the body and rituals of body decoration. In Africa, basket techniques of plaiting have also been used for straw hats, seed sieves, sleeping mats, and woven houses as counterparts to baskets with shared techniques. In addition, using hair in baskets could also be seen as part of a continuum from African plaiting techniques common to hair and basket decoration, as well as Western hair work jewelry of the nineteenth century that was made as keepsakes. All of these connections evoke the richness of craft methods inseparable from the body, decoration, and precious objects.

Additional symbolic and often gendered associations of baskets can be located in other literature. While Barrett's research (1976) suggests that both men and women made baskets in Pomo culture, he reminds us that the basket-weaving techniques employed by men and women were quite distinct. Specifically, "the men make no tightly woven baskets, and the women make very few openwork baskets" (p. 147). These tendencies frequently reflected the needs of basket makers for holding grain, fish, or even infants, so that the weave and pattern reflected those individual needs and purposes. Reichel-Dolmatoff (1985) writes that even in cultures where basket weaving is primarily done by men, baskets as food- and water-bearing vessels "have marked female association" (p. 30). In this way, food- and water-bearing baskets may relate symbolically to the life-giving female form even when they are not created by women. In addition, Heslop (2011) has suggested that baskets may have emerged from human hands drawing from inspiration of birds' nests. This gives baskets a special place as tiny structures or shelters or symbols of these objects, along with associations of bellies or vessels, all of which are provocative spatial and corporeal sites for curriculum to explore. In addition, it allows us to consider nature and history in explorations of how craft forms may endure.

The practical purposes of baskets in combination with patterns of trade and profit also impacted their evolution as forms created by females. During the early 1900s in Cherokee culture, the success of water-tight and finely woven baskets to hold food resulted in what Hill describes as an "autonomy [via] women's management of food... where the availability of provision could be uncertain" (p. 85). Hill also points out the connection of women's baskets and white colonization. Women's "ingenuity with food and baskets" (p. 54) impressed European settlers and traders, and the resulting alterations in the design and decoration of their weavings came to signify the level of assimilation of artistic and cultural norms. Miller (1996) notes a similar connection between basketry and colonization, arguing that Native Americans of the Plateau region "generally made baskets for their own use and for their families [but] baskets were also important as trade goods" (p. 43). For basket weavers like George, the sale of baskets was "a way to supplement [the] family's income" (p. 192).

But whenever assimilation occurs, the integrity of personal and cultural identity may be at stake. Shanks and Woo-Shanks (2010) hypothesize that Yokut makers (from a California Native American tribe) sometimes decorated their baskets with designs of human figures, perhaps due to European contact. The historical accounts of basket weaving in Hill's writings also reveal the colonial restraints on artistic styles to produce marketable baskets for traders. Additionally, as Hill writes, colonial records demonstrate "persistent neglect in recording the names of weavers [that] must be counted as a loss to history as well as to the weavers' descendants" (p. 243). In this way, the history of much Native American basketry is at times invisible and/or oral as opposed to written. This issue of documentation comprises another consideration for art educators to take into account within art historical content for students. By exploring objects that have been overlooked in the art education of art teachers, we can become co-learners with students and investigate gaps in documentation and indigenous art history. The overlap of consumption, tourism, and authenticity is interesting to question in this way, so that we can show students some of the complexities of craft and dimensionality of indigenous cultures by learning from indigenous makers.

As another educational aim, we can invite students to investigate where an outsider author may have (unintentional) bias or blind spots with reference to indigenous crafts. For example, Meilach's 1974 text on "Modern Basketry" is careful to specify in the preface that "each person's name accompanies his examples" (p. vii). However, it may be noted that the names of Native American basket weavers featured do not accompany the examples, nor are the majority of baskets appropriately "his," given the feminine nature of those names that are supplied. The structure and language of this book in and of itself is a generative topic for gender and culture politics associated with art history; for even in its emphasis on artistic credit, the book omits the names of Native American people and assumes masculine artistic identity throughout. Baskets can contain all of this provocative difficulty with classification and attribution that also extends to related areas of unsigned pottery and jewelry.

Weaving Baskets, Weaving Indigenous Mythology

Although the previous section argues that the presence of Native American women in basket weaving is lacking from colonial records as well as more recent literature, a fuller recognition of their roles can often be traced within Native American mythology. Beavert (1996) writes of the origins of basket weaving among her people, the Yakama Native Americans of the Plateau region. In this myth, S\inmi, or Grey Squirrel, acts as a teacher and challenges a young girl to make a basket that will not leak when dipped in water, encouraging her to accomplish this task with the enticement that "someday you will be famous for your work" (p. 36). Hill notes a prevailing Cherokee myth that rubbing "strong and shimmering webs" of industrious spiders as a sort of talisman will aid women in becoming successful basket weavers (p. 185). This is an evocative natural connection between the pattern and radial symmetry of the natural world and baskets.

Beyond theorizing the initial impetus to create baskets, additional mythology addresses basketry education and governs aesthetic choices such as design. For example, Barrett points out that several Native American tribes believed that Coyote had been the first basket-weaving instructor and that he taught basket weavers to leave breaks or gaps in designs or risk becoming blind. Legends exist that women weavers who neglected to leave openings in their basket patterns have "paid the penalty of blindness" (p. 171). Coyote's myth shows the importance placed on traditions of decoration, including an aesthetic of imperfection, humility, and humanity. Elsewhere in art education, this impulse continues in lesson plans like those of Allemand (1995) with suggestions that students can leave gaps and openings in a basket to add interest and character. The Native American myths also serve to connect weavers with heroic mythological figures, which is perhaps unsurprising, given the noble functions of baskets as ubiquitous storage vessels, memorials, and works of art. Educators can teach about such memorable and inspiring links between nature, myth, and making. Why might a maker want to include a mistake in their basket? What does that imperfection say about art and craft? These are the kinds of questions about the value and character of art that students can explore.

Shared Origins of Baskets and Pottery Vessels

As myths often address origins, so too basket weaving illuminates art history, particularly in terms of the origins of pottery. There are multiple references to shared techniques and histories between pottery and baskets. Barrett details the technique of coiling in basket making, a practice similar to using long coils of clay to form pottery. Beyond the radial symmetry in designs of both pots and baskets, Reichel-Dolmatoff (1985) points out similarities of universal phosphenes or optical sensations (in this case, images induced by ritual hallucinogenic drugs) in Tukanoan designs common to basketry and pottery, demonstrating the similarity in their design. Wyckoff (2001) notes the use of baskets and pots together in washing, cooking, and eating activities (p. 32). In addition, pots are often used for storing water and soaking reeds used in basket weaving. It would seem that while baskets serve as a metaphor for history, basketry histories overlap and give rise to pottery histories. Lee notes that "pottery had its beginning in an effort to make baskets watertight" (p. 2) by lining baskets with clay and exposing clay-filled baskets to cooking heat or fire, thus baking the clay and hardening it against porosity and leaking. In White's text, Blanchard reminds us that "ages before people had pottery to cook in they had basketry, which is, indeed, the oldest and most universally practiced handicraft known" and that pottery "evolved...directly from basketry" (p 191). Meilach (1974) also calls attention to the prevalence of basketry long before the evolution of pottery, showing the long history of this form of making. Cunningham and Terry (2006) observed how pots were also used in service of basket making for soaking reeds, storing materials, and other basketry preparations in Southern Africa. The idea of baskets engendering and supporting pottery offers parallels to the relationships of mother to daughter, providing an additional layering of history and metaphor.

We may also link the processes of pottery and basketry making, for both involve coiling. Some pottery employs a coiled texture in the finished pot (as opposed to other coiled pots where the coil is smoothed into a flat surface). Similarly, Woo and Woo-Shanks (2010) observed in California that Tubatulabal tribal baskets have snakeskin patterns, which perhaps underscores the formal similarity of coils of reeds and snakes. A practiced knowledge of the natural world is part of the basketmaker's work. Shanks and Woo-Shanks (2010) argue that "Native American women had to be anthrobotanists as well as artists. Basketry form and function also required that weavers have the analytical mind of the engineer when considering what materials to choose and which weaving techniques were needed to manage stresses, weight and wear" (p. 3). Meanwhile, Cunningham and Terry (2006) point out that English plant names are too general to describe the rich biodiversity of plant materials used in baskets of Southern Africa. These distinctions show linguistic as well as broader cultural differences, which touch on how indigenous craft entails scientifically rich and particularly interdisciplinary ways of knowing.

Within my own professional development as an educator, I once attended a pottery and ceramic sculpture workshop that was held in close proximity to a separate basket-making workshop (perhaps because of shared use of water and natural materials in contrast with areas like glassblowing). Surprisingly (and almost embarrassingly) I found myself more fascinated by the various baskets and basket weavers than many of the pots and potters I encountered in my designated studio. Although I was no less interested in pottery than I had been before the workshop, I felt a growing affinity for basketry. I perceived the formal quality of a container or vessel between the two crafts. I felt or suspected, to a certain extent, the rich history, gender associations, and connections to pottery that this research into basketry has communicated more specifically and in more varied indigenous women's voices. This is an area of dialog I invite other educators to explore: how is an art medium defined throughout history to its makers? As a Caucasian female educator, I have come to realize ways in which art and craft histories can be "white-washed" such that makers outside of European and white American experiences are overlooked. Meanwhile, even when indigenous peoples from these and other regions are included, this is done with a sense of isolation as marginal art, or exoticized so that culture is presented as monolithic, mythic, and trapped/enshrined as a sort of idealized, untouched commodity. So too, women's histories are frequently neglected among catalogs of educators and educational philosophers.

Given the overlap of pottery and basketry, it is almost surprising the two arts are not more frequently studied in correlation to bring shared cultural contexts and gender issues into teaching. Certainly, as a student of pottery, this was not the case in my own education. What studio and art history curriculum could emerge from the interdisciplinary crossroads of these two areas? This is a valuable curricular question in art and craft education that can serve to provide connections in curriculum as well as art history. Furthermore, basket weaving need not be seen as a purely functional craft, but as a symbolic and sculptural area of creation. Artists like Mary Butcher continue to apprentice to master basketmakers as was done in the past, even as they may create nonfunctional, asymmetrical, and experimental baskets. As art educators, we can push the boundaries of studio areas and conceptual links in this way. Those interested in sculptural baskets, or sculpture that is basket-like, might consult the work of Dorothy Gill Barnes. Her work includes forms that appear to be baskets transforming back into natural materials, as well as basket-hybrids of natural and man-made objects. The symbol and form of baskets has much to offer sculptural explorations.

Concluding Reflections on Baskets, Materiality, and Making

This chapter sought to investigate basket weaving as a form of art and craft, inseparable from evocations of family, gender, history, and culture. As Shanks and Woo-Shanks (2010) note,

> Californian Indian baskets remind us of our grandmothers. They have a gentle, loveliness about them and a sense of purpose and dignity that gains our respect. The beauty and the wisdom they represent is enhanced with age. Such baskets are honored and this is as it should be. (p. 1)

Writers like Hill (1997) also warn scholars and teachers from perceiving culture as a fixed and purely traditional entity, pointing out an evolving cultural balance maintained between tradition of the past and synthesis of the present. In order to bring crafts such as basketry into a more respectful, dynamic, and culturally nuanced educational space, we must be willing to push past oversimplified historical accounts and question what socialized perceptions of the Other—whether negative or idealized—shape educational approaches to looking and knowing. In this way, baskets can become accessible crafts and artifacts of great meaning to learners in art. Cunningham and Terry (2006) point out the unique sense of democracy of basket weaving, for it is inexpensive, few tools are needed, and special locations are not a prerequisite. Baskets can be seen as one of the first literally and symbolically grassroots activities, making it a political and personal art-making experience.

As part of addressing aspects such as nature, history, and myth mentioned earlier, we can also invite students to consider baskets in terms of place and space. As I am now a city dweller, my baskets are either made from purchased materials grown far away from my home or from local urban scraps like colorful telephone wires, old newspapers, or recycled plastic bags. Meanwhile, basket weavers in South Carolina may use sea grasses, and Japanese baskets are often made from bamboo. Art educator Allinder (1993) invited students to combine found natural materials like twigs with man-made fiberglass and wire. From these mixed supplies, students created asymmetrical, often large forms that become like aforementioned basket forms of wombs and nests. Although materials like fiberglass and telephone wire somewhat seem urban and Western, the Zulu people of South

Africa also utilize them in baskets, as a substitute for earlier wire baskets. We need not separate ourselves from family histories and local meanings of the materials we use to create our art, and to create our lives. Baskets offer a great deal of history and inspiration in terms of stories of makers and craft, the geographies and daily lives of users, and the enduring symbolism, materiality, and mystery of the objects. In a thoughtful interweaving of such cultural history, geographically specific materiality, and indigenous inquiry, we may collaboratively begin the rich and layered work of learning the art and craft of basket weaving.

14

An African Philosophy for Children: In Defense of Hybridity

Amasa Philip Ndofirepi

In this chapter, I present a theoretical argument for a hybridized Philosophy for Children program. I defend the contention that Africanizing education institutions should start from what is indigenous to Africa by arguing for a transcendence of Eurocentric education, acculturation, and socialization. I however acknowledge Matthew Lipman's initiative of doing philosophy with children in schools from an early age. For such a program to be relevant to the context, I submit that it must start from the existential circumstances of its consumers. But a hybridized Philosophy for Children project for Africa, which amalgamates the Western and traditional African ways of doing philosophy with children, is not dismissal of the Western paradigm.

The devaluation of traditional African cultures and the consequent intellectual subjugation has often been blamed on colonial and postcolonial education. Such forms of conquest have led to the entire neglect of African ways of thinking and of connecting with their world by "lighting Africa's tropics with temperate Euro-American educational torches" (Nsemanang & Tchombe, 2011, p. 7). Some African intellectuals have called for a reappropriation of precolonial forms of education to rediscover the roots of African identity (see Higgs, 2003, 2008; Kanu, 2007; Makgoba, 1997a, Odora-Hoppers, 2001a) especially given "the arrogance of modernisation and the conspiracy of silence in academic disciplines towards what is organic and alive in Africa" (Odora-Hoppers, 2001b, p. 1). Owolabi (2001) has, however, laid the blame on some Western-trained African scholars who have continued to deliberately ignore the methodological necessity of establishing African philosophical practice founded on indigenous culture. Hence "Africa's knowledge has increasingly ceased to be rooted in the African soil" (Ojiaku, 1974, p. 204). But the move suggested by the pro-Africanization agenda, critics would argue, will not only bring the standards down but is also incompatible with globalization and the accompanying modernization.

My case is premised on the following: (1) "education always occurs in a specific ecological and cultural context" (Nsemanang & Tchombe, 2011, p. 11); (2) philosophy begins in a cultural milieu and to philosophize, one starts from one's existential circumstances; and (3) the twenty-first-century Africa is fundamentally in a state of cultural flux because of the absence of a truly "traditional African" culture or the existence of Western culture living in a "third space" (Bhabha, 1996). On this basis, I examine the notion of hybridization and also defend a unique Philosophy for Children rooted in the existential circumstances of the African people.

What Is Philosophy for Children?

Philosophy for Children is a fairly recent educational development and a brainchild of Matthew Lipman, designed to promote philosophizing by children. Lipman came to the conclusion that there is a need for a philosophical curriculum that would help young people to improve their critical, creative, and caring thinking skills. For him, philosophy is the only means that can initiate the procedure of self-critical inquiry. Thus,

> If the schools could do more than teach children to exercise better judgment, it would protect them against those who would inflame them with prejudice and manipulate them through indoctrination. It would make them better producers and consumers, better citizens and better parents. (Lipman, 2003, p. 273)

Lipman criticized the traditional forms of school education for failing to teach students for critical reasoning by revealing that " while children of four, five and six are full of curiosity, creativity and interest and never stop asking for further explanations, by the time they are eighteen they are passive, uncritical and bored with learning" (1982, p. 37).

Lipman published the first of several philosophical novels for children in 1974 and established the Institute for the Advancement of Philosophy for Children (IAPC) at Montclair State University. His

An African Philosophy for Children

unique program created novels used to expose students to a variety of philosophical questions and ideas and to excite them into thinking philosophically. Lipman's novels are written in episodes designed to be read to and by children and depicting the various branches of philosophy. Philosophy for Children is not about teaching children philosophy or the philosophical ideas of great philosophers in history but is about doing philosophy with children till the age of 18. The program has been tried, tested, and implemented in many countries worldwide.

The Notion of Hybridization

Some scholars have highlighted that the concept of hybridity occupies a central place in social scientific discourses, especially in a cosmopolitan globalized world (Bhabha, 1996; Koopman, 2010; Pieterse, 2004). The concept originates from the science of plant species in which the word means mix, cross, amalgam, or crossbreed. While often used in a derogatory sense when referring to different race issues with hybrid races viewed as inferior races, the positive side of hybridity is in the acknowledgment that identity is a construct of a negotiation of difference. In the context of contemporary cultural discourse it is "celebrated and privileged as a kind of superior cultural intelligence owing to advantage of in-betweeness, the straddling of two cultures and the consequent ability to negotiate the difference" (Rutherford, 1990, p. 158).

The notion of hybridity is best explained in the construction of culture and identity within the milieu of antagonism and inequality (Bhabha, 1996; Odora-Hoppers, 2001b). Politically, hybridity is the process where authority undertakes to translate the identity of the colonized (the *other*) within a universal framework, but then fails to produce something familiar but rather new. It is out of the interweaving of the cultural elements of both the colonizer and the colonized that a new hybrid identity emerges thereby challenging the authority and legitimacy of any essentialist cultural identity. Hence a hybrid is a crossbreed of the local and the foreign to produce a unique "species."

Bhabha (1996) asserts that hybridity is an in-between space, what he refers to as a *third space*, where the cutting edge of translation and negotiation occurs. The third space becomes a form of expression and a gap that produces new possibilities. Those who occupy a hybrid space benefit from having an understanding of both local knowledge and global cosmopolitanism (Lone, 2000; Werbner, 1997). The concepts of hybridity and third space contribute to the development of "inclusionary, multifaceted, not dualistic, patterns of cultural exchange and maturation" (Coombes & Brah, 2000, p. 3). To this end, the hybrid discourse creates space for negotiation, which is not the assimilation of one culture by another. Hybridization, from the above, involves "the interpenetration of the universalisation of particularism and the particularisation of universalism" (Pieterse, 2001, p. 100) in some distinguished cultural synthesis. The indigenous and the exogenous interact to create a new distinct identity. But how can we situate the concept of hybridity in the African Philosophy for Children?

A Hybridized Philosophy for Children

At the mention of *"child"* and *"philosophy"* in *"Africa"* interested parties are both attracted and puzzled. For example, what is the notion of child in Africa? Can children in Africa do philosophy? The "child" in traditional Africa is perceived as a human *becoming* rather than human being, who, through the process of socialization, is to be shaped into a fully human adult being (James, Jenks, & Prout, 1998). Children are seen as in need of understanding, adult help, and protection and hence they are *not yet* ready. For traditional Africans, this stage of life implies an absence of responsibilities, the lack of autonomous thinking, and not having to deal with life's serious issues. But does this mean they cannot philosophize? Just like the inquisitive "child" elsewhere, the child in Africa is capable of wondering and asking philosophical questions.

Traditional African societies have often been criticized for their lack of appropriate impulsive character to sustained and philosophical inquiry. In this connection, Hamminga writes:

> From the African point of view, arguments are a sign of weakness, of lack of power and vitality. A good, forceful truth does not need arguments. Arguments are crutches only invalid opinions need. And truth is felt as a force coming from the speaking human. A strong man has strong truths. As far as truth is concerned, strength is not measured in muscles but in age and wisdom. Wisdom does not exist of stockpiles of arguments. It consists of wider and deeper understanding of the universe. Wisdom is felt as a force. (2005, p. 61)

This justifies how traditional Africans stunted the spirit of inquiry by emphasizing conformity for solidarity. However, Wiredu suggests that "to develop in any serious sense, we in Africa must break with our old uncritical habits of thought..." (1997, p. 323). Hence, my call for a hybrid Philosophy for Children in Africa will help resolve the continual struggle between its indigenous traditions and the modern and Western perspective of doing philosophy with children. Hence, the philosophical enterprise will originate from the actual social patterns of the child in the twenty-first-century Africa.

Despite the negatives that pervade traditional African epistemic and cultural schemes, Africa can still return to the past to move forward—a notion referred to in Akan language as *Sankofa*. The notion of *Sankofa* holds that we should reach back and gather the *best* of what our past has to teach us, so that we can achieve our full potential as we move forward (Kanu, 2007). This implies tradition as defending the process of transmitting something valuable or worthwhile by receiving it, preserving it, and passing it forward to those generations that come after the present.

If we consider Africa in the global context, we find the challenge of reconciling African culture and traditional values, on the one hand, and Western science and technology, on the other. Both no longer prevail in their pure form especially where Western sociocultural values conflict with those of traditional Africa. The question then is: in what context should African educational aims and objectives be fostered? I argue for a hybrid model that involves "indigenising what is foreign, idealising what is indigenous, nationalising what is sectional and emphasising what is African" (Mazrui, 1972, p. xvi). Hence, it is important for us to separate the philosophical enterprise that belongs to the universalist paradigm from that which belongs to the African particular. To deny children in Africa to practice doing philosophy in the African context in preference to the Western Lipmanian model is tantamount to "denying the presence of the particular, the local and its promise of political difference" (Osha, 2011, p.173), which I vehemently classify as racial, segregatory, and derogatory in its most raw form.

The pedagogical essence of philosophy will not change in the context of Africa since philosophy is universal. Traditional African cultural beliefs need to be taken on board and then critically interpreted to suit the present situations and priorities in Africa. Any philosophy that can be said to be African should be epitomized not by the mere recording of traditions and culture, but rather in the reconstruction of contemporary African experiences, challenges, and conditions. This will not only lift an African philosophy of education to the universal level that suits the specific existential conditions and priorities of Africa, but a hybrid Philosophy for Children is also a rejection of "the consecration of the normativeness of the West" (Kebede, 2011, p. 107) and hence a dismissal of the universal wholesale adoption of the Lipmanian model.

Africa needs to thoughtfully, inventively, and purposively cast the external in the context of the internal and "weave a cultural mesh" (Gyekye, 1997, p. 296). This implies knitting worthwhile aspects of traditional indigenous cultures with foreign ones to suit the present existential conditions. Accordingly, the African perspective cannot entirely reject the Lipmanian model that fuses children and philosophy. The novels and the instructional manuals for teachers have formed the wellspring of incontrovertible value for everyone interested in initiating Philosophy for Children in their own milieus. However, Wiredu's assertion that Africans "have no choice but to conduct their philosophical inquiries in relation to the philosophical writings of other peoples; for their own ancestors left them no heritage of philosophical writings" (1997, p. 326) should be treated with the highest contempt possible. Such a claim ignores the fact that

> Africans have their own ideas about the nature of the universe, time and space, about appearance and reality, and about freedom and necessity. The effort of the African to interpret man [and woman] in relation to the universe shows just as much intelligence [and rigor] as we find in the philosophy of the Greeks. (Van Hook, 1993, p. 29)

However, one needs to also acknowledge that we are living in the global world of which African is a constitutive part. Consequently, there is no way Africa can avoid the philosophical methods of their particular colonizers. There is no harm in recognizing ways of doing philosophy from other cultures especially where a certain richness of ideas derives from the comparative aspect of philosophizing.

An authentic African perspective of Philosophy for Children should begin with Africans and by Africans in cherishing and appreciating Africanicity in the forms of indigenous African institutions, knowledge systems, and techniques (Nsemanang & Tchombe, 2011). This would dismantle from an early age, "the racial hierarchy established by the colonial ideology" (Irele, 1990, p. 83), as well as ensure the emancipation and autonomy of children in Africa. As a result, a hybrid Philosophy for Children in Africa would dispel the idea that Africans play an inferior role in a world modeled and dominated by

Western rationality. It is therefore a matter of "if Euro-Americans can have their own Philosophy for Children which is purely western, Africans can equally have a hybridised programme of the same" rooted in the twenty-first-century African experience.

The notion of philosophizing as a critical activity is sensitive to context and does not have a place for forms of ready-made texts, concepts, methods, or values. If we are to develop a Philosophy for Children in schools that is "African," the reality of each school and the children who attend it should be the prime point of reference. The themes that form the content of the Philosophy for Children classes must start from the lives and experiences of the children and the school life. In this regard, the introduction of Lipman's texts and materials that do not concern the life and existential circumstances of the learners, teachers, and the school itself is inappropriate. Introducing Philosophy for Children in Ovamboland or deep parts such as KwaZulu Natal, for example, through the storybook *Harry Stottlemeier's Discovery* as well as picture books, videos, and films about dinosaurs would be an epistemological assault on the minds of the innocent learners. A hybrid Philosophy for Children that I propose develops culture-specific understanding of Africa's ethnical diversity.

Each time children form concepts around these daily experiences. Children in schools face insurmountable obstacles, social pressures, and values and challenges, among them competition, success, oppression, punishment, illness, hunger, and disease. Instead of imposing concepts from literature originating outside their African context, I suggest that an African Philosophy for Children should be initiated from the African context in the language and experiences of the participants. Such a philosophy does "not [expel] Europeans and their cultures" (Makgoba, 1997b, p. 571). Rather, it acknowledges the African tradition and its place in the global sphere by "incorporating, adapting and integrating other cultures into and through African visions" (ibid.).

Language is an element of life that improves philosophical competiveness especially if "it is within language that we dream, desire, have a consciousness and where images are located" (Nakusera, 2004, p. 131). In addition, "language affords a window into the views and beliefs of a people, and hence their philosophies" (Obotetukudo, 2001, p. 42). Consequently, the place of indigenous languages in education must form part of the rethinking of the philosophy of schooling in Africa in accordance with the 1951 UNESCO Meeting resolve that "the best medium for teaching a child is his mother tongue" (p. 11) *and* "in modern education a child should receive instruction in his mother tongue, and this privilege should not be withheld from the African child" (cited in Spencer, 1985, p. 168). Much as the use of the foreign language has a universal unifying effect, the language of a people and their historical circumstances remain crucial for their understanding of the world through interpretation (Ndofirepi, Shumba, & Musengi, 2012). Therefore, I propose that doing philosophy with children in Africa should adopt a positive attitude toward linguistic and cultural diversity since different languages represent different cultural knowledge and skills.

According to Lipman (1988, 1994) and Matthews (1984, 1994), the common practice is to engage children in philosophical discussion by introducing original philosophical stories as the stimulus and point of departure. Classes usually begin with students reading aloud or acting out part of a story. But the question remains: Whose stories? How does, or should philosophy travel across cultural divides? Do we bring philosophy to schools for transformation or for assimilation, especially the Lipmanian stories written in "a typically North American understanding of critical thinking and democracy."? (Rivage-Seul, 1987, p. 233) Hence I find Lipmanian texts lacking sensitivity to the history of the learners as well as the institutional contexts in which philosophizing takes place. Should the African school continue to remain "detached from the social thought, cultural traditions and livelihoods of African societies"? (Nsemanang & Tchombe, 2011, p. 8) Kohan argues that Philosophy for Children "should extend the criticism that it applies to thinking to the reality that has nurtured and contributed to forming those modes of thinking" (1995, p. 28). A hybridized African Philosophy for Children will involve critical thinking skills informed by relevant contextual detail. An African perspective of Philosophy for Children, while accepting in total the central role of critical inquiry, can only be authentic if it is interrogating the African existential situation both its past and the contemporary. A hybrid African Philosophy for Children paradigm would therefore embrace the Lipmanian pedagogy by advancing the critical perspective, on the one hand, with the African experience providing the content and context of the field, on the other.

The traditional African background is rich with ritual celebrations of community with the attendant emphasis on individual's selfless dedication to the welfare of the collective, empathic relations with others (*ukama*) (Ndofirepi, 2012) and the transformation of everyone's well-being. The traditional African worldview holds *community* in high esteem, and the Lipmanian constituent contributes the notion of critical rational *inquiry* to a new paradigm of Philosophy for Children in Africa. The stress of African holism with emphasis on the social whole is important in the scheme of the community of inquiry in that individuals dispose the holistic view in the community of inquirers as opposed to prioritizing individual parts. I challenge the Lipmanian model for stressing the analytical technique by focusing on the cultivation of technical proficiency while disregarding the social element. I therefore propose a new complementary weaving of both the critical/analytical component and the culturalist element as equally valuable constituents of a hybridized African perspective of Philosophy for Children. What alternatives are then left for African Philosophy for Children materials?

I foresee four alternatives: first to translate Lipman's novels in the main local languages including the manuals as well as supplementary proposals for discussion by teachers and children; second to adapt the content of Lipman's novels to the local culture through the transformation of certain incidents in ways that make them relevant to the culture, traditions, and context of the country concerned; third to write the new-look Lipman-style novels envisaged in terms of the same objectives for engaging in the same activity though founded in the specific culture of the country involved; fourth to produce new supporting material on the basis of Lipman's model including picture books, comic books, or other audiovisual materials. The common thread that cuts across the alternatives above, except the fourth, is that Philosophy for Children should be particular to a cultural context.

A Philosophy for Children in Africa should start from a recovery and reclamation of the cultural assets of traditional Africa, which then become the objects of its interpretation (Ndofirepi et al., 2012). As Wiredu and Kresse (2003, n.p.) reiterate, "just narrating is not good enough, we have to interpret. Trying to interpret is actually getting conceptual." But if we agree that philosophy is conceptual, then an African perspective of Philosophy for Children is not a repetitive narration of the African tradition but rather a critical interpretation of it. A synergy of the critical-analytical approach, with its inherent tenets of rigor, coherence, systemacity and rationality, and the comprehensive traditional narratives is crucial in the hybridization process of doing philosophy with children in Africa. Such an approach is "a hermeneutic procedure...the appropriate way to ensure an authentic encounter between the product of a cultural tradition and the demands of a rational understanding" (Ladriere, 1992, p. xxi).

Precolonial African culture was characterized by an oral tradition that found expression in stories, folktales, anecdotes, proverbs, and parables that provoked a great deal of reflection. Stories and proverbs are primary ways through which a great deal of African philosophical thought, knowledge, and wisdom has been taught. Scholars on African tradition, for example Chimhundu (1980), Gelfand (1965), and Gyekye (1997), have compared the wisdom paradigms of Western cultures against African cultures. Hence, Bodunrin maintains that

> There is no a priori reason why proverbs, myths of gods and angels social practices...could not be proper subjects for philosophical enquiry....The African philosopher cannot deliberately ignore the study of the traditional belief system of his people. Philosophical problems arise out of real life situations. (1991, pp. 76–77)

When used with children just as with adults, proverbs and stories allow the participants in the deliberative encounter to call to mind their reflectivity while making sense of the hidden meanings embedded within. The embedded meanings invite contests of ideas and knowledge as shared understanding results. Proverbial lore, like all other forms of orality in traditional societies, follows implicit rules of performance, sequencing, content appropriateness, and timeliness. For example, adults would gather youngsters around a fire at night and tell them great stories and legends about the past, which helped the youngsters to grasp the prevailing ethical standards of their community. Key moral as well as philosophical debates then ensued coupled with exploration of contestable and central concepts such as greed, egotism, disobedience, honesty, faithfulness, justice, responsibility, love, hatred, beauty, to mention a few. Such themes may form the basis of a classroom community of philosophical inquiry with children, for example in a rural setting.

Riddles, among others, constitute a plethora of ways through which traditional Africans not only sharpen the reasoning skills of the young but also provide entertainment to participants. Through the search for solutions to riddles, children are challenged to think more theoretically with depth and breadth, while their figurative language gives the child the chance to uncover their meaning through a reasoning process. The answer to a given riddle acts as a conclusion of the logical process and it is often a one-word answer that is both precise and clear to the participants. Among the Shona "riddles promote logical skills and the one who is capable of solving many riddles is arguably more mentally sophisticated than the one who is less capable" (Gwaravanda & Masaka, 2008, p. 194). Riddles are a crucial tool in imparting and sharpening reasoning and memory skills. Being able to provide correct answers to the tribal riddles was considered a sign of wit.

A hybridized Philosophy for Children for Africa, while responding in terms of content and pedagogy(Gyekye, 1997), should be deliberative through self-criticism and self-reflection as benchmarks of rationality on the African experience. Hence "a critical touchstone is needed if the traditional wisdom is to be sifted" (Giddy, 2012, p. 15). However, such a philosophy should guard against an "apist attitude" (Waghid, 2004, p. 40) where African philosophy looks to the West or even to the traditional African sage packages for inclusion in the twenty-first century. Rather the hybrid philosophy should be an alloy of racial, cultural, and ethnic metals (McCarthy, 1998). To this end, a Philosophy for Children program for Africa should anchor children in Africa in the security of their past and present cultural background.

Conclusion

The twenty-first-century Africa is unique seen from its traditional past. It is neither a wholly traditional Africa nor a replica of a European Africa. Africa is now a *third space*, a cultural universe, which continues to forge *some* of the values of traditional. To that end, education in Africa should mirror these values. Indeed, there are criticisms against hybridization as an ideal. However, hybridity neither essentializes the West nor the African traditional past. It proposes a new weaving devoid of cultural supremacy. It symbolises the values of a twenty-first-century African. A hybridized Philosophy for Children acknowledges that neither the Lipman's model nor the traditional African paradigm is overarching. Consequently, I have maintained that Philosophy for Children amalgamates the rational, systematic, and analytic view of the Lipmanian model and the traditional African ethos of community coupled with the virtues of solidarity, respect for others, reciprocity, and mutuality. I therefore recommend that the African existential circumstances, priorities, and challenges centered on the perennial questions of poverty, famine, HIV/AIDS, underdevelopment, corruption, dictatorships, and violence, among others, would provide the stimulus for inquiry by children from an early age.

15

Language Ideology and Policy in an American "Hot Spot": Perspectives on Native American Language Education

J. Taylor Tribble

Native American tribes within the state of Oklahoma are faced with the loss of their heritage language at an alarming rate, much to do with monolingual English language ideologies that have been promoted within schools. This chapter is informed by document and policy analysis of Native American language education within the state of Oklahoma. It begins by examining the history of language ideology, policy, and language immersion programs both at the state and national level. The chapter then discusses an analysis of policy texts and government reports that relate to Native American language education and highlights a clash of ideology and a confusing disconnect between policy intentions and actions on the ground. The chapter yields further contributions to the dialog on Native American language education and language policy planning by highlighting the relationship between language ideology, policy, and educational practices that impact student outcomes.

Over the past century, prevailing monolingual language ideologies and policies in the United States and abroad have played an enormous role in language loss and obsolescence (Garrett, 2004). In many instances, schooling practices and educational policies have been the common ideological space by which this language loss and obsolescence have been explicitly and implicitly promulgated through overt and symbolic violence (Adams, 1997; Bourdieu & Thompson, 1999; Bourdieu & Passeron, 1990; Menken, 2008; Menken & Garcia, 2010).

In 2007, National Geographic and the Living Tongues Institute's Enduring Voices Project named Oklahoma as a "Language Hotspot."

A language hotspot is a geographic region with a combination of high levels of genetic diversity, high levels of language endangerment, and low levels of language documentation (Living Tongues Institute, 2007). Oklahoma has the highest density of spoken Native American languages in the United States (Reese, 2011; National Geographic Society, 2007b). Yet very few native speakers remain of each of these languages, and relatively minimal language documentation is taking place within the state (National Geographic Society 2007a, b). Approximately 40 native languages are spoken in the state of Oklahoma, and of the 38 federally recognized tribes in the state, only 18 have fluent tribal language speakers (Linn, 2007).

Although there is a small yet growing movement within Oklahoma to preserve and/or revitalize these languages, many policy actors at the national and state levels, through hegemonic monolingual language ideology and consequent educational policy, are discouraging bilingualism and language revitalization efforts (Gandara & Hopkins, 2010). Since the 1980s, over half of the states in the United States have passed legislation declaring English the official language of their state, and Oklahoma on November 2, 2010, joined the growing number of states declaring English as the official language through the passage by 75.5 percent popular vote of State Question 751 (SQ 751) (NewsOK, 2010). Although there is a provision in the law to use Native American languages "if necessary," the discouraging ideologies expressed through the English as official language policy negatively impacted the state's English language learners, indigenous communities, and native English speakers alike (Gandara and Hopkins, 2010; Linn, Naranjo, Nichola, Slaughter, Yamamoto, & Zependa, 2002; Menken, 2008). As schools are primary ideological spaces in which the transmission of culture and language ideology occurs (Bourdieu & Thompson, 1999; Bourdieu & Passeron, 1990; Menken, 2008; Menken & Garcia, 2010), a necessary component of Native American language revitalization efforts must involve an in-depth understanding of the primary actors, ideologies, and issues involved in creating and implementing language policy in the field of Native American language instruction.

Language Policy and Ideology in the United States: A Historical Background

Although language ideology has been a "contemporary battleground" in the United States (Olson, 2009), the United States has been and currently is a nation of numerous indigenous communities and immigrants rich in bilingualism and multilingualism, which historically has been an economic, academic, military, and societal asset. In 1968, the US Congress passed the Bilingual Education Act, which provided competitive grant funding for schools (Lessow-Hurley, 2005), and in 1974, the US Supreme Court ruled in *Lau v. Nichols* that students who are learning English must receive special language services in order to help them be able to access academic content in English. In 2001, the Bilingual Education Act was subsumed and renamed under Title III of the No Child Left Behind Act of 2001 (NCLB) with the term bilingual education stripped from the act's terminology. In 1990 a national policy precedent was set in the Native American Languages Act, which recognized the need to "preserve, protect, and promote the rights and freedom of Native Americans to use, practice, and develop Native American languages." Additionally, the Esther Martinez Native American Languages Preservation Act 2006 furthered the goals of the Native American Languages Act by tying funding grants to language preservation and revitalization programs. Although these policies are a step in the right direction, and many tribes in Oklahoma have developed language preservation programs, much needs to be done on the national, state, and local policy level to support and promote bilingualism and to reverse the "language shift" (Fishman, 2001) that has occurred in our nation and to a greater extent in the state of Oklahoma.

For approximately two centuries, English has been the common language of the present-day United States and has functioned alongside pockets of linguistic diversity as attitudes toward bilingualism and linguistic diversity have vacillated over time according to multidimensional ideological and political beliefs regarding immigration, national security, diversity, and education. Currently, there is a continued movement toward establishing English as the official language of many states as well as the nation. These monolingual ideologies negatively impacted work toward Native American language revitalization.

Some advocates of linguistic diversity and bilingual education suggest that official English laws have little impact on language usage and school programs (Linton, 2009; Menken & Garcia, 2010). Some might also argue that the Oklahoma official English amendment is a lenient policy in that it states that "Native American language could be used" (Ballotopedia, 2010). While it is possible that a state may proclaim English as the official language and simultaneously allow schools implementation space to promote linguistic diversity through language revitalization and bilingual education programs, the assertion that language policy has little influence discounts the impact that the attitudes and behaviors of majority language speakers (dominant speech communities) have on minority language speakers (nondominant speech communities) (de Bres, 2008; Philips, 2004). Peoples' attitudes toward language often have a stronger impact on the future of minority languages than official language policies (Linn et al., 2002), but oftentimes attitudes of linguistic intolerance are most strongly felt, represented, and perpetuated through the democratic passage of official English policies. Thus, the attitudes, beliefs, and behaviors dominant speech communities hold regarding minority language(s) can have and have had a significant impact on the value and status that Native American language speech communities place on their own language (de Bres, 2010).

Attitudes of dominant speech communities impact nondominant speech communities and the perceived value of minority languages through legislation, school, and social norms (de Bres, 2010). Langauge and education policies send a clear message regarding the perceived value of minority languages. Language speakers and policy actors are social actors who use words and policy to create social action (Duranti, 1997). School teachers and administrators, albeit primarily subconsciously, also take part in this social action and promotion of the valuation of language (Philips, 1972; Philips, 1983). This process oftentimes plays a major role in the societal inequalities that exist today, as stated by Philips (2004):

> At the heart of the relationship between language and social inequality is the idea that some expressions of language are valued more than others, in a way this is associated with some people being more valued than others and some ideas expressed by people through language being more valued than others. (p. 474)

Through the process of language valuation, speech communities are built and evolve over time, while members of nondominant speech communities must negotiate power structures through communication with dominant speech communities. Nondominant speech communities must be able to communicate in the dominant speech communities' language and dialect in order to achieve status and power in any society (Morgan, 2004). Therefore, some policies and linguistic valuation processes perpetuate the cycle of linguistic and social inequality (Hill, 2008). Few speakers of the dominant speech community are explicitly aware of the advantages that specific policies provide for the dominant speech community as many policy actors have more seemingly altruistic motives such as cutting costs for state services and promoting the social, political, and economic unity of the state's citizens. In this way, cultural and linguistic hegemony is sustained in society at large, and in schools, as ill-informed communities construct a worldview that devalues nondominant speech communities' language and culture. Policies that promote English as the official language support the same attitudes that were promoted by J. D. C. Atkins, commissioner of Indian Affairs from 1885 to 1888, regarding the need for indigenous language instruction and use. Atkins stated:

> The instruction of the Indians in the vernacular is not only of no use to them, but is detrimental to the cause of their education and civilization, and no school will be permitted on the reservation which the English language is not exclusively taught. (1887, pp. xxi–xxiii)

Atkins' statements support the present notion held by some that the language and culture of Native Americans has little value in society and schools. Conversely, the assumptions discussed in this chapter are driven by the viewpoint that language attitudes, language policy, and school systems, to a great extent, have contributed to the loss of Native American languages. Although there has been much progress in promoting alternative and positive viewpoints toward the use of Native American languages in recent decades, much work remains to be done.

Current Language Policy Issues

The Esther Martinez Native American Languages Preservation Act 2006 focuses on and encourages language maintenance and revitalization; however, there are a number of other national, state, and local policies that impact Native American language education in schools as well. The NCLB Act 2001 that aims to measure student performance in reading and math; The Race to the Top (US Department of Education, 2010) initiative and incentive to reform; and state education laws and local policies *all* have had various effects on Native American language instruction in K-12 schools. At times, all of the previously mentioned policies are in competition with one another as the various policy actors work toward promoting and perpetuating their own agendas and ideologies. Therefore, as US states control public education decisions, the outcomes of Native American language policy on the ground may vary greatly from state to state.

This chapter discusses the four distinct yet interrelated levels: nation, state, local, and tribal nation. Each level in this chapter is considered as a distinct interpretive community—holding unique perceptions, beliefs, and values that result in part from their particular involvement in the language and education policy environment. The perceptions, beliefs, and values of one interpretive community may compete with, contradict, and/or reinforce that of other interpretive communities. Multiple policy documents, resolutions, congressional hearings, meeting notes, reports, and media coverage demonstrate the challenges that we face in relation to the implementation of language revitalization programs in schools. The multiple and various data sources discussed in this chapter give depth to the understanding of the interaction between language policy and the implementation of Native American language education in Oklahoma.

Federal, State, Local, and Tribal Nation Policy Documents

US federal, state, local, and tribal nation documents help us understand the goals and ideologies that are represented in the various realms of the policy process. Language and education policies from the past and present were included in a document analysis as a means for providing a background and context for the current issues related to language policy and planning. Additionally, proposed language and education policy and legislation were included in the analysis in order to contemplate the potential outcome and efforts of the various language policy actors.

At the national level, the following documents relate to indigenous language education:

- English Language Unity Act (proposed legislation 2011)
- NCLB 2001
- Esther Martinez Native American Language Preservation Act 2006
- Native American Language Act (NALA) 1990

At the state level, the following documents differ in their level of support toward policy goals at the national level:

- School Laws of Oklahoma 2011
- Oklahoma State Constitution Amendment 2010
- Oklahoma Indian Language Heritage Protection Act 2001

In addition to federal and state policies, local school district and tribal nation polices demonstrate the challenge we face within the state regarding language revitalization. At the school district level within the state, Tahlequah Public Schools in one of only a few districts have policies addressing Native American language education. Additionally, of the 38 federally recognized tribes in Oklahoma, fewer than 7 percent have official policies regarding the revitalization and/or preservation of their language.

By comparing and analyzing these policies, we can answer questions that relate to the following general themes:

- Beliefs about language in general
- Beliefs about Native American language teaching and learning
- Impact on other relevant policies that may support or conflict with state, local, and/or tribal nation efforts that support language preservation

The master list of themes (see Tables 15.1–15.4) presented below helps further contextualize relevant policies.

Table 15.1 Master list—categories and themes from national-level documents

1. Beliefs about language in general

   Language as a problem
   English Language Unity Act (proposed 2011)
   NCLB (2001)
   Language as a right/resource
   Esther Martinez Native American Language Preservation Act (2006)
   NALA (1990)

2. Beliefs about Native American language teaching and learning

   NALA (1990)-Remove barriers of teaching native american languages
   NCLB (2001)- Academic assessment must be conducted in English

3. Impact of other relevant policies that support or conflict with language preservation efforts

   Creates barriers for language preservation efforts
   English Language Unity Act (proposed 2011)
   NCLB (2001)
   Supports language preservation efforts
   Esther Martinez Native American Language Preservation Act (2006)
   NALA (1990)

Table 15.2 Master list—categories and themes from state-level documents

1. Beliefs about language in general
    Language as a problem
    School Laws of Oklahoma (2011)
    Language as a resource
    Oklahoma *Senate Concurrent Resolution No. 37* ([SCR 37] 2001)
2. Beliefs about Native American language teaching and learning
    School Laws of Oklahoma (2011)- mixed messages and barriers for teaching Native American languages
    Oklahoma SCR (2001)- seeks to remove barriers from teaching Native American language
3. Impact on other relevant policies
    Creates barriers for language preservation efforts
    School Laws of Oklahoma (2011)
    Supports language preservation efforts
    Oklahoma SCR (2001)

Table 15.3 Master list—categories and themes from local-level documents

1. Beliefs about language in general
    Language as a problem
      no policy data found
    Language as a right/resource
      few districts take a policy stance
      Tahelquah Public Schools has policy that supports Native American language perservation
2. Beliefs about Native American language teaching and learning
      few districts have developed methods to support language preservation
3. Impact on other relevant policies
    Creates barriers for language preservation efforts
      lack of policy suggests unspoken barriers
    Supports language preservation efforts
    TPS Board Policies(2007)

Table 15.4 Master list—categories and themes from tribal nation-level documents

1. Beliefs about language in general
    Language as a problem
      no policy data found
    Language as a resource
      few tribes have explicit policy that addresses their language
      Approximately 6% of tribal nations in Oklahoma have policy addressing language preservation

continued

Table 15.4 Continued

2. Beliefs about Native American language teaching and learning
    many tribal nations have developed approaches for teaching their language
3. Impact on other relevant policies
    Creates barriers for language preservation efforts
        lack of policy suggests that efforts towards langauge policy creation might support overall language revitalization efforts
    Supports language preservation efforts
        various tribal policy and resolustions (ex. Chiasaw Nation *General Resolution Number 22-042*[2005], Joint Council of Cherokee Nation and The Eastern Band of Cherokee Indians *Resolution #02-08* [2008])

Future Directions: Implications for Practice

The future of Native American languages is at a critical point in history, and many tribes and nations within the state of Oklahoma are faced with the possible loss of their language. The perceptions, beliefs, and values held by policy actors at the national, state, local, and tribal nation levels ultimately have some level of impact on the outcome of language preservation and revitalization efforts in Oklahoma and beyond (de Bres, 2010). Within the US policy environment, we have institutional schizophrenia. On the national stage, we proclaim that we should support the preservation, protection, rights, and freedom of Native Americans to use, practice, and develop Native American languages, while on the other hand we believe that common language (English) "is the most powerful unifying force known throughout history" (Fox, 2012). At the state level, we propose the opposition to barriers to the instruction and learning of Native American languages, but are adamant that English is the common and unifying language of the State of Oklahoma. It is understandable in this policy environment why local and tribal nation policy actors might have difficulty accomplishing mutual goals of language preservation.

NCLB, which terminated the Bilingual Education Act, requires all public school teachers to be "highly qualified," meaning that teachers must have a bachelor's degree, state teacher certification, and verifiable knowledge of their subject matter. This creates a major barrier for many fluent speakers of Native American language who do not possess teaching credentials and/or university degrees in their native language. Conversely, NALA requires that the state remove obstacles to the teaching and learning of Native American languages, but many tribal nations and school districts have difficulty convincing state department of education authorities to accept the required NALA exemption for certification.

Currently, according to the School Laws of Oklahoma, "The board of education of each school district shall employ and contract in writing...only with persons certified or licensed to teach by the State Board of Education in accordance with the Oklahoma Teacher Preparation Act" (Oklahoma State Department of Education (OSDE), 2011, §180.10). In order to become a certified teacher in Oklahoma, an individual must hold a minimum of a bachelor's degree, a teacher preparation program and/or specified number of education credit hours, and complete the required competency examinations (OSDE, 2011, §180.10).

Although there have been discussions with the department of education regarding exemptions to these regulations, to date (more than 30 years after NALA, and over 10 years since NCLB) there have been no exemptions made to certify Native American language instructors in Oklahoma. Tribal nations have tried creative solutions to these challenges, but students are only able to get core credit for taking Native American language in very few circumstances. The Cherokee Nation, for example, has worked with the Northeastern State University and the OSDE to develop a Cherokee language teacher certification program (NSU, 2012; Certification Examinations for Oklahoma Educators, 2012). The Cherokee Nation has also worked with Tahlequah Public Schools to coordinate policies and classes that support Cherokee language preservation (Tahlequah Public Schools, 2012). But this type of collaboration is currently not the norm; the Cherokee language certification is the only Native American language certification offered in the state. Other Native American language classes are offered in public schools, through the Choctaw Nation for example, as an elective/enrichment credit, but these credits do not qualify as a world language graduation credit requirement. Most Native American language programs in the state are offered through tribal nations—online, after school and/or during the summer, or in master-apprentice programs—but for the most part are not recognized by the public school system.

NCLB also requires state-standardized student achievement testing, which is to be conducted entirely inEnglish. This creates challenges for immersion schools such as the Cherokee Nation language immersion school in Tahlequah, which operates on a language immersion model instructing students almost entirely in the target language and later introduces English to students in the upper elementary grades.

The process of learning two languages initially limits the acquisition of English, and for this reason, students may not perform as well on standardized assessments as they would if they were in a monolingual environment, but by the end of their education, students become speakers of both their native language and English. NCLB policy does not recognize the value of bilingualism and does not allow for any flexibility in regard to student assessment, which is tied to federal funding for schools.

The educational policies and language ideologies that support reforms such as NCLB trickle down to the state, local, and then institutional level—schools—where the intentions of such reform efforts are oftentimes muddled, making it difficult to interpret the true intents of such reform policies. Why does national ideologically monolingual educational policy, such as NCLB, continue to usurp the power of national probilingual policy such as NALA? Amidst the conflict and confusion, hegemonic monolingual language ideologies continue to take hold in schools, while most tribal nations within the state continue to lose fluent speakers of their language.

Conclusions and Recommendations

With the knowledge of the historical use of educational policy within the United States, one might speculate that there may be hidden agendas when reading between the lines of educational policies such as NCLB and School Laws of Oklahoma. When there is substantial research to demonstrate the positive impacts of bilingualism and the negative impacts of high-stakes testing reforms on minorities (Au, 2009; Johnson & Johnson, 2006; Jones, Jones, & Hargrove, 2003; Menken, 2008; Rothstein, 2004; Taylor, 2004), why do we continue to base many of our educational decisions on the ideologically monolingual paradigm?

As stated by Kroskrity (2004, p. 501), "language ideologies represent the perception of language and discourse that is constructed in the interest of a specific social or cultural group." Expressed differently, the language of our educational policies is a means to express thoughts, ideas, feelings, hopes, and goals of the educational policy actors who are sociopolitical language users who construct and perpetuate their worldview through language and law (Duranti, 1997). There is a significant interplay between the worldview of policy makers and their role in the continuation and manipulation of their worldview through policy (Bahktin, 1982; Bourdieu & Passeron, 1990;

Duranti, 1997). Social structure emerges and maintains itself through individuals applying native methods of understanding and communicating to modern-day concerns (Duranti, 1997), and in education these concerns are expressed by the policy elite through educational policies such as NCLB and the School Laws of Oklahoma.

A language-ideology emphasis on the sociocultural interests of the educational policy maker allows the reader of such policies to recognize interests that are purported to leave no child behind, but instead do quite the opposite. It is also true that the language ideologies that manifest in education policy are grounded in social experience and thus are "profitably conceived as multiple" (Kroskrity, 2004, p. 503), meaning that the educational policies serve multiple interests of various interpretive communities while disproportionally representing the interests of specific groups. This helps to explain the apparent tension and conflict between policies like NCLB, NALA, and the School Laws of Oklahoma. The understanding of the multiplicity of divergent perspectives of educators and policy makers helps explain the wide variety of outcomes relating to the implementation of educational policy. For this reason, it is imperative to frame the analysis of educational policies and reform around outcomes on the ground, rather than the intent of the policy. The overall outcome of our current educational policies on the ground in Oklahoma is the continued promotion of a monolingual ideology, which is to the detriment of Native American language preservation and revitalization.

It may be presumed that few policy makers are explicitly aware of the advantages that their language ideologies and assessment policies such as NCLB and the School Laws of Oklahoma provide language-dominant communities, but these policies are dominant culture artifacts that are both hegemonic and epistemologically defined. As stated by Solano-Flores (2011), education policy is

> part of a complex set of culturally established instructional and accountability practices; they are created with the intent to meet certain social needs or to comply with mandates and legislation established in a society; they are written in the language (and the dialect of that language) used by those who develop them; their content is a reflection of the skills, competencies, forms of knowledge, and communication styles valued by a society.

In the most hopeful sense, one would trust that the majority of policy makers must have more seemingly altruistic motives for educational reform, but NCLB and the School Laws of Oklahoma are explicit examples of how cultural and linguistic hegemony is sustained in society at large and in schools, as ill-informed policy elites construct a worldview that devalues nondominant communities and languages while nondominant communities oftentimes comply with such reforms. While language and education polices cannot "fix" the current state of indigenous languages, they do play a part in the problem and the solution. Some might argue that the problem of language loss is a problem to be solved by tribal nations, and it is best addressed at that "endoglossic" level (Ruiz, 1995), but the majority of the 38 recognized tribal nations in Oklahoma are not organized on reservations, and tribal nation citizens in Oklahoma generally live among culturally and linguistically heterogeneous communities that are spread out amidst the general population. Consequently, the vast majority of the state's Native American students are attending public schools where each day they hear and speak English for at least 7–8 hours; for this reason, tribal nation language preservation efforts must be supported by local district-level policies.

We have a unique problem that requires a unique solution within the state of Oklahoma. In order to achieve the goal of preserving the linguistic resources that exist in Oklahoma, we must make use of mixed approaches to language preservation (Ruiz, 1995) at the national, state, local, and tribal nation levels. Some courses of action that need to take place within the state of Oklahoma are listed below.

- Host an ongoing state-level campaign to engender greater awareness, among all state residents, regarding the challenges we face in regard to Native American language loss and preservation within the state. This campaign must focus on building knowledge, among both policy actors and the general public alike, as to why it is important to preserve the Native American languages spoken in the state.
- Develop a state-level position for a language preservation leader to guide and represent the process. Part of the campaign for greater language preservation awareness must be directed by a leader who makes learning Native American language a priority in the public school system.
- Develop a state-level Native American language education framework to guide the goal of making language learning an option for all students in Oklahoma public schools. When possible consider using bilingual education models that support advanced levels of proficiency in English and at least one Native American language.
- Maintain a balance between centralized and decentralized measures to support Native American language preservation efforts. In this way,

school systems will have flexibility to implement programs under the general framework of national and state policy and funding initiative.
- Develop and implement ongoing professional learning opportunities to support Indian Education directors and teachers in their efforts toward language preservation.
- Collaborate across all interpretive and professional learning communities. Best practices in language preservation, instruction, and learning must be shared to develop programs that lead to specified language learning outcomes.
- Promote stronger efforts of collaboration between universities and tribes to integrate Native American language teaching education programs at all universities in the state.
- Collaborate with tribal nations to support the development of comprehensive language and education policy that fosters language preservation.
- Use culturally based education methods within all levels of schooling in the state to promote deeper understanding in regard to Native American culture and language.
- Cultivate collaboration among the school, families, and tribal nations.
- Promote district-level policies that address issues related to Native American language preservation.
- Remove teacher certification barriers for Native American language teachers.
- Allow *all* students to gain high-school world languages core course credit for taking Native American language classes.
- Develop a method to allow students to demonstrate mastery in a Native American language that is not taught in the student's school system as a means to allow the student to gain high-school world language course credit for their mastery of a Native American language.
- Conduct further research in the state that continues to focus on the success and challenges of preserving Native American language in the state.

These recommendations, of course, are not an exhaustive list and should be supplemented by continued research and collaboration among national, state, local, and tribal nation policy actors. Ultimately, it will take the efforts and collaboration of multiple national, states, local, and tribal nation policy actors and stakeholders to achieve the goal of language preservation within the state. But, I am hopeful that the specified goals and recommendations of this chapter will contribute to the greater community of individuals who are working to ensure that our linguistic resources are preserved within Oklahoma and beyond.

Bibliography

Abbott, A. (2010). Education for humanity: A challenge within globalization. *International Journal of the Humanities, 5(7)*, 223–228.
Adams, B., Adam, A. S., & Opbroek, M. (2005). Reversing the academic trend for rural students: The case of Michelle Opbroek. *Journal of American Indian Education, 44(3)*.
Adams, D. (1997). *Education for extinction: American Indians and the boarding school experience 1875–1928*. Lawrence: University of Kansas Press.
Ade, K. S. (1998). Odu. [CD]. Produced by Andrew C. Frankel. New York: Atlantic Recording Corporation.
Agosto, V., Dias, L., Kaiza, N. McHatton, P., & Elam, D. (2013). Culture-based leadership and preparation: A qualitative meta-synthesis of the literature. In Linda C. Tillman & James J. Scheurich (Eds.), *Handbook of research on educational leadership for equity and diversity* (pp. 625–650). Routledge/Taylor Francis.
Al-Attas, M. N. (1977). The concept of education in Islam. Keynote Address, First World Conference in Muslim Education. Makkah: Umm al-Qurah University.
Al-Attas, M. N. (2005). Islam and secularism. *Journal of Islamic Philosophy, 1*, 11–43.
Alaska Department of Education and Early Development (2006). "Spring 2006 Standards Based Assessment" retrieved from: http://education.alaska.gov/TLS/Assessment/AsmtVer2006/SchoolAsmtVerSupd.cfm?do=37
Alawi, A. (2010). Re-islamising the world. In W. M. Wan Daud & M. Z. Uthman, (Eds.). *Knowledge, language, thought and the civilization of Islam* (pp. 59–82). Kuala Lumpur: Penerbit.
Alfred, T. (1999). *Peace, power, righteousness: An Indigenous manifesto*. Don Mills, ON: Oxford University Press.
Alfred, T., Couthard, G., & Simmons, D. (September–October 2006). *New Socialist*, Special issue on Indigenous Radicalism. Retrieved June 14, 2011, from http://www.newsocialist.org/attachments/128_NewSocialist-Issue58.pdf.
Allemand, J. (1995). Funtastic fibers & fabrics. *Arts & Activities, 11(8)*, 20–23.
Allinder, M. (1993). Beyond baskets: Natural materials and fiberglass create challenge. *Arts & Activities, 11(4)*, 28–29.

Archibald, J. (2008). *Indigenous storywork: Educating the heart, mind, body, and spirit.* Vancouver: UBC Press.

Atkins, J. D. C. (1887). *Annual Report of the Commissioner of Indian Affairs.* Washington DC: Government Printing Office.

Au, W. (2009). *Unequal by design: High-stakes testing and the standardization of inequality.* New York: Routledge, Taylor and Francis Group.

Austin-Broos, D. (2009). *Arrernte present, Arrernte past: Invasion violence and imagination in indigenous Central Australia.* Chicago and London: University of Chicago Press.

Bagele, C. (2012). *Indigenous research methodologies.* Los Angeles: Sage.

Bakhtin, M.M. (1982). *The dialogic imagination: Four essays.* Austin, TX: University of Texas Press.

Ballotopedia. (December 2, 2010). Oklahoma state question 751 (2010). Retrieved March 7, 2011, from http://ballotpedia.org/wiki/index. php/Oklahoma_State_Question_751_(2010)#cite_note-8.

Bang, M., Medin, D. L., & Altran, S. (2007). Cultural mosaics and mental models of nature. *Proceedings of the National Academy of Sciences, 104,* 13868–13874.

Barber, K. (1991). *I could speak until tomorrow: Oriki, women, and the past in a Yoruba town.* Edinburgh: Edinburgh University Pres.

Barnard, A. (1992). *Hunters and herders of South Africa. A comparative ethnogragpy of the Khoisan peoples.* Cambridge, MA: Cambridge University Press.

Barnard, A. (2004). Mutual aid and the foraging mode of thought: Re-reading Kropotkin on the Khoisan. *Social Evolution & History, 3(1),* 3–21.

Barreto, A. A. (1998). *Language, elites, and the state: Nationalism in Puerto Rico and Quebec.* Westport, CT: Praeger.

Barreto, A. A. (2009). Enlightened tolerance or cultural capitulation: Contesting notions of American identity. In A. McCoy & F. Scarano (Eds.), *Colonial crucible: Empire in the making of the modern American state* (pp. 145–162). Madison: University of Wisconsin Press.

Barrett, S. A. (1976). *Pomo Indian basketry.* Glorieta, NM: Rio Grande Press.

BasketMakers. *BasketMakers.* n.p., n.d.

Basso, K. (1996). *Wisdom sits in places.* Albuquerque: University of New Mexico Press.

Battiste, M. (2002). *Indigenous knowledge and pedagogy in First Nations education: A literature review with recommendations.* Ottawa: Indian and Northern Affairs Canada.

Beavert, V. (1996). Creation. In L. Ackerman (Ed.), *A song to the creator: Traditional arts of Native American women of the plateau.* London: University of Oklahoma Press.

Benhabib, S. (2011). *Dignity in adversity: Human rights in troubled times.* Cambridge, MA: Polity Press.

Bennett, J. (2010). *Vibrant matter: A political ecology of things.* Durham and London: Duke University Press.

Berman, M. (1981). *The reenchantment of the world.* Ithaca, NY: Cornell University Press.

Bhabha, H. K. (1996). *Cultures in between: Questions of cultural identity.* London: Sage.

Bish, R. L., & Cassidy, F. (1989). *Indian government: Its meaning in practice.* British Columbia: Oolichan Books and the Institute for Research on Public Policy.

Bodunrin, P. O. (1991). The question of African philosophy. In T. Serequeberhan (Ed.), *African philosophy: The essential readings* (pp. 63–86). St Paul, MN: Paragon House.

Boske, C. (2011). Using the senses in reflective practice: Preparing school leaders for non-text-based understandings. *Journal of Curriculum Theorizing, 27(2),* 82–100.

Boske, C. (2012). Aspiring school leaders addressing social justice through art making. *Journal of School Leadership, 22(1),* 116–146.

Bourdieu, P., & Passeron, J. (1990). *Reproduction in education, society, and culture.* Thousand Oaks, CA: Sage.

Bourdieu, P., & Thompson, J. (1999). *Language and symbolic power.* Cambridge, MA: Harvard University Press.

Brayboy, B. (2005). Toward a tribal critical race: Theory in education. *Urban Review, 37(5),* 425–446.

Briggs, L. (2002). *Reproducing empire: Race, sex, science, and U.S. imperialism in Puerto Rico. American crossroads,* 11. Berkeley: University of California Press.

Brown, W. (2011). Occupy Wall Street: Return of a repressed Res-Publica. In *Theory & Event, 14(4),* supplement. Retrieved October 15, 2012, from http://muse.jhu.edu/.

Bryant, Levi R. (2011). *The democracy of objects.* Ann Arbor: Open Humanities Press.

Cagan, E. (1978). Individualism, collectivism, and radical educational reform. *Harvard Educational Review, 48,* 227–266.

Cajete, G. (2004). Philosophy of Native science. In A. Waters (Ed.), *American Indian thought* (pp. 45–57). Malden: Blackwell.

Cajete, G. (2005). American Indian epistemologies. In M. Tippeconnic, S. Fox, S. Lowe, & G. McClellan (Eds.), *Serving Native American students* (pp. 69–78). San Francisco, CA: Jossey-Bass.

Calderón, D. (2011). Locating the foundations of epistemologies of ignorance in education ideology and practice. In E. Malewski & N. Jaramillo (Eds.), *Epistemologies of ignorance in education* (pp. 105–128). Charlotte, NC: Information Age.

Canada, Minister of Supply and Services. (1996). Perspectives and realities. Report of the Royal Commission on Aboriginal Peoples.

Canada, Minister of Supply and Services. (1996). Restructuring the relationship. Report of the Royal Commission on Aboriginal Peoples.

Cantu, C. O. (2004). Toy alternatives: Crafts and fine motor development. *Exceptional Parent, 34(10),* 28–29.

Cazden, C. (1988). *Classroom discourse: The language of teaching and learning.* Portsmouth, NH: Heinemann.

Center for New England Culture, University of New Hampshire, Contemporary Indigenous New England Artists. n.p., n.d.
Certification Examinations for Oklahoma Educators. (2012). *Certification Requirements.* Retrieved December 6, 2012, from http://www.ceoe.nesinc.com/CE16_certificationrequirements.asp.
CHE (Council on Higher Education). (2007). *Review of Higher Education in South Africa: Selected Themes.* CHE: Pretoria.
Chimhundu, H. (1980). Shumo, Tsumo and socialization. *Zambezia, VIII(1),* 37–51.
Christie, M. (1993). "Exploring Aboriginal alternatives to Western thinking" and "constructing a Galtha curriculum." *Education Australia, 6–8,* 15–18.
Churchill, W. (2003). Acts of rebellion: The Ward Churchill reader. New York: Routledge.
Clark, H. H., & Brennan, S. A. (1991). Grounding in communication. In L.B. Resnick, J.M. Levine, & S.D. Teasley (Eds.). *Perspectives on socially shared cognition.* Washington: APA Books.
Clement, J. (2009). University attainment of the registered Indian population, 1981–2006: A cohort approach. In J. P. White, J. Peters, D. Beavon, & N. Spence (Eds.), *Aboriginal Education: Current crisis and future alternatives* (pp. 69–103). Toronto, ON: Thompson Education.
Coombes, A. E., & Brah, A. (2000). Introduction: The conundrum of mixing. In A. Brah & A. E. Coombes (Eds.), *Hybridity and its discontents: Politics, science, culture* (pp. 1–16). London: Routledge.
Crenshaw, K. (1991). Mapping the margins: Intersectionality, identity politics, and violence against women of colour. *Stanford Law Review, 43,* 1241–1299.
Cunningham, A. & Terry, M. (2006). African basketry: Grassroots art from Southern Africa. Fernwood Press: Black Point, Nova Scotia.
Davie, L. (2012). *Sarah Baartman, at rest at last.* Updated May 14, 2012.
Davis, O. J. (1997). Editorial: Beyond "best practices" toward wise practices. *Journal of Curriculum and Supervision, 13(1),* 92–113.
De Bres, J. (2008). Planning for tolerability in New Zealand, Wales and Catalonia. *Current Issues in Language Planning, 9(4),* 464–482.
De Bres, J. (2010). Promoting a minority language to majority language speakers: Television advertising about the Maori language targeting non-Maori New Zealanders. *Journal of Multilingual and Multicultural Development, 31(6),* 515–529.
De Haan, M. (2002). Distributed cognition and shared knowledge of the Mazahua: A cultural approach. *Journal of Interactive Learning Research, 13(1).*
De Costa, R. (2005). Indigenism. Retrieved August 2, 2011, from Globalization & Autonomy, http://www.globalautonomy.ca/global1/glossary_entry.jsp?id=CO.0027.
Declaration of the Rights of Indigenous Peoples. (2007). The United Nations Permanent Forum on Indigenous Issues. Retrieved December 3, 2012, from http://social.un.org/index/IndigenousPeoples/DeclarationontheRightsofIndigenousPeoples.aspx.

Deleuze, G., & Guattari, F. (1987). *A thousand plateaus: Capitalism and schizophrenia*. London: Athlone Press.

Deloria, V. Jr. (1999). *Spirit and reason: The Vine Deloria reader*. In B. Deloria, K. Foehner, & S. Scinta (Eds.). Golden, CO: Fulcrum.

Deloria, V. Jr. (2001a). Knowing and understanding. In V. Deloria Jr. & D. R. Wildcat, *Power and place in Indian education in America* (pp. 7–20). Golden, CO: Fulcrum.

Deloria, V. Jr. (2001b). Power and place equal personality. In V. Deloria Jr. & D. R. Wildcat, *Power and place in Indian education in America* (pp. 21–28). Golden, CO: Fulcrum.

Deloria, V. Jr., & Wildcat, D. (2001). *Power and place: Indian education in America*. Golden, CO: Fulcrum.

Delos Reyes, P., & Mulinari, D. (2005). *Intersektionalitet: Kritiska reflektioner över (o)jämlikhetenslandskap*. Norstedts, Häfstad, Sweden.

Diamond, C. T., Patrick, & Mullen, C. A. (1999). *The postmodern educator: Arts-based inquiries and teacher development*. New York: Peter Lang.

Douglas, S. L., & Shaikh, M. A. (2004). Defining Islamic education: Differentiation and applications. *Current Issues in Comparative Education*, 7(1), 5–18.

Drewal, M. T. (1992). *Yoruba ritual: Performers, play, agency*. Bloomington: Indiana University Press.

Du Preez, M. (2008). *Of tricksters, tyrants, and turncoats—more unusual stories from South Africa's past*. Cape Town: Zebra Press.

Duany, J. (2002). *The Puerto Rican nation on the move: Identities on the island and in the United States*. Chapel Hill: University of North Carolina Press.

Dunlop, R. (1999). Beyond dualism: Toward a dialogic negotiation of difference. *Canadian Journal of Education*, 24(1).

Duranti, A. (1997). *Linguistic anthropology*. Cambridge, MA: Cambridge University Press.

Edwards, W. H. (Ed.) (1998). *Traditional aboriginal society* (2nd ed.). Melbourne: Macmillan Education Australia.

Ellison, R. W. (1952). *Invisible man*. New York: Random House.

Elsie Allen: Pomo Basketweaver (1980). YouTube, September 18, 2011.

Farrand, L. (1900). Traditions of the Chilcotin Indians. In F. Boaz (Ed.), *Memoirs of the American museum of natural history: The Jesup North Pacific expedition. Part IV* (page #s). New York: American Museum of Natural History.

Fenelon, J., & LeBeau, D. (2006). Four directions for Indian history. In I. Abu-Saad & D. Champagne (eds.), *Indigenous education and empowerment* (pp. 21–68). New York: Rowman & Littlefield.

Fishman, J. (Ed.). (2001). *Can threatened languages be saved? "Reversing Language Shift" Revisited*. Clevendon: Multilingual Matters.

Fishman, J. (1982). Whorfianism of the third kind: Ethnolinguistic diversity as a worldwide societal asset. *Language in Society*, 11, 1–14.

Fixico, D. (1997). *Rethinking American Indian history*. Albequerque: University of New Mexico Press.

Fixico, D. (2003). *The American Indian mind in a linear world: American Indian studies and traditional knowledge*. New York: Routledge.

Flannery, T. (2012). *After the Future: Australia's New Extinction Crisis. Quarterly Essay* 48, November 2012. Black Inc: Melbourne.

Fox, L. (2012). Congressman Steve King Strives to Make English the Official Language of U.S. U.S. News.com. Retrieved from U.S. http://www.usnews.com/news/articles/2012/08/02/congressman-steve-king-strives-to-make-english-the-official-language-of-us.

Furi, M., & Wherrett, J. (2003). *Indian status and Band membership issues.* (Library of Parliament publication no. BP-410E). www.parl.gc.ca/Content/LOP/ResearchPublications/bp410-e.htm#bchangestx.

Gammage, B. (2012). *The biggest estate on Earth. How aborigines made Australia.* Sydney: Allen & Unwin.

Gandara, P., & Hopkins, M. (2010). *Forbidden language: English learners and restrictive language policies.* New York: Teachers College Press.

Garrett, P. (2004). Language contact and contact languages. In A. Duranti (Ed.), *A Companion to Linguistic Anthropology* (pp. 47–72). Malden, MA: Blackwell.

Gaztambide-Fernández, R., & Murad, Z. (2011). Out of line: Perspectives on the "browning" of curriculum and pedagogy. *Journal of Curriculum and Pedagogy, 8(1),* 14–16.

Gelfand, M. (Ed.). (1965). *African background: The traditional culture of the Shona-speaking people.* Cape Town: Juta.

Glatigny, P. D. & Maré, E. A. (2002). "Inter se nulli fines": the Khoi in seventeenth-century European representations of Khoi habitation at the Cape of Good Hope.

Giddy, P. (2012). "Philosophy for children" in Africa: Developing a framework. *South African Journal of Education, 32,* 15–25.

Giroux, H. (2012). *Education and the crisis of public values: Challenging the assault on teachers, Students, and Public Education.* New York: Peter Lang.

Goncalves, P., & Araujo-Olivera, S. (2009). Achieving quality education for indigenous peoples and Blacks in Brazil. In J. Banks (Ed.), *Routledge international companion to multicultural education* (pp. 526–540). New York: Routledge.

Grande, S. (2000). American Indian geographies of identity and power: At the crossroads of Indigena & Mestizaje. *Harvard Educational Review, 70(4),* 467–499.

Grande, S. (2004). *Red pedagogy.* New York: Rowman & Littlefield.

Grisoni, L., & Collins, B. (2012). Sense making through poem houses: An arts-based approach to understanding leadership. *Visual Studies, 27(1),* 35–47.

Guerra, L. (1998). *Popular expression and national identity in Puerto Rico: The struggle for self, community, and nation.* Gainesville: University Press of Florida.

Gwaravanda, E. T., & Masaka, D. (2008). Shona reasoning skills in Zimbabwe: The importance of riddles. *Journal of Pan African Studies, 2(5),* 193–208.

Gyekye, K. (1997). *Tradition and modernity: Philosophical reflections on the African experience.* New York: Oxford University Press.

Hale, T. A. (1998). *Griots and griottes: Masters of words and music.* Bloomington: Indiana University Press.

Hall, M. (2010). Nothing is different, but everything's changed. In D. I. Featherman, M. Hall, & M. Krislov (Eds.), *The next 25 years: Affirmative action in higher education in the United States and South Africa* (pp. 355–370). Scottsville, South Africa: University of KwaZulu Natal Press.

Hallett, R. (1974). *Africa since 1875*. Ann Arbor, MI: University of Michigan Press.

Hamminga, B. (2005). Epistemology from the African point of view. In B. Hamminga (Ed.), *Knowledge cultures: Comparative Western and African epistemology* (pp. 57–84). New York: Radopi.

Harvey, L. (1990). *Critical social research*. London: Unwin Hyman.

Havelock, E. A. (1982). *Preface to Plato*. Cambridge, MA: Harvard University Press.

Havelock, E. A. (1996). *The muse learns to write: Reflections on orality and literacy from antiquity to the present*. New Haven, CT: Yale University Press.

Henderson, Y. J. S., Benson, M. L., & Findlay, I. M. (2000). *Aboriginal tenure in the Constitution of Canada*. Scarborough, ON: Carswell Thomson Professional.

Heslop, S. (2011). Introduction. In *Basketry: Making human nature*. Norwich, UK: Sainsbury Centre for Visual Art.

Hewlett, E. S. (1973). The Chilcotin uprising of 1864. *BC Studies, 19*, 50–72.

Higgs, P. (2003). African philosophy and the transformation of educational discourse in South Africa. *Journal of Education, 30*, 5–22.

Higgs, P. (2008). Towards an indigenous educational discourse: A philosophical reflection. *International Review of Education, 54*, 445–458.

Hill, J. H. (2008). *The everyday language of White racism*. Hoboken, NJ: Blackwell.

Hill, J. H. (2008). Expert rhetoric in advocacy for endangered languages: Who is listening and, what do they hear? *Journal of Linguistic Anthropology, 12(2)*, 119–133.

Hill, S. H. (1997). *Weaving new worlds: Southeastern Cherokee women and their basketry*. London: University of North Carolina Press.

Hinton, L., & Hale, K. (Eds.).(2001). *The green book of language revitalization in practice*. San Diego, CA: Academic Press.

Hornberger, N. (2006). Frameworks and models in language policy and planning. In T. Ricento (Ed.), *Language policy: Theory and method* (pp. 24–41). Malden: Blackwell.

Horsthemke, K. (2004). "Indigenous knowledge"—conceptions and misconceptions. *Journal of Education, 32*, 31–48.

Hotep, U. (2010). African centered leadership-followership: Foundational principles, precepts, and essential practices. *Journal of Pan African Studies, 3(6)*, 11–26.

Huntley, D. L. (2008). *Ancestral Zuni glaze-decorated pottery: Viewing Pueblo IV regional organization through ceramic production and exchange*. Tucson: University of Arizona Press.

IAPC. (1987). *Philosophy for Children 1987*. New Jersey: Institute for the Advancement of Philosophy for Children.

Irele, A. (1990). *The African experience in literature and ideology*. Bloomington: Indiana University Press.

Jacobs, H. H. (2010). *Curriculum 21: Essential education for a changing world.* Alexandria, VA: ASCD.
Jah, O. (2010). Al-Balagh. In W. M. Wan Daud & M. Z. Uthman (Eds.), *Knowledge, language, thought and the civilization of Islam* (pp. 83–96). Kuala Lumpur: Penerbit.
James, A., Jenks, C., & Prout, A. (1998). *Theorising childhood.* Cambridge, MA: Polity Press.
Jansen, J. (2010). Moving on Up? The Politics, Problems, and Prospects of Universities as Gateways for Social Mobility in South Africa. In D.I. Featherman, M. Hall, and M. Krislov (Eds.), *The Next 25 Years: Affirmative Action in Higher Education in the United States and South Africa* (pp. 129–136). Scottsville: University of Kwazulu Natal Press.
Jennings, M. (2004). *Alaska Native political leadership and higher education: One university, two universes.* Walnut Creek, CA: Altimira Press.
Johnson, D. D., & Johnson, B. (2006). *High stakes: Poverty, testing, and failure in American schools.* New York: Rowman & Littlefield.
Jones, M. G., Jones, D. J., & Hargrove, T. Y. (2003). *The unintended consequences of high-stakes testing.* New York: Rowman & Littlefield.
Joseph, P. B. (2011). Conceptualizing curriculum. In P. B. Joseph (Ed.), *Cultures of curriculum* (pp. 3–22), New York: Routledge.
Kamsteeg, F. (2008). In search of a merged identity: The case of multi-campus North-West University, South Africa. *TD—The Journal for Transdisciplinary Research in Southern Africa, 4(2),* 431–451.
Kanu, Y. (Ed.). (2006). *Curriculum as cultural practice: Postcolonial imaginations.* Toronto, ON: University of Toronto Press.
Kanu, Y. (2007). Tradition and educational reconstruction in Africa and global times: The case for Sierra Leone. *African Studies Quarterly:The Online Journal For African Studies, 9(3),* 56–84.
Kanu, Y. (2011). *Integrating Aboriginal perspectives into the school curriculum: Purposes, possibilities and challenges.* Toronto, ON: University of Toronto Press.
Kawagley, A. O. (1995). *A Yupiaq worldview: A pathway to an ecology and spirit.* Prospect Heights, IL: Waveland Press.
Kawageley, O. (2001). Tradition and education. In K. James (Ed.), *Science and Native American communities: Legacies of pain visions of promise* (pp. 51–56). Lincoln: University of Nebraska Press.
Kebede, M. (2011). African development and the primacy of mental decolonisation. In L. Keita (Ed.), *Philosophy and African Development: Theory and Practice* (pp. 97–114). Dakar: Council for the Development of Social Science Research in Africa.
Kirkness, V.J. & Barnhardt, R. (1991). First Nations and higher education: the four r's – respect, relevance, reciprocity, responsibility. *Journal of American Indian Education, 30(3),* 1–15.
Klein, S. R., & Diket, R. M. (1999). Creating artful leadership. *International Journal of Leadership in Education, 2(1),* 23–30.
Klug, B., & Whitefield P. (2003). *Widening the circle: Culturally relevant pedagogy for American Indian children.* New York: Routledge.

Kohan, W. O. (1995). The Origin, nature and aim of philosophy in relation to Philosophy for Children. *Thining: The Journal of Philosophy for Children, 12(2)*, 25–31.

Koopman, N. (2010). Towards a pedagogy of hybridity, reconciliation and justice. Retrieved October 3, 2011, from http://www.soliustitiae.co.za/insights/2010/11/22/towards-a-pedagogy-of-hybridity-reconciliation-and-justice/.

Kovach, M. (2010). *Indigenous methodologies: Characteristics, conversations, and contexts*. Toronto, ON: University of Toronto Press.

Kroskrity, P. V. (2004). Language ideologies. In A. Duranti (Ed.), *A companion to linguistic anthropology* (pp. 3–22). Malden: Blackwell.

Kunkel, T., Schorcht, B., & Brazzoni, R. (2011). Aboriginal business capacity building programs in Central Interior of British Columbia: A collaborative project between the university and communities. *Canadian Journal of University Continuing Education, 37(1)*, 1–11.

Ladriere, J. (1992). Preface to Madu. In R. Madu (Ed.), *African symbols, proverbs and myths: The hermeneutics of destiny* (pp. xxi). New York: Peter Lang.

Lane, R. (1953). *Cultural relations of the Chilcotin Indians of West Central British Columbia*. PhD dissertation, University of Washington, Washington, DC.

Langdon, J. (2009). *Indigenous knowledges, development and education*. Rotterdam: Sense.

Lappan, G., Fey, J. T., Fitzgerald, W. M., Friel, S. N., & Phillips, E. D. (2002). *Getting to know connected mathematics: An implementation guide*.

Lave, E., & Wenger, E. (1991). *Situated learning: Legitimate peripheral participation*. New York: Cambridge University Press.

Lee, M. L. (1948). *Basketry and related arts*. New York: Van Nostrand.

Lerman, S. (2000). The social turn in mathematics education research. In J. Boaler (Ed.), *Multiple perspectives on mathematics teaching and learning*. Westport, CT: Ablex.

Lessig, L. (2011). #OccupyWallSt, then #OccupyKSt, then #OccupyMainSt., retrieved on October 15, 2012, from http://www.huffingtonpost.com/lawrence-lessig/occupywallst-then-occupyk_b_995547.html.

Lessow-Hurley, J. (2005). *The foundations of dual language instruction* (4th ed.). New York: Longman.

Lévi-Strauss, C. (1966). Scope of anthropology. *Current Anthropology, 7(2)*, 112–123.

Linn, M. S., Naranjo, T., Nichola, S., Slaughter, I., Yamamoto, A., & Zependa, O. (2002). The language. Challenges of enduring language programs: Field reports from 15 programs from Arizona, New Mexico, and Oklahoma. Retrieved from EBSCO*host*.

Linn, M. (2007). Oklahoma Native languages at the centennial. *World Literature Today, 81(5)*, 24–25.

Linton, A. (2009). Language politics and policy in the United States: Implications for the immigration debate. *International Journal of the Sociology of Language, 199*, 9–37.

Lipka, J. (Ed.). (1998). *Transforming the Culture of Schools: Yup'ik Eskimo Examples*. Mahwah, NJ: Lawrence Erlbaum.
Lipka, J., Brenner, B., & Sharp, N. (2005). The relevance of culturally based curriculum and instruction: The case of Nancy Sharp. *Journal of American Indian Education*, 44(3).
Lipka, J., Kisker, E. E., Adams, B. L., & Millard, A. R. (2007). *The effects of a culturally based math curriclum on Alaska Native students' academic performance*. Fairbanks: University of Alaska Fairbanks.
Lipman, M. (1982). Philosophy for Children *Thinking: The journal for Philosophy for Children*, 3.
Lipman, M. (1988). *Philosophy goes to school*. Philadelphia. PA: Temple University Press.
Lipman, M. (1994). *Thinking in education*. New York: Cambridge University Press.
Lipman, M. (2003). *Thinking in education* (2nd ed.). New York: Cambridge University Press.
Lippard, L. (1990). *Mixed blessings: New art in a multicultural America*. New York: Random House.
Living Tongues Institute. (2007). Living Tongues Language Hotspots. Retrieved December 7, 2012, from http://www.livingtongues.org/hotspots.html.
Lomawaima, K. T. (2004). Educating Native Americans. In J. Banks & C. Banks (Eds.), *Handbook of research on multicultural education* (pp. 441–461). San Francisco, CA: Jossey-Bass.
Lomawaima, K. T., & McCarty, T. (2006). *To remain an Indian: Lessons in democracy from a century of Native American education*. New York: Teachers College.
Lone, M. H. (2000). Does philosophy for children belong in school at all? *Analytic Teaching*, 2(1), 151–156.
Lorde, A. (1984). The master's tools will never dismantle the master's house. In A. Lorde (Ed.), *Sister outsider: The crossing press feminist series* (1st ed.), (pp. 110–113). New York: Ten Speed Press.
Maake, N. (2011). *Barbarism in higher education—Once upon a time in a university*. Johannesburg: Ekaam Books.
MacDonald, V.-M. (2004). *Latino education in the United States: A narrated history from 1513–2000*. New York: Palgrave Macmillan.
Makes Marks, L. F. (2007). Natures of the sacred: On Native North American sacred lands and places. Retrieved from ProQuest Digital Dissertations. (UMI 3264334).
Makgoba, M. W. (1997). *Mokoko: The Makgoba affair; A reflection on transformation*. Florida: Vivlia.
Malpas, J. E. (2007). *Place and experience. A philosophical topography*. Cambridge, UK: Cambridge University Press.
Mamdani, M. (1997). From justice to reconciliation: Making sense of the African experience. Lecture in the Crises and Reconnstruction, African Perspective Series—Two Lectures. Nordiska Afrika Institutet.
Mamdani, M. (May 13, 1998). When does a settler become a Native? Reflections of the colonial roots of citizenship in Equatorial and Southern Africa. New Series No. 28—Inaugural Lecture. University of Cape Town.

Matthews, G. B. (1984). *Dialogues with children*. Cambridge, MA: Harvard University Press.
Matthews, G. B. (1994). *The philosophy of childhood*. Cambridge, MA: Harvard University Press.
Mazrui, A. (1972). *Cultural engineering and nation-building in East Africa*. Evanston, IL: North West University Press.
McCarthy, C. (1998). *The uses of culture: Education and the limits of ethnic affiliation*. New York: Routledge.
McCarty, T. L. (2002). *A place to be Navajo : Rough Rock and the struggle for self-determination in indigenous schooling*. Mahwah, NJ: Lawrence Erlbaum.
Meilach, D. Z. (1974). *A modern approach to basketry with fibers and grasses using coiling, twining, weaving, macramé, crocheting*. New York: Crown.
Meléndez, M. M. (1916). *Estado social del campesino portorriqueño*. San Juan, PR: Tip. Cantero Fernández.
Meléndez, M. M., & Huyke, J. B. (1927). *Ensayos: El niño, la escuela y el hogar; El pauperismo en Puerto Rico; Ventajas e inconvenientes del lujo*. San Juan, PR: Negociado de Materiales, Imprenta y Transporte.
Meléndez, M. M. (1963). El jibaro en el siglo XIX: Cultura, analfabetismo y vida social. In M. M. Meléndez (Ed.), *Obras completas de Miguel Meléndez Muñoz* (pp. 490–503). San Juan de Puerto Rico: Instituto de Cultura Puertorriqueña.
Meléndez, M. M. (1966). *El jíbaro en el siglo XIX: Ensayo mínimo sobre una realidad máxima*. Barcelona: Ediciones Rumbos.
Menken, K. (2008). *English learners left behind: Standardized testing as language policy*. Clevedon: Multlingual Matters.
Menken, K., & Garcia, O. (2010). *Negotiation language policies in schools: Educators as policymakers*. New York: Routledge.
Mihesuah, D. A. (2005). *So you want to write about American Indians? A guide for writers, students, and scholars*. Lincoln: University of Nebraska.
Miller, J. R. (1996). *Shingwauk's vision: A history of Native residential schools*. Toronto, ON: University of Toronto Press.
Miller, L. (1996). Basketry styles of the plateau region. In L. Ackerman (Ed.), *A song to the creator: Traditional arts of Native American women of the plateau*. London: University of Oklahoma Press.
Miller, A. G., & Thomas, R. (1972). Cooperation and competition among Blackfoot Indian and urban Canadian children. *Child Development, 43*, 1104–1110.
Milloy, J. S. (1999). *A national crime: The Canadian government and residential school system; 1879 to 1986*. Winnipeg: University of Manitoba Press.
Mills, C. H. (1997). *The racial contract*. Ithaca, NY, & London: Cornell University Press.
Mixer, K. (1926). *Porto Rico: History and conditions social, economic and political*. New York: Macmillan.
Monture-Angus, P. (1999). *Journeying forward: Dreaming First Nations' independence*. Nova Scotia: Fernwood.

Moore, K. D., Peters, K., Jojola, T., & Lacy, A. (Eds.). (2007). *How it is: The Native American philosophy of V.F. Cordova*. Tucson: University of Arizona Press.

Moral, S. (2006). *Race, science, and nation: The cultural politics of schools in colonial Puerto Rico, 1917–1938*.

Moral, S. (2009). Negotiating colonialism: "Race", class and education in early-twentieth-century Puerto Rico. In A. McCoy & F. Scarano (Eds.), *Colonial crucible: Empire in the making of the modern American state* (pp. 135–144). Madison: University of Wisconsin Press.

Morales, C. A., Babín, M. T., & American Association for State and Local History. (1983). *Puerto Rico: A political and cultural history*. New York: W. W. Norton.

Moreton-Robinson, A. (2000). *Talking up to the white woman*. St. Lucia: University of Queensland Press.

Moreton-Robinson, A. (2002). The possessive investment in patriarchal Whiteness: Nullifying Native title. In C. Bacch (Ed.), *Left directions*. Perth: University of Western Australia Press.

Moreton-Robinson, A. (2003). The possessive logic of patriarchal White sovereignty. In S. Schech & B. Wadham. (Eds.), *Placing race and localising whiteness conference*, Flinders University, Adelaide, October 1, 2003.

Moreton-Robinson, A. (2004). *Whitening race: Essays in social and cultural criticism*. Canberra: Aboriginal Studies Press.

Moreton-Robinson, A. (2007). *Sovereign Subjects: Indigenous Sovereignty Matters*. Australia: Allen & Unwin.

Morgan, M. (2004). Language and social inequality. In A. Duranti (Ed.), *A companion to linguistic anthropology* (pp. 3–22). Malden: Blackwell.

Morphy, H. (1995). Landscape and the reproduction of the ancestral past. In E. Hirsh & M. O'Hanlon (Eds.), *The anthropology of landscapes: Perspectives on place and space* (pp. 184–209). New York: Oxford University Press.

Morris, J. (2012). Leadership of the San. *Kalahari People's Network*. July 4, 2012.

Morris, M. (2004). *Every step of the way: The journey to freedom in South Africa* (pp. 43–44). Cape Town: HSRC Press (Commissioned by the Department of Education).

Mostert, N. (1993). *Frontiers: The epic of South Africa's creation and the tragedy of the Xhosa people* (2nd ed.). Johannesburg: Pimlico.

Msila, V. (2009). Ubuntu and peacemaking in schools. *International Journal of Educational Policies, 3(1)*, 51–66.

Minister of Supply and Services, Canada. (1996). Looking forward, looking back. Report of the Royal Commission on Aboriginal Peoples.

Nakusera, E. (2004). Rethinking higher education transformation in terms of an African(a) philosophy of education. *South African Journal of Higher Education, 18(3)*, 127–137.

National Geographic Society. (2007a). Special Projects. Retrieved March 19, 2010, from http://www.nationalgeographic.com/donate/projects.html.

National Geographic Society. (2007b). Language Hotspots Map. Retrieved March 19, 2010, from http://travel.nationalgeographic.com/travel/enduring-voices/.
Navarro, J.-M. (2002). *Creating tropical yankees: Social science textbooks and U.S. ideological control in Puerto Rico, 1898–1908*. Latino communities. New York: Routledge.
Navarro-Rivera, P. (2009). The imperial enterprise and education policies in colonial Puerto Rico. In A. W. McCoy & F. A. Scarano (Eds.), *The colonial crucible: Empire in the making of the modern American state* (pp. 163–174). Madison: University of Wisconsin Press.
Ndofirepi, A. P. (August 15–18, 2012). *Ukama—a contribution to Philosophy for Children in Africa*. Paper presented at the International Network of Philosophers of Education 13th Biennial Conference, Addis Ababa, Ethiopia.
Ndofirepi, A. P., Shumba, A., & Musengi, M. (2012). *Philosophy for children in Africa: Is the hermeneutic–narrative approach the answer?*
Negrón, M. A. (1977). *La americanización de Puerto Rico y el sistema de instrucción pública, 1900–1930*. Río Piedras: Editorial Universitaria, Universidad de Puerto Rico.
Nettle, D., & Romaine, S. (2000). *Vanishing voices: The extinction of the world's languages*. New York: Oxford University Press.
NewsOK. (November, 2010). Oklahoma English-only measure challenged. Retrieved November 21, 2010, from http://newsok.com/oklahoma-english-only-measure-challenged/article/3513258.
Nicoll, F. (October 2004). Are you calling me a racist? Teaching critical whiteness theory in indigenous sovereignty. In D. Riggs. (Ed.), *Why whiteness studies? 3(2)*, borderlands e-journal, Canberra.
Northeastern State University (NSU). (2012). Cherokee language education, B.A. Retrieved December 6, 2012, from http://academics.nsuok.edu/languagesliterature/DegreePrograms/CherokeeLanguageEducationBA.aspx.
Norton-Smith, T. M. (2010). *Dance of person and place*. New York: SUNY.
Nsemanang, A. B., & Tchombe, T. M. S. (2011). Introduction: Generative pedagogy in the context of all cultures can contribute scientific knowledge of universal value. In A. B. Nsemanang & M. S. Tchombe (Eds.), *Handbook of African educational theories and practices: A generative teacher education curriculum*. Bamenda: Human Resources Development Centre.
Null, W. (2011). *Curriculum: From theory to practice*. Lanham, MD: Rowman & Littlefield.
Nussbaum, M. (1996). Patriotism and cosmopolitanism. In J. Cohen, (Ed.), *For love of country: Debating the limits of patriotism* (pp. 3–20). Boston, MA: Beacon Press.
O'Sullivan, S. (2006). *Art encounters Deleuze and Guattari: Thought beyond representation*. New York: Palgrave Macmillan.
Obotetukudo, S. (2001). The African philosophy of development: When localism And traditionalism collide with globalism. Is "tele"communication the answer?, 39–57. Retrieved from http://www.jsd-africa.com/Jsda/Fallwinter2001/articlespdf/ARC.

Odora-Hoppers, C. A. (2001a). Introduction. In P. Higgs, N. C. G. Vakalisa, T. V. Mda, & N. T. Assie-Lumumba (Eds.), *African voices in education: Retrieving the past, engaging the present and shaping the future* (pp. 1–11). Cape Town: Juta.

Odora-Hoppers, C. A. (2001b). *Indigenous knowledge and the integration of knowledge systems: Toward a conceptual and methodological framework. A comparative study of the development, integration and protection of knowledge systems in the Third World.* Pretoria: Human Sciences Research Council.

Odora-Hoppers, C. A. (2002). Indigenous knowledge and the integration of knowledge systems: Towards a conceptual and methodological framework. In Odora-Hoppers, C. (Ed.), *Indigenous knowledge and the integration of knowledge systems: Towards a philosophy of articulation* (pp. 2–22). Claremont: New Africa Books.

Ojiaku, M. O. (1974). Traditional African social thought and western scholarship. *Présence africaine: Revue culturelle du monde noir, 90*, 204–214.

Oklahoma State Senate (proposed, 2001). *Oklahoma Indian Language Heritage Protection Act*, SCR No.37.

Oklahoma State Department of Education. (2011). *School Laws of Oklahoma.*

O'Loughlin, M. (1996). Ways of thinking about being: Explorations in ontology. *Studies in Philosophy and Education, 15.*

O'Loughlin, Marjorie. (1997). Listening, heeding, and respecting the ground at one's feet: Knowledge and the arts across cultures. *Philosophy of Music Education Review, 5(1)*, 14–24.

O'Loughlin, M. (2006). *Embodiment and education. Exploring creatural existence.* Dordrecht: Springer.

Olatunji, O. O. (1984). *Features of Yoruba oral poetry.* Ibadan: University Press.

Olson, L. (2009). The role of advocacy in shaping immigrant education: A California case study. *Teachers College Record, 111(3)*, 817–850.

Olu, D., & Jeje, A. (1995). *Awon asa ati Orisa Ile Yoruba.* Ibadan: Onibon-Oje Press.

Ong, W. J. (1982). *Orality & literacy: The technologizing of the Word.* New York: Methuen.

Osha, S. (2011). Appraising Africa: Modernity, decolonisation and globalisation. In L. Keita (Ed.), *Philosophy and African development: Theory and practice* (pp. 169–176). Dakar: Council for the Development of Social Science Research in Africa.

Osuna, J. J. (1949). *A history of education in Puerto Rico.* Rio Piedras, PR: Editorial de la Universidad de Puerto Rico.

Owolabi, K. A. (2001). The quest for method in African philosophy: A defence of the hermeneutic-narrative approach. *Philosophical Forum, XXXII(2)*, 147–163.

Paci, C. D. J. (2006). Decolonizing Athabaskan education: Aboriginal treaty rights in Denendeh. In I. Abu-Saad & D. Champagne (Eds.), *Indigenous education and empowerment* (pp. 81–112). New York: Rowman & Littlefield.

Palmater, P. D. (2011). *Beyond blood: Rethinking indigenous identity.* Saskatoon, SK: Purich.

Parekh, B. (2000). Rethinking Multiculturalism. *Cultural Diversity and Political Theory.* Hampshire and London: Macmillan Press.
Patrick, J. (2011). Plaited paper baskets. *Arts & Activities, 150(4),* 16–18.
Pew Forum on Religion and Public Life. (2011). *The future of the global Muslim population: Projections for 2010 – 2030* (Washington, DC: Pew Research Center).
Philips, S. U. (1972). Participant structures and communicative competence: Warm Springs children in community and classroom. In C. B. Cazden, V. T. John, & D. Hymes (Eds.), *Functions of language in the classroom* (pp. 370–394). New York: Teachers College Press.
Philips, S. U. (1983). *The invisible culture: Communication in classroom and community on the Warm Springs Indian Reservation.* New York: Longman.
Philips, S. (2004). Language and social inequality. In A. Duranti (Ed.), *A companion to linguistic anthropology* (pp. 474–495). Malden, MA: Blackwell.
Pieterse, J. N. (2001). Hybridity, so what? The anti-hybridity backlash and the riddles of recognition. *Theory, Culture & Society, 18(2–3),* 219–245.
Pieterse, J. N. (2004). *Globalisation and culture: Global interchange.* London: Rowman & Littlefield.
Pinar, W. F. (1975). The method of currere. Paper presentation, AERA.
Pinar, W. F. (2011). *What is curriculum theory?* (2nd ed.). Hoboken, NJ: Taylor & Francis.
Pinxten, R. (1997). Applications in the teaching of mathematics and the sciences. In A. B. Powell & M. Frankenstein (Eds.), *Ethnomathematics: Challenging eurocentrism in mathematics education.* Albany, NY: SUNY.
Poelzer, G. (1996). Through a theory of Native self-government: Canada and Russia in comparative perspective. Unpublished doctoral dissertation, University of Alberta, Edmonton, Alberta.
Prakash, M., & Esteva, G. (2008). *Escaping education: Living as learning within grassroots cultures.* New York: Peter Lang.
Putnam, R., & Borko, H. (2000). What do new views of knowledge and thinking have to say about research on teacher learning? *Educational Researcher, 29(1).*
Ramos, A. (1998). *Indigenism: Ethnic politics in Brazil.* Madison: University of Wisconsin Press.
Rasmussen, L. B. (1998). Learning cultures. *AI & Society, 12(3),* 134–154.
Reese, S. (2011). Teaching and preserving native languages. *Language Educator, 6(5),* 42–48.
Reichel-Dolmatoff, G. (1985). *Arts and crafts of the Desana Indians of the Northwest Amazon.* Los Angeles, CA: Museum of Cultural History.
Reif, N., & Grant, L. (2010). Culturally responsive classrooms through art integration. *Journal of Praxis in Multicultural Education, 5(1),* 100–115.
Ridenour, C. S. (2004). Finding the horizon: Education administration students paint a landscape of cultural diversity in schools. *Journal of School Leadership, 14(1),* 4–31.
Rigney, Lester-Irabinna (1999). Internationalization of an Indigenous anticolonial cultural critique of research methodologies: A guide to Indigenist research methodology and its principles.

Rivage-Seul, M. (1987). Critical thought or domestication? Paper presented at the Philosopical studies in Education, Ohio Valley Philosophy of Education Society, Terre Haute, Indiana.

Rogoff, B. (1990). *Apprenticeship in thinking: Cognitive development in social context*. New York: Oxford University Press.

Rose, D.B. (2000). *Dingo Makes us Human. Life and Land in an Australian Indigenous Culture*. Cambridge University Press: Cambridge, UK.

Rothstein, R. (2004). *Class and schools: Using social, economic, and educational reform to close the black—white achievement gap*. Washington, DC: Economic Policy Institute.

Ruiz, R. (1995). Language planning consideration in indigenous communities. *Bilingual Research Journal, 19(1)*, 71–81.

Rutherford, J. (1990). *The third space: Interview with Homi Bhabha; identity, community, culture, difference*. London: Lawrence & Wishart.

Saltman, K. (2000). *Collateral damage*. Lanham, MD: Rowman & Littlefield.

Sampson, E. E. (1988). The debate on individualism: Indigenous psychologies of the individual and their role in personal and societal functioning. *American Psychologist, (1)*, 43.

Schell, P. (2010). Eugenics Policy and Practice in Cuba, Puerto Rico, and Mexico. In A. Bashford & P. Levine (Eds.), *The Oxford handbook of the history of eugenics* (pp. 477–492). New York: Oxford University Press.

Schnarch, B. (October 2005). Ownership, control, access, and possession or self determination applied to research. Retrieved February 6, 2010, from http://www.researchutoronto.ca/ethics/pdf/human/nonspecific/OCAP%20principles.pdf.

Schnarch, B. (January 2004). Ownership, control, access, and possession (OCAP) or self-determination applied to research: A critical analysis of contemporary First Nations research and some options for First Nations communities. *Journal of Aboriginal Health*.

Schneider, N. (2011). From Occupy Wall Street to occupy everywhere. Retrieved October, 15, 2012, from http://www.thenation.com/article/163924/occupy-wall-street-occupy-everywhere.

Sefa Dei, G. J. (2002). Learning culture, spirituality and local knowledge: Implications for African schooling. *International Review of Education, 48(5)*, 335–360.

Semali, L., & Kincheloe, J. L. (1999). *What is Indigenous knowledge? Voices from the academy*. New York: Falmer Press.

Shaetti, B. F., Ramsey, S. J., & Watanabe, G. C. (2008). From intercultural knowledge to intercultural competence. In M. A. Moodian (Ed.), *Contemporary leadership and intercultural competence: Exploring the cross-cultural dynamics within organizations* (pp. 125–138). Thousand Oaks, CA: Sage.

Shanks, R., & Woo-Shanks, L. (2010). *California Indian baskets: San Diego to Santa Barbara and beyond to the San Joaquin valley, mountains and deserts (Indian Baskets of California and Oregon)*. Novato, CA: Costano Books.

Sharp, N. (1994). Caknernarqutet. *Peabody Journal of Education, 69(2)*.

Smith, L. T. (2012). *Decolonizing methodologies: Research and indigenous peoples*. New York: Zed Books.

Smith, R. (2008). Proteus Rising: Re-Imagining Educational Research. *Journal of Philosophy of Education*, 42(S1), 183–198.

Solano-Flores, G. (2011). Assessing the cultural validity of assessment practices. In M. Rosario Basterrra, E. Trumbull, & G. Solano-Flores (Eds.), *Cultural Validity in Assessment: Addressing Linguistic and Cultural Diversity*. New York: Routledge.

Solís, J. (1994). *Public school reform in Puerto Rico: Sustaining colonial models of development*. Contributions to the study of education, no. 60. Westport, CT: Greenwood Press.

Some, M. P. (1995). *Of water and spirit: Ritual, magic, and initiation in the life of an African shaman*. New York: Penguin.

Spencer, J. (1985). Language and development in Africa: The unequal equation. In N. Wolfson & J. Manes (Eds.), *Language of inequality* (pp. 123–143). New York: Mouton.

State of Oklahoma. (2010). Constitution of the state of Oklahoma. Retrieved December 7, 2012, from http://www.oklegislature.gov/ok_constitution.html.

Stankiewicz, M. A., Amburgy, P., & Bolin P. (2004). Questioning the past: Contexts, functions and stakeholders in 19th century art education. In E. Eisner & M. Day (Eds.), *Handbook of research and policy in art education* (pp. 35–55). Reston, VA: NAEA & London, UK: Lawrence Erlbaum.

Stanner, W. E. H. (2009). *The Dreaming and other essays* with an introduction by Robert Manne. Melbourne: Black.

Statistics Canada. 2006 Census: Aboriginal Peoples in Canada in 2006: Inuit, Métis and First Nations, 2006 Census: First Nations people. http://www12.statcan.ca/census-recensement/2006/as-sa/97-558/p16-eng.cfm.

Stavenhagen, R. (1996). *Ehnic conflicts and the nation-state*. London: Macmillan.

Sterling, S. (1997). *The grandmother stories: Oral tradition and transmission of culture*. PhD dissertation, University of British Columbia.

Stocek, C. & Mark, R. (2009). Indigenous research and decolonizing methodologies: Possibilities & opportunities. In Jonathan Langdon (Ed.), *Indigenous knowledges, development and education* (pp. 73–96). Rotterdam: Sense.

Stubington, J. (2007). *Singing the land: The power of performance in Aboriginal life*. Foreword by Raymattja Marika. Sydney: Currency House Press.

Sullivan, M., Schwartz, D., Weiss, D., & Zaffran, B. (1996). *The Native American look book: Art and activities from the Brooklyn Museum*. New York: New Press.

Sutherland, I., & Gosling, J. (2010). Cultural leadership: Mobilizing culture from affordances to dwellings. *Journal of Arts Management, Law, and Society*, 40, 6–26.

Sutherland, L. (1995). Citizen minus: Aboriginal women and Indian self-government, race, nation, class and gender. Unpublished master's thesis, University of Regina, Regina Saskatchewan.

Sutton, P. (2011). *The Politics of Suffering. Indigenous Australia and the End of Liberal Consensus*. Melbourne University Press: Melbourne.

Swain, T. (1993). *A place for strangers: Towards a history of Australian Aboriginal being*. Cambridge, UK: Cambridge University Press.

Swanson, D. M. (2009). Where have all the fishes gone? Living Ubuntu as an ethics of research and pedagogical engagement. In D. Caracciolo & A. M. Mungai (Eds.), *In the spirit of Ubuntu: Stories of teaching and research* (pp. 3–21). The Netherlands: Sense.

Tahlequah Public Schools. (2012). TPS Board Policies. Retrieved December 6, 2012, from http://www.tahlequah.k12.ok.us/BOE/Documents/5000.pdf.

Taliaferro-Baszile, D. (2010). In Ellisonian eyes, what is curriculum theory? In Malewski, E. (Ed.), *Curriculum studies handbook: The next movement* (pp. 483–495). New York: Routledge.

Taylor, C. (1985). *Philosophy and the human sciences: Philosophical papers 2*. Cambridge, MA: Cambridge University Press.

Taylor, G. S. (2004). *Impact of high-stakes testing on the academic futures of non-mainstream students*. Lewistion, NY: Edwin Mellen Press.

Taylor, S. S., & Ladkin, D. (2009). Understanding arts-based methods in managerial development. *Academy of Management Learning and Education, 8(1)*, 55–69.

TCP: Canadian Institutes of Health Research, Natural Sciences and Engineering Research Council of Canada, and Social Sciences and Humanities Research Council of Canada. (2010). *Tri-Council Policy Statement: Ethical conduct for research involving humans*. pp. 105–33.

Teit, J. (1906). The Lillooet Indians. The Jesup North Pacific Expedition: Memoir of the American Museum of Natural History, *II(V)*, 195–300.

Terrance, L. L. (September–October 2011). Resisting colonial education: Zitkala-Ša and Native feminist archival refusal. *International Journal of Qualitative Studies in Education, 24(5)*, 621–626.

Tharp, R., Estrada, P., Dalton, S., & Yamauchi, L. A. (2000). *Teaching transformed: Achieving excellence, fairness, inclusion and harmony*. Colorado: Westview Press.

The Guardian. (2007). The Hottentot Venus: Sarah Baartman (1789–1816). Saturday, March 31, 2007.

The Economist. (2005). The global housing boom: In come the waves. Retrieved December 7, 2012, from http://www.economist.com/node/4079027?story_id=4079027.

Theal, G. M. (1910). *History and Ethnography of Africa South of the Zambezi, from the Settlement of the Portuguese at Sofala in September 1505 to the Conquest of the Cape Colony by the British in September 1795*. Perth: Cowan & Co. Ltd.

Thomas, J. (2007). *Leading an extraordinary life: Wise practices for an HIV prevention campaign with Two-Spirit men*. Toronto, ON: Two-Spirited People of the First Nations.

Trevors, J. T., & Saier, M. H. (December 5, 2009). Water, air, and soil pollution, National Center for Biotechnology Information, *Education for Humanity Series*, http://www.ncbi.nlm.nih.gov/pmc/articles/PM3252885/.

Tuck, E. (2009). Theorizing back: An approach to participatory policy analysis, *Eve Tuck* personal reflection. In J. Anyon. (Ed.), *Theory and educational research: Toward critical and social explanation* (pp. 111–130). New York: Routledge.

Bibliography   241

Tuhiwai Smith, L. (1999). *Decolonizing methodologies: Research and Indigenous peoples*. New York: Zed Books.
Tufvesson, I. (December 2005). *They ought to be (t)here! but...: An intersectional study of racialised academic women's marginalisation in Australia, South Africa, and Sweden*. Doctoral Thesis, University of New South Wales, Sydney.
Tufvesson, I. (December 2012). The politics of loyalty: Accountability, transformation, and redress in South African higher education. *Critical Race and Whiteness Studies, 8(2)*, 1–23.
Tutu, D. (1999). *No future without forgiveness*. New York: Doubleday.
UC Davis Fact Sheet, December 2011.
US Congress. (1990). Native American Languages Act. S.1781. ES. 101st Cong.
US Congress. (2006). Esther Martinez Act. H.R. 4766. 109th Cong.
US Congress (proposed 2011). English Language Unity Act. H.R. 997. 112th Cong.
US Department of Education. (1968). Bilingual Education Act.
US Department of Education. (2001). No child left behind act of 2001.
US Department of Education. (2010). Race to the top program: Executive Summary. Retrieved December 7, 2012, from http://www2.ed.gov/programs/racetothetop/executive-summary.pdf.
US Supreme Court. (1974). *Lau V. Nichols*. 414 U.S. 563, 94S. Ct. 786, 39L. Ed.2dl.
Välimaa, J. (1998). Culture and identity in higher education research. *Higher Education, 36(2)*, 119–138.
Vallance, E. (1983). Hiding in the hidden curriculum: An interpretation of the language of justification in nineteenth century educational reform. In H. Giroux & D. Purpel (Eds.), *The hidden curriculum and moral education* (pp. 9–27). Berkeley: McCutchan.
Van Hook, J. M. (1993). African philosophy: Its quest for identity. *Quest, VII(1)*, 28–43.
Van der Westhuizen, C. (2007). *White power & the rise and fall of the National Party*. Cape Town: Zebra Press.
VanStone, J. W. (1993). Material culture of the Chilcotin Athapaskans of West Central British Columbia: Collections in the Field Museum of Natural History. *Anthropology New Series (20)*. Field Museum of Natural History.
Van Wyk, B., & Higgs, P. (2007). The call for an African university: A critical reflection. *Higher Education Policy, 20(1)*, 61–71.
Vavrus, M. (2002). *Transforming the multicultural education of teachers*. Teachers College Press.
Venter, E. (2008/9). The *Paidea* Project Online. http://www.bu.edu/wcp/Papers/Educ/EducVent.html.
Vinnicombe, P. (1986). Rock Art, territory and land rights. In M. Biesele, R. Gordon, & R. Lee (Eds.), *The past and future of Kung Ethnography: Critical Reflections and Symbolic Perspectives. Essays in Honour of Lorna Marshall* (pp. 275–325). Hamburg: Helmut Buske Verlag.
Wa Thiong'o, N. (2009). Foreword. In D. Caracciolo & A. M. Mungai (Eds.), *In the spirit of Ubuntu: Stories of teaching* (pp. ix–xi). Rotterdam, The Netherlands: Sense.

Wahlman, M. S. (2001). *Signs and symbols: African images in African American 1uilts*. Atlanta, GA: Tinwood Books.
Walters, J. (2011). *Occupy America: Protests against Wall Street and inequality hit 70 cities*. Retrieved October 15, 2012, from http://www.guardian.co.uk/world/2011/oct/08/occupy-america-protests-financial-crisis.
Waghid, Y. (2004). Revisiting the African-Africana philosophy of education debate: Implications for university teaching. *Journal of Education, 34*, 127–142.
Waghid, Y. (2011). *Conceptions of Islamic education: Pedagogical framings*. New York: Peter Lang.
Wan Daud, M. W. (2009). Attas' concept of *ta'dib* as true and comprehensive education in Islam. Retrieved September 19, 2010, from http://www.seekersguidance.org.za.
Warner, L. S., & Grint, K. (2006). American Indian ways of leading and knowing. *Leadership, 2(2)*, 225–244.
Waters, A. (2004). Introduction. In A. Waters, *American Indian thought* (pp. xv–xxxviii). Malden: Blackwell.
Watson-Gegeo, K., & Gegeo, D. (2001). "How we know": Kwara'ae rural villagers doing Indigenous epistemology. *Contemporary Pacific, 13(1)*, 55–88.
Watson-Gegeo, K., & Gegeo, D. (2004). Deep culture: Pushing the epistemological boundaries of multicultural education. In G. S. Goodman & K. Carey (Eds.), *Critical multicultural conversations* (pp. 235–256). Creskgill, NJ: Hampton Press.
Watt, D. L., Lipka, J., Parker Webster, J., Yanez, E., Andrew-Ihrke, D., & Adam, A. S. (2006). *Designing patterns: Exploring shapes and area*. Calgary, AB: Detselig.
Webster, J. P., Wiles, P., Civil, M., & Clarke, S. (2005). Finding a good fit: Using MCC in a "Third Space." *Journal of American Indian Education, 44(3)*.
Werbner, P. (1997). Introduction: The dialectics of cultural hybridity. In P. Werbner & T. Modood (Eds.), *Debating cultural hybridity: Multicultural identities and the politics of anti-racism* (pp. 1–26). London: Zed Books.
Wesley-Esquimaux, C., & Calliou, B. (2010). *Best practices in Aboriginal community development: A Literature review & Wise practices approach*. Banff, Alberta: The Banff Centre.
White, M. (1901). *How to make baskets*. New York: Doubleday, Page.
White J. P., and Peters, J. (2009). A short history of Aboriginal education in Canada. In J. P. White, J. Peters, D. Beavon, & N. Spence (Eds.), *Aboriginal education: Current crisis and future alternatives* (pp. 13–31). Toronto: Thompson Education.
Wicazo Sa Review. (1999). Emergent Ideas in Native American Studies, 14(2), 109–121. http://www.jstor.org/stable/1409555
Wildcat, D. (2001). Indigenizing education. In V. Deloria Jr. & D. R. Wildcat, *Power and place in Indian education in America* (pp. 7–20). Golden, CO: Fulcrum.
Wilkins, I., & Strydom, H. (2012). *The super Afrikaners: Inside the Afrikaner broderbond* (3rd ed.). Jeppestown: Jonathan Ball.

Wilson, S. (2008). *Research is ceremony: Indigenous research methods.* Halifax, NS: Fernwood.
Wiredu, K. (1997). How not to compare African traditional thought with western thought. *Transition: The Anniversary Issue; Selections from Transition,1961–1976, 75/76*, pp. 320–327.
Wiredu, K., & Kresse, K. (2003). Language matters: Decolonisation, multiculturalism, and African languages in the making of African philosophy. Kwasi Wiredu in dialogue with Kai Kresse. Retrieved October 19, 2010, from http://them.polylog.org/2/dwk-en.htm.
Wraga, W. (2006). Curriculum theory and development and public policy making. *Journal of Curriculum & Pedagogy, 3(1)*, 83–87.
Wroth, W. (1994). The Hispanic craft revival in New Mexico. In J. Kardon (Ed.), *Revivals! Diverse traditions 1920–1945: The History of twentieth-century American craft.* New York: Harry N. Abrams, in association with the American Craft Museum.
Wyckoff, L. (2001). *Woven worlds: Basketry from the Clark Field Collection.* Tulsa, OK: Philbrook Museum of Art.
Ylimaki, R. M. (2012). Curriculum leadership in a conservative era. *Educational Administration Quarterly, 48(2)*, 304–346.
Young, I. M. (1990). *Justice and the politics of difference.* Princeton, NJ: Princeton University Press.
Young, I. M. (1997). *Intersecting voices: Dilemmas of gender, political philosophy, and policy.* Princeton, NJ: Princeton University Press.
Zuma, J. G. (February 9, 2012). *State of the Nation Address.* South Africa: African National Congress. http://www.info.gov.za/speech/DynamicAction?pageid=461&tid=55960.

Contributors

Dolapo Adeniji-Neill is assistant professor at Ruth S. Ammon School of Education, Adelphi University, Garden City, New York. She is an ascendant of Chief Sapakin of Ikoti, Loro Gbenla, and Olufunmilayo Odanye of the Yoruba people in Nigeria and worldwide. Her research interests and work include Sociological and cultural implications influencing individual and group educational opportunities in the U.S and internationally; Class and gender influences in K-12 and higher education settings; Immigrant education; Multiculturalism.

Vonzell Agosto is assistant professor in the Department of Educational Leadership and Policy Studies. She is of African American and Mexican American descent. Her research interests are curriculum, curriculum leadership, culturally relevant leadership preparation in relationship to anti-oppressive education and equitable excellence.

Nuraan Davids is lecturer in the Department of Education Policy Studies at Stellenbosch University. Her interests include democratic citizenship education, Islamic education, and educational leadership and management.

Donna Elam is a nationally recognized authority in diversity and cultural competence research and training for governmental, business, community, and educational agencies. She and her family is Caribbean, from the island of Antigua. She is of Irish, African American, and Cherokee descent.

Frances Kay Holmes is a recent graduate of the University of California, Davis, from the School of Education with a Masters in Native American Studies. Of Muscogee (Creek) ancestry, Kay is currently employed with the Ione Band of Miwok Indians in Northern California.

Melissa Kagle is assistant professor of Educational Studies and coordinator of Math and Science Teacher Preparation at Colgate University.

Her research focuses on the incorporation of Indigenous knowledge in math and science teaching.

Titi I. Kunkel is a woman from the Yoruba tribe of West Africa. She spent a considerable number of her formative years in Lagos, Nigeria, where she learned the Yoruba culture as passed down to her by her grandmother. She has been teaching and doing research work with the Aboriginal communities in the province of British Columbia, Canada, since 2005.

Carol D. Lee is Edwina S. Tarry Professor of Education and Social Policy at Northwestern University. She is a renowned international scholar, and has developed a theory of cultural modeling that provides a framework for the design and enactment of curriculum that draws on forms of prior knowledge that traditionally underserved students bring to classrooms. She was the 2009/2010 AERA President; just one of her many notable achievements.

Georgina Martin from the Faculty of Education, University of British Columbia, is both *Secwepemc* and a member of Lake Babine Nation. She fosters reciprocal relationships between communities and researchers, advocates for Indigenous communities in relation to health and social issues, Indigenous self-determination, Indigenous education, and Indigenous voice.

Amasa Philip Ndofirepi is a Zimbabwean of Shona origins and resident in South Africa. He is a Postdoctoral Research Fellow in the Faculty of Education at the University of Johannesburg, South Africa. His PhD thesis titled *Philosophy for Children: A Quest for an African Perspective* has generated a wide range of international, peer-reviewed journal articles on African philosophy of education and critical thinking. Currently Amasa has developed research insights into epistemologies in higher education in Africa.

Bethsaida Nieves is a PhD candidate in the Department of Curriculum and Instruction at the University of Wisconsin-Madison. Her research interests include international and comparative education.

Marjorie O'Loughlin is involved in Aboriginal teacher education at the Koori Centre, University of Sydney. She is a philosopher and social scientist and has published widely on themes of identity, embodiment, and citizenship, having carried out significant research on understandings of place, self, and notions of belonging.

Omar Salaam is a graduate student earning his PhD in Educational Leadership and Policy Studies at the University of South Florida. He is the son of descendants of the Trans-Atlantic slave trade. He has been a formal educator and administrator within public and private schools in America and abroad for 20 years.

Joyce Schneider, Kicya7 is Samahquamicw of the Stl'atl'imx and carried her grandmother's ancestral name of Kicya7 since December of 2008. She is a PhD candidate in the Educational Studies program at the University of British Columbia and has been an instructor in the Aboriginal Bridge Programs at Simon Fraser University since 2007.

Blanca Schorcht is dean of the College of Arts, Social and Health Sciences at University of Northern British Columbia (UNBC). She specializes in First Nations literatures, oral and written traditions, and auto-ethnography. As the Regional Chair of UNBC's South Central campus, Blanca was instrumental in the planning and delivery of the Tsilhqot'in language and culture program for the communities.

J. Taylor Tribble is a doctoral candidate in the Department of Educational Leadership and Policy Studies, Jeannine Rainbolt College of Education, University of Oklahoma. His heritage includes both Caucasian and Native American (Lakota) ancestry. His research interests include Native American language revitalization/language policy planning.

Ingrid Tufvesson recently ended her employment at North-West University. She coined the notion of a *politics of loyalty* by which one can understand the paradoxical persistence of the past in the South African presence. Her insight is presented from the subaltern position as *outsider within*, and she continues to write on the subjects of Indigenous ontology/ontologies.

Berte van Wyk is an ascendant of the First Nation Griqua tribe of the Khoisan people of South Africa. He is associate professor in the Department of Education Policy Studies at Stellenbosch University. His research interests include African philosophy, Khoisan conceptions of education, and institutional culture in higher education.

Yusef Waghid is distinguished professor of philosophy of education at Stellenbosch University. His research foci include: analytical inquiry, democratic citizenship education, African education, and religious education.

Courtney Lee Weida is associate professor of Art Education at Adelphi University, New York. She is interested in feminism, digital learning communities, and contemporary craft as models for activism (craftivism).

Index

Page numbers in bold indicate figures and tables.

Abolition of the Slave Trade Act, 29–30
Aboriginal Affairs and Northern Development Canada (AANDC), 56–7
Aboriginal knowledge/practices, 76–7
 and avoidance of West/non-West dichotomy, 83
 diversity of, 73
 kinship, 79–80, 148
 nonindigenous interface with, 72–4, 83–5
 and postcolonial framework, 73–4
 sense of place and, 77–9
 time, 82
 Western misinterpretation of, 79–80
 worldview, 7
Aboriginal people
 percent of Australian population, 74–5
 and reclamation of individual/collective identities, 59–60
 worldview of, 76–7
academia. See also universities
 inherent characteristics of, 150
Ade, King Sunny, 12, 177, 179
Adeniji-Neill, Dolapo, 4, 12
Africaans language, Khoi adoption of, 147

African cultures
 devaluation of, 197
 precolonial, 206–7
African identity(ies), precolonial education and, 197
African National Congress (ANC), 28
 Khoisan land issues and, 24
African Philosophy for Children, 197–207
 and African traditional culture *versus* Western science, 201
 and dismantling of colonial ideology, 202–3
 hybridized, 198–207
 and integration with Lipmanian pedagogy, 204–5
 and reconstruction of contemporary African experience, 201–2
 Sankofa and, 201
 traditional African worldview in, 204–7
African societies, and perceptions of wisdom, 200–1
Afrikaner Broederbond, influence of, 151–2, 155n9
Agosto, Vonzell, 9
Alaska, village teaching in, 161–9. See also Math in a Cultural Context (MCC)

Allen, Elsie Comanche, 187–8
American Craft Revival, 187–8
American Indians. *See also* Native American languages; specific tribes
 leadership among, 117
Americanization, of Puerto Rican education, 33–4, 38–9
Anangu culture, The Dreaming and, 79–80
animals
 relatedness with, 92
 totemic, 77
apartheid
 Khoisan resistance to, 22
 land issues and, 24
 legislation enforcing, 145–6
 South African universities and, 150–3
assimilation, risk of, 130
Atkins, J. D. C., 213
Australia. *See also* Aboriginal knowledge/practices
 Aboriginal peoples in, 145
 contemporary intellectual/social context in, 74–5
 The Dreaming in (*see* The Dreaming)
 Indigenous concepts/practices in (*see* Indigenous concepts/practices)
 and policies disrupting kinship, 79

Baartman, Saartjie (Sarah), 5, 26–30, 147
Band membership, 6
 aboriginal views on, 59–60
 Bill C31 amendment and, 56–7, 60, 67
 blood quantum requirement for, 64–5, **64**
 code for, 63–4, **63**, 68
 debate over, 60–1
 dual citizenship and, 65–6, **65**
 Indian Act of 1876 and, 55
 (*see also* Indian Act of 1876)

 portability issue and, 66, **66**
 RCAP and, 61
 and return to traditional practices, 68
Bantu Education Act 47 of 1953, 151
Barnes, Dorothy Gill, 194
basketry, 12–13, 185–96
 in Africa, 189
 Cherokee, 186, 188–90, 192
 concluding reflections on, 195–6
 female symbols in, 186
 gender and, 189–91
 historical roles of family and education in, 186–9
 Indigenous mythology and, 191–2
 place and space and, 195
 Pomo, 186–8, 190
 shared origins with pottery, 185–6, 192–4
 Zulu, 195–6
Beans, Winifred, 158–9, 164
Bennett, Jane, 83
Berré, Baptiste, 27
Biggest Estate on Earth, The: How Aborigines Made Australia (Gammage), 81
Bilingual Education Act, 211
bilingualism
 NCLB and, 219
 policy deterrents to, 210
Bill C-31 amendment, 56, 57, 60, 67
Billy, Susan, 187
Blainville, Henri de, 27
Boas, Franz, 47
Bradley, Rowena, 188
British Columbia. *See also* Canim Lake Bank; Tsilhqot'in language and culture courses
 First Nations cultures in, 43
 Indian Act of 1876 and (*see* Indian Act of 1876)
Brumbaugh, Martin, 34
Bryant, Levi R., 83
Burke, Annie, 187–8
Butcher, Mary, 194

Index

campesino children
  eugenic discourse and, 36–7
  imagined geographies and, 37–40
campesino identity, 5
  common-law marriage and, 37
  construction of, 31–41
Canada
  Constitution Act of 1867 and, 55–6
  Indian Act of 1876 in (*see* Indian Act of 1876)
  and legislative authority over aboriginal people, 55–7 (*see also* Indian Act of 1876)
  native education in, 52–3
Canadian Aboriginal Aids Network (CAAN), 128–9
Canadian Constitution, section 91(24) of, 60
Canim Lake Band, 55
  Band membership study and, 62–7, 63, 64, 65, 66
  Indigenous identity and, 55
  research problem and, 58–9
Carrier people, 46
Catholic Church, and Americanization of Puerto Rican education, 33–4
Cherokee basketry, 186, 188–90, 192
Cherokee families, matriarchal relationships of, 189
Cherokee language, certification program for, 218
children. See also *campesino* children
  African philosophy for (*see* African philosophy for children)
  and development of critical reasoning, 198–9
  traditional African perceptions of, 200
Choctaw language, instruction in, 218
Churchill, Ward, 130–1
circular thinking, in Indigenous epistemologies, 89

Cissoko, Tiemoko, 175–6
citizenship
  aboriginal views on, 59–60
  Canim Lake Band study and, 62–7
  debate over, 60–1
  RCAP and, 61
clan system, of First Nations people, 57
classroom, incorporating Indigenous knowledge into, 10–11. *See also* Math in a Cultural Context (MCC)
clay-molding, role in theory building, 117–18, 123
Cloete, Willem, 25
colonization
  basketry and, 12, 190–2
  Canadian Aboriginal peoples and, 61
  TribalCrit Theory and, 9, 114
colonizing mandate, internalization of, 67–8
"Coloured" registration, 146–7
common-law marriage, *campesino* identity and, 37
community, Khoisan people and, 19–21, 26
consciousness, in Indigenous epistemology, 92
consensus-making, in Stl'atl'imicw knowledge seeking, 135–6
Constitution Act of 1867, aboriginal people and, 55–6
corporatization
  Indigenous epistemologies and, 93–4
  relatedness and, 7–8
cosmopolitanism, identity and, 111–12
creation stories, land in, 90
critical engagement (*ta'lim*), 101, 108, 110
Cruikshank, George, 28
cultural emancipation, 9
  leadership and, 114, 121–2

cultural imperialism, 113–14, 117–18
culturally competent leadership, 9
culture
    deep, 88–9
    definitional differences and, 11–12
    TribalCrit Theory and, 9
curriculum, Indigenous knowledge and, 2–3, 119–20, 122–3
curriculum leadership
    creation of, 113–14
    culturally emancipatory, 114, 121–2, 124
Curriculum Theory course, 113–24
    clay-molding in (professor's perspective), 117–18, 123
    culturally emancipatory leadership in (student perspective), 119–21
    development of, 115–16
    Indigenous perspectives in, 116–18
    pottery analogy and, 118
Cuvier, Georges, 27, 28

Dakelh language, 54n1
Dakelh (Southern Carrier) people, 43
Damon, Saul, 22
Davids, Nuraan, 8
Davison, Patricia, 189
Declaration for the Rights of Indigenous Peoples, 9, 122–3
deep culture, 88–9
Designing Patterns unit, 158
    expert-apprentice modeling and, 159–60
    joint productive activity and, 160
    translating indigenous knowledge into, 159–60
District Six, 24
Dreaming. *See* The Dreaming
Dreaming Law, 80–1
Dreaming Time, 80–1
Dunlop, William, 26

Dutch, first encounter with Khoisan people, 22–3
Dutch-Khoikhoi wars, 23

economic societies, and Americanization of Puerto Rican education, 33–4
education. *See also* African Philosophy for Children; Khoisan educational system; Muslim education; Puerto Rican education
    assimilation supported by, 114
    constitutive meanings of, 4
    cultural imperialism in, 9, 113–14, 117–18
    cultural norms in, 109
    defunding of, 94
    hegemonic notions of, 150–3
    for humanity, 150–4
    identity and, 4–6
    Indigenous knowledge and, 2–3, 119–20, 122–3
    Indigenous *versus* Western notions of, 4
    South African, repressive legislation and, 151
    through observation, 11, 165
    transcending Indigenous/nonindigenous divide in, 111–12
    Western model of, 18, 95
education laws, state, 213
educational policy, Native American languages and, 13–14. *See also* language policy
educational settings, relatedness and Indigenous perspectives, 94–7
    mainstream perspectives, 97–9
Elam, Donna, 9
elders
    Aboriginal, 80–1
    of Camin Lake Band, 58
    Sankofa and, 116, 120, 121

Stl'atl'imicw, 126–8, 134
Tsilhqot'in, 44, 47–8, 50–3
Yoruba, 173
Yup'ik, 157–61
elitnauristet maklagtutulit, 11, 157, 170
Ellison, Ralph, 114
English language, official status of, 210, 211
English Language Unity Act, 214
epistemology. *See* Indigenous knowledges
defined, 88
Eskimo culture, observation *versus* questioning in, 11, 165
Esther Martinez Native American Languages Preservation Act 2006, 214
provisions of, 211, 213–14
eugenic discourse, 5, 33–6
campesinos and, 33, 36–7, 40–1
jibaros and, 40–1

Farrand, Livingston, 45, 47
Fasseke, Balla, 177
First Nations
Canadian government policies and, 52–3
and right to self-determination, 61
First Nations identity(ies)
Indian Act of 1876 and, 56–7
versus traditional Indigenous laws, 57
First Nations languages, 43–4. *See also* Tsilhqot'in language and culture courses
and transmission of culture, 6
First Nations people. *See also* Canim Lake Band; Tsilhqot'in language and culture courses; Tsilhqot'in people
contemporary cultural forms of, 6
homogeneity and, 59–60
research ethics code and, 48–9
Fixico, Donald, 96

Gammage, B., 81
George, Lucy (Nola), 188
gifting, Stl'atl'imicw knowledge seeking and, 133
Gitksan people, 46
Glatigny, Pascal Dubourg, 4, 18
Gods Must Be Crazy, The, 142, 147
griot
defined, 175
origin of term, 184n1
Oriki and, 175–7
roles of, 176–7

Haley, Alex, 184n2
Harvey, Lee, 3–4
health education, racial regeneration agenda and, 5–36
Heslop, Sandy, 186
higher education
inherent characteristics of, 150
South African, and colonization of knowledge, 140, 143
Higher Education Transformation Network, 140
Hill, Sarah, 188, 191, 195
Holmes, Frances Kay, 7
Honour, Hugh, 28
"Hottentot Venus," 26–7, 29. *See also* Baartman, Saartjie (Sarah)
Huet, Nicolas, 27
humanity, education for, 150–4
humble togetherness, 117, 120–1
hybridization
and absence of cultural supremacy, 207
notion of, 199–200

identity(ies). *See also under* specific groups
African, precolonial education and, 197
constitutive meanings of, 4
cosmopolitanism and, 111–12
education and, 4–6

identity(ies)—*Continued*
  sense of place and, 77–9
  social and biological construction of, 5
identity politics
  Aboriginal culture/experience and, 74
  failure of, 148–9
illiteracy issue, in Puerto Rico, 36–9
Iluvaktuq's story, MCC and, 159
imperialism, cultural, 9, 113–14, 117–18
Incantation for Self-protection, 178–9
Indian Act of 1876
  Bill C-31 amendment to, 56–7, 60
  and determination of Indian identity, 56–7
  identity loss and, 6
  impact on Indigenous women, 57
  sections 2(1) and 6 of, 56
  self-determination and, 55–69
Indigenist, defining, 129–30
Indigenist approach to research, 125–37
  consensus-making and, 135–6
  frameworks for, 129–31
  noninterference and, 125–8
  reflecting in, 134–5
  Stl'atl'imicw knowledge-seeking protocols and, 132–3
  Stl'atl'imicw research processes and, 131–2
  Stl'atl'imicw ways of knowing and, 127–8
  visualizing in, 133–4
  versus Western practices of, 129
  wise approaches/practices and, 128–9
Indigenist discourse, themes of, 130
Indigenous, *versus* Indigenist, 130
Indigenous basket weaving. *See* basketry
Indigenous concepts/practices
  Australian context of, 73–5
  constitutive meanings of, 3
  contexts studied, 2
  country/place in, 73
  and education for humanity, 10
  usefulness and implications of, 2
Indigenous cultures, and interactions with postmodern Western cultures, 1–2
Indigenous education. *See also* education
  transcending divide with nonindigenous education, 111–12
Indigenous identity(ies)
  Canim Lake Band and, 55
  Canim Lake community survey and, 62–7
  challenging federal authority over, 67–9
  defragmentation of, 146
  erosion of, 6
  Indian Act of 1876 and, 55–69
  (*see also* Indian Act of 1876)
  and internalization of colonizing mandate, 67–8
Indigenous knowledge in classroom, 10–11, 119–21, 157–70. *See also* Math in a Cultural Context (MCC)
  potential for, 169–70
Indigenous knowledges/epistemologies, 88, 7–11
  characteristics/concepts of, 102–4
  industrialization/corporatization and, 93–4
  land in, 89–90
  language in, 90–1
  mainstream dismissal of, 8
  role of, 2
  similarities across nations, 89
  time and circular thinking in, 89
  two leggeds and four leggeds in, 91–2, 99n2
  Western dismissal of, 87–9
  versus worldviews, 88

Indigenous languages. *See also*
  Native American languages
  in education, 203–4
Indigenous mythology, basketry and,
  191–2
Indigenous no man's land, of South
  Africa, 140, 154n3
Indigenous peoples, rights of, 122–3
Indigenous relatedness, 87–99
  concepts of, 7–8
  in indigenous educational settings,
    94–7
  intersectionality of, 93
  in mainstream educational
    settings, 97–9
Indigenous science, 76
Indigenous sovereignty
  and hegemonic notions of
    education, 151–3
  importance of, 144–5
  Khoisan concept of, 139
  South African barriers to, 140–2
  South African legislation
    enforcing, 145–6
Indigenous university staff, racist
  acts against, 151, 154n7
individualism
  market economy and, 93
  white colonist notions of, 147–8
industrialization
  Indigenous epistemologies and, 93–4
  relatedness and, 7–8
InInupiaq village, MCC and, 161–9
Initiate-Respond-Evaluate (IRE)
  structure, 168–9
*Integrating Aboriginal Perspectives
  into the School Curriculum*
  (Kanu), 119
intelligence, race and, 33
intersectionality, Crenshaw's concept
  of, 149
Inuit peoples, homogeneity and,
  59–60
Islam
  knowledge of, 8

versus Muslim education, 106
  reduction of, 106–7
  prevalence by country, 108
  Qur'an's authority in, 105, 107
  Sunnah in, 107

Jackson, Michael, 176
jibaro identity, 5
  construction of, 31–41
  eugenic discourse and, 36–7, 40–1

Kagle, Melissa, 10–11
Khoisan (Khoi-San; KhoiSan),
  nomenclature debate and, 154n1
Khoisan (Khoi-San; KhoiSan)
  educational system
  basis of, 148
  characteristics of, 4, 18
  community and, 26
  key notions in, 17
  kinship and, 148
  leadership and, 26
  organization of, 5
Khoisan (Khoi-San; KhoiSan)
  identity(ies)
  defragmentation of, 146–7
  educational system and, 17–30
  identity politics and, 148–9
  land and, 25
Khoisan (Khoi-San; KhoiSan) land
  philosophy, European response
  to, 23
Khoisan (Khoi-San; KhoiSan) people
  "Coloured" registration and, 146–7
  community and, 19–21
  Eurocentric views of, 4–5, 17
  and first encounter with Dutch,
    22–3
  indigeneity and, 143–50
  Land Act of 1913 and, 144
  land question and, 22–6
  name variations, 17–18
  public recognition of, 143–4
  traditional leadership and, 21–2
  World War II service by, 25

Kicya7, Joyce Schneider, 9
kinship. See also Indigenous relatedness
   in Aboriginal ways of knowing, 79–80
   in Koi-San culture, 148
knowledge. See also Aboriginal knowledge/practices
   Horsthemke's types of, 104
   interrelational forms of, 114
   in Islam, 8
knowledge systems, Indigenous nature of, 102–3
Kouyate, Djeli Mamoudou, 175
Kunkel, Titi I., 6
Kwame Ture Leadership Institute, 116

land
   Aboriginal relationship with, 76–7
   Aboriginal ways of knowing and, 80
   in creation stories, 90
   in Indigenous epistemologies, 89–90
   Khoisan people and, 22–6, 145
   Tsilhqot'in people and, 45, 51
   Land Act of 1913, 24
   and dispossession of Khoisan people, 144
Land Restitution Act of 1994, 146
Lane, Robert, 45
language hotspots, defined, 210
language loss, of Native Americans in Oklahoma, 13–14. See also entries under Oklahoma
language policy
   current issues in, 213–14
   federal, 210–14, **215**, 217–19
   influence of, 212
   local, 213, 215, **216**, 218
   state, 213–15, **216**, 217–18
   tribal, 215, **216–17**, 218
language preservation, recommendations for, 221–2

languages. See also Tsilhqot'in language and culture courses; specific languages
   First Nation, 6, 43–4
   ideologies and policies of, 209
   impacts on thinking, 90–1
   Indigenous, in education, 203–4
   in Indigenous epistemologies, 90–1
   minority, attitudes toward, 212
   monolingual ideologies of, 209–10, 219
   Qur'anic Arabic, 108
   Secwepemc, 54n1
   Yoruba, characteristics of, 174
Lau v. Nichols, 211
leadership
   culturally competent, 9
   culturally emancipatory, 121–2
   Khoisan education and, 26
   Khoisan people and, 21–2
   as technocratic process versus artful experience, 114–15
leadership practices
   Ourobouros, 116–17, 120, 124
   Sankofa, 116, 120, 124
   Ubuntu, 117, 120–1, 124
Lillooet peoples. See Stl'atl'imicw knowledge seeking
linguistic intolerance/inequality, 212–13
Lipka, Jerry, 157
Lipman, Matthew, 13, 197–9, 202
Living Tongues Institute's Enduring Voices Project, 210
loyalty, politics of. See politics of loyalty
Lumley, Henri de, 29
Luthuli, Albert, 21–2

Mabandla, Brigitte, 29
Makgoba, Malegapuru, 153
Malthus, Thomas, 36
Mandela, Nelson, 28
Maré, Estelle Alma, 4, 18

marginalized communities, everyday
lives of, 2
market economy
education and, 95
individualism and, 93
marriage, common-law, *campesino*
identity and, 37
Martin, Georgina, 6
Math in a Cultural Context (MCC),
11, 157–70. See also *Designing
Patterns* unit
analysis segment in, 167–9
Indigenous content knowledge in,
158–9
individual exploration in, 163–7
in InInupiaq village, 161–9
learning to teach with, 160–1
lesson introduction, 162–3
potential for, 169–70
mathematics, indigenous conceptions
of, 159. See also Math in a
Cultural Context (MCC)
Matisse, Henri, 28
matrilineal system, of First Nations
people, 57
Mbeki, Thabo, 29
MCC curriculum. See Math in a
Cultural Context (MCC)
McCarty, Teresa, 94
McKinley, William, 34
meal sharing, Stl'atl'imicw
knowledge seeking and, 132–3
Métis people, 46, 59–60
Miller, Paul G., 38
Mitchell's Plain, 24
Mitterand, François, 28
monolingual ideologies, 209–10, 219–20
Monture-Angus, Patricia, 59–60
Morata, Olympia, 186
Moreton-Robinson, A., 141–2, 144–5
Muskogee Creeks, 90
Muslim education, 101–12
certainty concept and, 105–6
as Indigenous, 109–11
indigenous knowledge and, 103

key epistemological/ethical
practices in, 101, 108
knowledge concept in, 104–8
versus knowledge of Islam, 106
memorization in, 109–10
moral purpose in, 109
nonbifurcationist nature of, 105
Muslim knowledge
globalization and, 107–8
as Indigenous, 107–8
Mustapha, Adefunke, 180

narrative, European *versus*
Aboriginal, 78
Native American Language Act
(NALA) 1990, 214, 217–18
Native American language
education, 209–22. See also
language policy
Native American languages
Bureau of Indian Affairs and, 213
future directions for, 217–19
number in Oklahoma, 210
recommendations for preserving,
221–2
teaching barriers and, 217–18
Native American tribes, in
Oklahoma, 13–14
Native Land Act of 1913, 145, 146
Native Peoples, defined, 99n1
natural world
Aboriginal approaches to, 7
San relationship with, 23–4
Ndofirepi, Amasa Philip, 13
neoliberalism, impacts of, 93–4
Ngubane, Ben, 19
Nieves, Bethsaida, 5
Nisga'a people, 46
No Child Left Behind 2001 (NCLB),
214
Bilingual Education Act and, 211
and English requirement for
achievement testing, 218–19
language policy and, 213
teacher requirements of, 217

no man's land, Indigenous, in South Africa, 140, 154n3
North-West University (NWU), characteristics of, 139

observation, in Eskimo culture, 11, 165
Occupy Wall Street, 94, 97
Ojibway people, 92
Oklahoma
  as language hotspot, 210
  Native American languages in, 210
  Native American tribes in, 13–14
  School Laws of, 215, 218, 220–1
Oklahoma Indian Language Heritage Protection Act 2001, 215
Oklahoma State Constitution Amendment 2010, 215
O'Loughlin, Marjorie, 7
oral tradition
  Khoisan, 18
  Oriki and, 177–9
  Tsilhqot'in language and culture diploma and, 45–8
Oriki (praise poetry)
  of Brazilian Yorubas, 184n3
  chanters of, 180
  of chiefs and kings, 182
  as chronicle of heroic deeds, 182–3
  contemporary performance venues of, 175–6
  continuing significance of, 178–9
  dancing and, 184
  family inheritance of, 181–2
  during funerals, 177–8
  griot and, 175–7
  Incantation for Self-protection, 178–9
  oral culture and, 177–9
  in preservation of culture, 180–1
  as reflection of oral culture, 180
  repetition in, 179–80
  role of, 12, 173
  urbanization/immigration impacts and, 183–4
  Yoruba worldview and, 173–84
Oriki performers, specialties of, 177–8
Ourobouros leadership practice, 116–17, 120, 124
Ownership, Control, Access, and Possession (OCAP), 48–9

Philosophy for Children (Lipman), 202. *See also* African Philosophy for Children
  hybridized, 13, 197–9
  inappropriateness for African children, 202–4
Pinar, William, 114
place, significance of, 77–9, 90
politics of loyalty, 139–55
  dynamics of, 141–3
  and education for humanity, 150–3
  intersectionality and, 149–50
  Khoi-San people and, 143–50
  and maintenance of status quo, 141–2
  push-in and push-act factors and, 152–3
  transformation and, 139, 151–3, 154n2
Pomo basketry, 186–8, 190
Potchefstroom University for Christian Higher Education, 140, 151
pottery, shared origins with basketry, 185–6, 192–4
prayer, Stl'atl'imicw knowledge seeking and, 132
property, white colonist notions of, 147–8
puberty ritual, Stl'atl'imicw, 131–2
Puerto Rican education. See also *campesino* children; *campesino* identity; *jibaro* identity

Americanization of, 38–9
and *campesino* and *jibaro*
children, 36–7
campesino versus *jibaro* identities
and, 5
"elite" Puerto Rican teachers and,
33
English language textbooks and, 32–3
eugenic discourses and, 34–6
Home Economics Clubs and, 35
Red Cross and, 35
teacher training and, 32–4
US colonial rule and, 31–41

questioning, Eskimo culture and,
165, 167–9
Qur'an. *See also* Muslim education
Islamic knowledge and, 105, 107
Qur'anic Arabic, role in Islam, 108

race
eugenic discourse of, 5, 33–6
intelligence and, 33
Race to the Top, language policy
and, 213
racialization, social, cultural
processes of, 33
racism
Indigenous university staff and,
151, 154n7
scientific, 38–9
reflecting, in Stl'atl'imicw knowledge
seeking, 134–5
relatedness. *See also* Indigenous
relatedness
absence in dominant systems, 87
religious institutions, and
Americanization of Puerto
Rican education, 33
research
Indigenist approach to (*see*
Indigenist approach to research)
Stl'atl'imicw ways of knowing
and, 9–10
Western approach to, 129

research ethics code, First Nations
and, 48–9
researchers, Whitestream, 8
resistance movements, 94
Restitution of Land Rights Act of
1994, provisions of, 24
rhizomatic thinking, 118
riddles, and development of
reasoning skills, 206–7
ritournelle, 124
Roessel, Ruth Wheeler, 94–5
Rose, Deborah Bird, 79–81
Rowlandson, Thomas, 28
Royal Commission on Aboriginal
Peoples (RCAP), 61
rural space, *versus* urban, 37–41

Saint-Hilaire, Étienne, 27
Salaam, Omar, 9
San (Bushmen), 17, 19–20. *See also*
entries under Khoisan (Khoi-
San; KhoiSan)
relationship with nature, 23–4
traditional leadership and, 21–2
Sankofa leadership practice, 116,
120, 124
and African Philosophy for
Children, 201
Schorcht, Blanca, 6
science, Indigenous, 76
scientific racism, 38–9
Secwepemc language, 54n1
Secwepemc (Shuswap) people, 43
contemporary communities of,
57–8
self-determination
and challenge to federal authority,
67–9
First Nations' rights to, 61
Indian Act of 1876 and, 55–69
Sharp, Nancy, 157
Sherman, Marlon, 95–6
Sherman, Richard, 95–6
Shona people, and education
through riddles, 206–7

Shuswap People in Story, 58
Smith, Adam, 36
Smith, Linda Tuhiwai, 188–9
smudging, Stl'atl'imicw knowledge seeking and, 132
social activism (*ta'dīb*), 101, 108, 109, 110
socialization (*tarbiyyah*), 101, 108, 109
South Africa
 Aboriginal people of, 143–50 (*see also* entries under Khoi-San; KhoiSan)
 and barriers to Indigenous sovereignty, 140–2
 cultural revolution in, 18–19
 and dismissal of Indigenous ways of being, 10
 Indigenous no man's land of, 140, 154n3
 racialized monocultural norm in, 140–1
 repressive education legislation in, 151
 university impacts in, 140
South African Constitution, 144
space. *See also* third space
 urban *versus* rural, 37–41
"spotlighting," 168–9
Stanner, W. E. H., 79–80
State Question 751, 210
Stl'atl'imicw knowledge seeking
 consensus-making in, 135–6
 processes of, 131–2
 protocols of, 132–3
 reflecting in, 134–5
 research and, 9–10, 127–8, 131–2
 visualizing and, 133–4
Stolen Generation, 145
story telling, in precolonial African culture, 206–7
success
 concepts of, 143
 conceptualizations of, 10
Sundiata, Epic of, 177

Sunset Clauses, 146
Susag, Dorothea, 119
Sutherland, Linda, 67
Swayney, Zona' Nick, 188

ta'dīb (social activism), 101, 108, 109, 110
Tahdooahnippah/Warner American Indian Leadership Model, 117
Tahlequah Public Schools, 215, 218
ta'lim (critical engagement), 101, 108, 110
tarbiyyah (socialization), 101, 108, 109
Taylor, Charles, 3
Teit, James, 45, 133
The Dreaming (Tjukurrpa), 7, 77, 79–82
 discussing with students, 82
 role in Aboriginal life, 79–81
 theoretical framework, guiding questions for, 3
thinking, rhizomatic, 118
third space
 Africa as, 207
 contemporary Africa as, 13
 discourse patterns within, 165
 hybridized Philosophy for Children and, 199–200
 between Indigenous culture and mainstream school, 11
 MCC program and, 158, 161–9
time, in Indigenous epistemologies, 89
Titus, D. A., 22
Tjukurrpa. *See* The Dreaming (Tjukurrpa)
TNG, 44, 49
Tobias, Philip, 28
totemic animals, 77
transformation, politics of loyalty and, 139, 151–3, 154n2
TribalCrit Theory
 interrelational forms of knowledge in, 114
 tenets of, 9

Index

Tribble, J. Taylor, 13
Tsilhqot'in Culture: Sadanx, Yedanx, K'andzin—The Ancient, The Past, and the Present, 46–8, 51, 53
Tsilhqot'in language, 54n1
Tsilhqot'in language and culture courses, 43–54
  barriers to participation in, 51–2
  community member involvement in, 44–5
  English translations and, 47–8, 50
  first delivery of, 50–1
  impacts of, 53
  informed consent and control issues in, 48–9
  language teaching certification and, 49
  lessons learned and recommendations, 51–3
  oral tradition and, 45–8
  research ethics code and, 48–9
  textbook for, 46–7, 51, 53
  and translation and validation of oral narratives, 49–50
  Tsilhqot'in elders and, 47–8, 50–1, 53
Tsilhqot'in Language Group (TLG), members of, 44–5
Tsilhqot'in people, 43
  contemporary practices of, 45–6
  language preservation and, 6
  oral traditions of, 45–6
  and resistance to settler activities, 45
Tsimshian people, 46
Tubatulabal basketry, 193
Tufvesson, Ingrid, 10
Tukanoan basketry, 192
two leggeds/four leggeds (peoplehood), in Indigenous epistemologies, 91–2, 99n2

Ubuntu leadership practice, 117, 120–1, 124
Ucwalmicw languages, 137n1
Ucwalmicw people, 125
Uluru formation, 80
United States
  language policy and ideology in, 210–13, 217–18
  Native Peoples in history of, 98
universities
  inherent characteristics of, 150
  South African, and colonization of knowledge, 140, 143, 150
University of Cape Town (UCT), 151
  characteristics of, 139
University of KwaZulu Natal (UKZN), 153
urban space, *versus* rural, 37–41

Valandra, Edward, 96–7
van Riebeeck, Jan, 17–18, 22–3
van Wyk, Berte, 4
van Wyk, Maria, 20
VanStone, James, 45
Vibrant Matter: A Political Ecology of Things (Bennett), 83
visualizing, Stl'atl'imicw knowledge seeking and, 133–4

Waghid, Yusef, 8
Wailly, Léon de, 27
Watkins, William, 120
Weida, Courtney Lee, 12–13
White Australia Policy, 145
Whitestream researchers, 8
Williams Lake Indian Band, 58
wisdom, African perception of, 200–1
wise practices
  versus best practices, 128
  characteristics of, 128–9
Witbooi, Hendrik, 144–5
worldviews, *versus* ontologies/epistemologies, 8

Yakama basketry, 191–2
Yarralin people, 80–1
Yokut basketry, 190–1

Yoruba culture, oriki's role in, 12
Yoruba language, characteristics of, 174
Yoruba people, in Brazil, 184n3
Yoruba poetry, patterns of, 174
Yoruba worldview, Oriki (praise poetry) and, 173–84. *See also* Oriki (praise poetry)
Yup'ik elders, MCC program and, 157–61

Yup'ik people, and conservation of resources, 160–1
Yup'ik schools, nonindigenous teachers in, 157

Zulu basketry, 195–6
Zulu language, university requirement for, 153
Zuma, Jacob Gedleyihlekisa, 143–4

GPSR Compliance
The European Union's (EU) General Product Safety Regulation (GPSR) is a set
of rules that requires consumer products to be safe and our obligations to
ensure this.

If you have any concerns about our products, you can contact us on

ProductSafety@springernature.com

In case Publisher is established outside the EU, the EU authorized
representative is:

Springer Nature Customer Service Center GmbH
Europaplatz 3
69115 Heidelberg, Germany

www.ingramcontent.com/pod-product-compliance
Lightning Source LLC
LaVergne TN
LVHW051914060526
838200LV00004B/138